GW01376842

# The RDS Forex System

Founded in 1807, John Wiley & Sons is the oldest independent publishing company in the United States. With offices in North America, Europe, Australia, and Asia, Wiley is globally committed to developing and marketing print and electronic products and services for our customers' professional and personal knowledge and understanding.

The Wiley Trading series features books by traders who have survived the market's ever changing temperament and have prospered—some by reinventing systems, others by getting back to basics. Whether a novice trader, professional, or somewhere in-between, these books will provide the advice and strategies needed to prosper today and well into the future.

For a list of available titles, visit our web site at www.WileyFinance.com.

# The RDS Forex System

## A Breakthrough Method to Profiting from Market Turning Points

**MICHAEL RADKAY**
**STEPHANIE RADKAY**

WILEY

John Wiley & Sons, Inc.

Copyright © 2012 by Michael Radkay and Stephanie Radkay. All rights reserved.

Published by John Wiley & Sons, Inc., Hoboken, New Jersey.
Published simultaneously in Canada.

No part of this publication may be reproduced, stored in a retrieval system, or transmitted in any form or by any means, electronic, mechanical, photocopying, recording, scanning, or otherwise, except as permitted under Section 107 or 108 of the 1976 United States Copyright Act, without either the prior written permission of the Publisher, or authorization through payment of the appropriate per-copy fee to the Copyright Clearance Center, Inc., 222 Rosewood Drive, Danvers, MA 01923, (978) 750-8400, fax (978) 646-8600, or on the Web at www.copyright.com. Requests to the Publisher for permission should be addressed to the Permissions Department, John Wiley & Sons, Inc., 111 River Street, Hoboken, NJ 07030, (201) 748-6011, fax (201) 748-6008, or online at http://www.wiley.com/go/permissions.

Limit of Liability/Disclaimer of Warranty: While the publisher and author have used their best efforts in preparing this book, they make no representations or warranties with respect to the accuracy or completeness of the contents of this book and specifically disclaim any implied warranties of merchantability or fitness for a particular purpose. No warranty may be created or extended by sales representatives or written sales materials. The advice and strategies contained herein may not be suitable for your situation. You should consult with a professional where appropriate. Neither the publisher nor author shall be liable for any loss of profit or any other commercial damages, including but not limited to special, incidental, consequential, or other damages.

For general information on our other products and services or for technical support, please contact our Customer Care Department within the United States at (800) 762-2974, outside the United States at (317) 572-3993, or fax (317) 572-4002.

Wiley also publishes its books in a variety of electronic formats. Some content that appears in print may not be available in electronic books. For more information about Wiley products, visit our web site at www.wiley.com.

*Library of Congress Cataloging-in-Publication Data:*

Radkay, Michael, 1967–
   The RDS Forex system : a breakthrough method to profiting from market turning points / Michael Radkay, Stephanie Radkay.
      p. cm. – (Wiley trading series ; 537)
   Includes bibliographical references and index.
   ISBN 978-1-118-09668-0 (cloth); ISBN 978-1-118-26199-6 (ebk);
   ISBN 978-1-118-23698-7 (ebk); ISBN 978-1-118-22366-6 (ebk)
  1. Foreign exchange market.   2. Foreign exchange futures.   I. Radkay, Stephanie, 1968–   II. Title.
   HG3851.R28 2012
   332.4'5–dc23
                                                                                               2011043891

Printed in the United States of America

10  9  8  7  6  5  4  3  2  1

*This book is dedicated to the remaining floor traders and aspiring new traders; may you have the courage to ask questions when you trade on the computer.*

# Contents

**Preface** ix

**Acknowledgments** xiii

**CHAPTER 1** Introduction to Today's Forex Market 1

**CHAPTER 2** Comparing Forex to Other Markets 13

**CHAPTER 3** Finding the New Edge 19

**CHAPTER 4** The Long and Short of Fundamental Analysis 35

**CHAPTER 5** Price Never Lies 47

**CHAPTER 6** Play at Peak Times 61

**CHAPTER 7** Preparing for Known Events 75

**CHAPTER 8** Risk Tolerance and Developing a Feel for Price Movement 87

**CHAPTER 9** Why Technical Analysis Works 109

**CHAPTER 10** Defining the Rotating Directional System 123

**CHAPTER 11   Putting It All Together**                 **159**

**CHAPTER 12   Evaluating Your Performance**             **197**

**Resources**                                             **215**

**About the Authors**                                     **217**

**Index**                                                 **219**

# Preface

In the spring of 1991, we lived within a block of each other in the Lincoln Park neighborhood of Chicago. Every morning, we met at the corner of Orchard and Drummond to ride the "El" to work together. Our trading careers kicked off our relationship and then life happened and solidified the bond. Twenty years later, we are looking back at two careers on the trading floor, transitions to the computer screen, and several education firms built, all of which have brought us to the decision to write this book.

These days we can take our computer anywhere so we opted for about 280 days more of sunshine per year and now live in Los Angeles. We focus on trading currencies and educating those that dare enter this business. Our mission over the years has been simple, which is to help others become independent traders, thinkers, and decision makers.

When we reminisce about our lives it seems that we have always been traders and coaches in some respect, whether it was Mike helping a fellow football teammate with his studies or Steph tutoring students through high school and college. We try to give in any way we can whether offering a friend or family member a place to stay until they got back up on their feet or holding a banner that shouted a friend's message to voters to elect him to a local political office. Living from a standpoint that life is abundant with plenty to go around for all became a mode that we wanted to live by.

The trading arena has tested our giving attitude to the core, but we've persevered. In the late 1980s and early 1990s we entered into the pits at the Chicago Board of Trade (CBOT) and the Chicago Mercantile Exchange (CME), two of the world's leading derivatives markets that later merged to become the CME Group.

Steph found her home at the CME in the S&P 500 and NASDAQ pits as a broker, one that executed customer buys and sells and traded proprietary funds for Timber Hill, now known as Interactive Brokers. Her acronym on the floor was TIGR. Mike found his home at the CBOT in the 30 Year Bond Pit in 1989. He was a broker from 1993 to 1997 at the CBOT working with one of the largest independent broker firms in the business. He eventually became an independent self-funded trader referred to as a *local* in June of

1997. A local is somebody who trades for his or her own individual account and takes 100 percent of the profits and losses. His acronym is RDS, which initially was just an abbreviation of our last name. Many called him "Rads" but the real meaning behind the badge will reveal itself as the *Rotating Directional System* in this book.

These badges let people know two things. The first was that it let everybody know on the trading floor that you were a member of the exchange and had the right to trade in your respective pit. The second was that the acronym was in a sense your address and how colleagues identified you when you traded with them on their trading cards. As you made a trade you would write the acronym and three digit numbers so the trade could be entered in the trader's account.

Fear and greed dominated the landscape and we saw all walks of life hopped up on adrenaline and crammed together in the trading pits. They had a locker room smell and an atmosphere where verbal abuse was commonplace and expected. You had to get used to it and use some street smarts and quick wit of your own or go home. The adrenaline rush of this business was so powerful; after all, fortunes could be made or lost in a matter of seconds. There were no time-outs, crying, or take backs. Our eyes witnessed first-hand that trading literally didn't stop for injuries, heart attacks, or fights. Putting the extreme aside, the pulse of the pit was extremely orderly and quite an efficient mechanism to establish a fair and honest market price for all traders, although it was never easy.

As we made our way in the trading world, we saw a tremendous need for an education model to help others compete in this rugged climate and culture. We partnered with Steph's dad in the beginning, Mickey Hoffman, now Senior Vice President of Dowd Westcott, to build an environment to help nourish the skills and provide the tools that a new trader would need entering the pit-trading arena. The CME and CBOT took notice and began hiring us to run and develop their open-outcry mock trading environments through the 1990s. After a long day in the pits our day didn't end as we went right back to some of the very spots we just left and taught our students after hours the lessons we experienced daily while competing in the markets.

As computerized trading started to take over 25 percent of the daily volume from the open-outcry markets in 2002, Mike began to make a transition and build trading models focusing on the Screen Trader. Mike was the best candidate to build the program as he was one of the first groups of local traders to bring a hand-held computer in the trading pit. The writing was on the wall for the open-outcry pit trader and Mike had learned a big lesson one year earlier—to follow the money. As the volume shifted to 80 percent computerized and with Mike doing nearly 100 percent of his round turns on the computer, he left the trading floor at the end of 2004 and never looked back.

As our new screen-trading education model took shape, firms started to ask us to help them enhance their environments. We were asked to deliver our skills and do on-site classes and webinars as featured educators for the CME Group and the Intercontinental Exchange (ICE). In addition we were routinely asked for help by high-ranking officers of firms like MF Global, Dorman, Goldenberg Heymeyer (now Penson), PFG, Mirus Futures, Dowd Wescott, and most recently Global Futures. Platform vendors like Trading Technologies (X-Trader), Pats Systems, and CQG wanted experienced traders to help their customers with trading plans and since we were using their software at the time, they asked us for our help as well. NinjaTrader powered by Zenfire or Kinetick also took notice and added us as an educational partner for their software. On-line webinar groups like Trader Kingdom, FX Instructor, and Forex Connect regularly ask for our content so we help them as well. We just live and breathe this industry.

After solidifying our sought-after model in the Commodity Futures Industry we turned our focus and applied it to the growing Forex arena in 2005. Our education now helps firms add Forex as an investment class to their books as we have introduced thousands to FX Solutions, FXCM, and Gain Capital. DTI Trader, a highly accredited Futures and Options Education Firm, in 2010 asked us to help them build their non-existent Forex arm, which we gladly accepted.

Our commitment runs deep to help the trader as we see so much of the trading education out there today that acts as though this business is as easy as a dollar-store purchase. You may have even heard some of their shouts that they have the secret formula to help you gain fortunes in minutes. It just isn't that easy; nothing is for that matter. If it was, everybody would be doing it. It takes a special breed of person who can get knocked down and bounce back up in moments to try again. These fly-by-night educators fall so in love with their product that they forget to do one thing, which is to listen to your questions. Everybody is different. The markets for the most part are the same; they go up or they go down but the person who shows up and gets in the driver's seat might be angry, sad, happy, tired, highly capitalized, or undercapitalized to name a few. We know that there is no specific perfect formula that a high, low, open, or close can deliver. The missing piece of the formula comes from your ability to balance instincts and emotions with fundamental and technical knowledge. We just become the facilitator to open up your eyes and bring out what type of trader you can be or want to be. The ability to think and act under pressure becomes the magic formula and that is up to you. We want to give you a realistic shot at trading for a living. There is no better feeling than being your own boss and owning your own business.

Since nobody cares more about your money than you do, we have written this book for those of you who want to take charge of your own financial decisions. The speed of today's technology forces our hand to be real-time and the time it takes to call your broker to get you in on the action means that you are already a step behind. Having a finger on the pulse is necessary, but before you enter this arena we thought it wise to give you some of our insights that have helped us navigate through the financial waters. Since there are a million strategies out there that have even confused us in the beginning, we have drawn our focus into not reinventing the wheel but organizing and simplifying concepts. First we want to express a need to know the key fundamentals that strengthen or weaken our economy, to build our market bias and technically time our entries and exits with five simple rules.

We are not the policy makers, so we understand that in order to compete a method for the individual to handle today's investment speed is vital. As we had to adjust from the open-auction environment to the computerized world, you will as well. The computer is here to stay as our society will never accept going slower. We as humans need to embrace, learn, and understand the technology being used. *Do not step into the investment world unless you really have read the prospectus to its core.* Just as you have, we have taken some lumps while investing in today's turbo-speed economy and felt the need to write a book to help you find a way to handle today's wired-in world.

# Acknowledgments

Even for us, success doesn't come without the help of others. We would like to thank our parents, as they were the instrumental force that helped us become who we are today, and our brother and sister, who helped us with our sense of humor and gave us a sibling's shoulder to lean on along the way. Mike would like to give a special thanks to his high school football coach Frank Lenti for being a strong adult male role model that he so desperately needed at that time in his life. As a trader, Mike wants to give special recognition to JTN for hiring him out of college to work with NANCO at the CBOT and also to ANI who believed in Mike and opened some invaluable doors along the way. To the brokers that filled orders and risked dollars at NANCO a special okay sign (they will know) to JCN, TIF, PLI, TCL, PLZ, TNI, PAB, AZE, NAW, KPC, To the boys to our side DHO, OUX, PPS, RBE, PSN, SP, and HAT, it was fun running through all of the ups and downs together. When the pushing and shoving got to be too much, the shout from SP saying "What's the Hang-Up", kept it light. Laughing every time he answered his own question; "it's a Bar on Elm". When we moved to the new financial room; KOD, DGL, ESR, GTK, MID, WGE, TGL, BDF, TTX, BTZ, RVO, CON, DKD, PUF, JYC, and TGS thanks for keeping it light, fun, and real.

Steph would like to give a special thanks to Timber Hill and those guys that she worked with that were kind enough to treat her as a lady but professional enough to treat her as an equal, so a special thanks to Thomas Peterffy, Dave Downey, DRUM, GURU, SAGE, XLI, WEX, and PUG.

As trading educators we have built some deep, long-lasting friendships and would like to give a special thanks to NOX, JYP, and of course to TEQ who gave us both an arena to show what we were capable of sharing with other traders educationally, which was our knowledge and passion for the game we call "the markets."

Mike and Stephanie Radkay<br>
February 2012

# CHAPTER 1

# Introduction to Today's Forex Market

Algorithmic trading, high-frequency trading, computer trading—regardless of the name you choose to use for this type of trading, is it really to blame for global chaos?

Some suggest high-frequency, quick-buck artists are the cause for the pillaging of our financial system since the turn of the century. Everybody needs to have a culprit it seems, and a group to finger point at as the source. Flash crashes, tech booms, bubbles, and bankruptcies are monthly events these days. The financial system was placed on steroids when the computer was introduced into our open-auction pit trading society at the end of the twentieth century. Entire nations are now being traded like penny stocks on a minute to minute basis. There are price moves so volatile that they make the 1987 crash look like a mediocre event. When the finger is pointed at computer traders as the source of the economic evil, we have to agree to a point, but we agree with a smile. Do you see the world pointing the finger at Henry Ford for the cause of the air pollution problem and global warming? Our culture demands a timely and efficient mode of getting from point A to B. As Maverick and Goose stated in *Top Gun*, "We have a need for speed."

## A NEW PLAYING FIELD

The introduction of the computer into our business wasn't welcome at first. We liked the person-to-person deal making in the open-auction environment. But if we wanted to stay in our business, we needed to embrace the new era as every industry does. Just as technology in automobiles improved to make cars go farther and faster, our trading industry decision makers embraced the new technology to help it reach farther and faster. The computer and Internet would give all a chance to receive real-time information from their own home or office via the computer and Internet. With every invention, the initial use of it brings chaos, then adaptation and growth as society implements it into their routines. What the decision makers in our industry didn't bargain for was the volatility. Human-to-human speed was reasonable, but computer speed in trading is like upgrading from a bike to an X-15 fighter jet.

The public cried for a leveling of the playing field in the investment community to give everybody a fair and equal chance to compete, not just those in the trading pits. Be careful what you wish for. The computer was a game changer. Joe the Plumber could now actually compete for top position in line with the likes of Goldman Sachs or receive the same real-time information as former Treasury Secretary Hank Paulson. It's enough to rattle the nerves of any of today's high-powered chief executive officers (CEOs). So we hear and understand the cries of blogger Mark Cuban who wrote on May 9, 2010:

> *To traders, whether day traders or high frequency or somewhere in between, Wall Street has nothing to do with creating capital for businesses, its original goal. Wall Street is a platform. It's a platform to be exploited by every technological and intellectual means possible. The best analogy for traders; they are hackers. Just as hackers search for and exploit operating system and application shortcomings, traders do the same thing. A hacker wants to jump in front of your shopping cart and grab your credit card and then sell it. A high frequency trader wants to jump in front of your trade and then sell that stock to you. A hacker will tell you that they are serving a purpose by identifying the weak links in your system. A trader will tell you they deserve the pennies they are making on the trade because they provide liquidity to the market.*
> —*Blog Maverick*; The Mark Cuban Weblog by Mark Cuban, http://www.blogmaverick.com

Cuban has a point because market crashes are painful and today's volatility is eye-popping. Now the original intention of the Forex, Futures, and Options markets that are populated by a huge portion of day traders was to create a place of liquidity and a place for an individual to hedge against an economic downturn. When there are floods, bankruptcies, defaults, or just the plain old uncertainty of what tomorrow might bring, most are pretty glad that there always seems to be a buyer and a seller in all conditions. The price may not always be pleasing, but Forex, Futures, and Options help the buy-and-hope players in the market with a place to go to protect their fortunes, whether they rest in currencies, treasuries, equities, grains, energies, softs, or metals. In the trading pits you used to know where the buying or selling was coming from; now you don't know if it's coming from an overseas hedge fund or your neighbor down the street. Regulations and controls are getting better and better as technology advances, but there is always room for improvement as we press forward.

We don't blame Cuban for his concern as we are sure his portfolio—much like the S&P 500—has seen swings of 50 percent or more from 2000 to 2011 during some of the hair-raising moments witnessed over this time span. Entering into the markets at the end of the 1990s left a feeling of invincibility as there was a nothing-could-go-wrong mentality in the air. People had long forgotten the 1987 crash at this point—let alone the Great Depression. "We are much better equipped" was a common shout, but fear and greed are inherited and inescapable by-products in our global culture. With markets soaring to unheard of levels, the drop only gets more expensive. Warren Buffett says it best, "Be fearful in greedy times and be greedy in fearful times." Greenspan's word for greed was "over-exuberance." Losing retirement or investment dollars is enough to get anyone's heart rate pumping, whether you have billions or thousands invested. Heads need to roll! Education about what to do in turbulent times is completely necessary in this day and age, especially when the speed of technology is certainly only going to get faster.

So in true finger-pointing fashion we are here to tell you that the need for growth as human beings is the culprit. As Oliver Stone's Gordon Gekko says "Greed is good." The greed for life, greed for money, and the greed to be the best are to blame. We didn't bring the computer and Internet to the trading industry; it was brought on a silver platter by Microsoft, IBM, and Dell to name a few. We personally were introduced to computers in high school and used them in college but a computer didn't enter our home until 1997. Now they are in kindergarten classrooms across the world. You call us hackers; it will only be child's play when the kids of today enter the adult workforce and financial markets of tomorrow. Computers are being exploited just as Internet satellites are being exploited to broadcast news around the world to everybody in real time. The need for speed even creates a release of unconfirmed events before they are fact. Do you remember when Gore won Florida, no Bush won Florida, and, we don't know who won Florida. Do we now know for sure who won Florida? Information these days is one "Hanging Chad" after another. Real-time information is the current cry as newspapers become yesterday's trash.

Sending a letter—forget about it; e-mail and texting are the new form of thank you.

The need for speed by us all is the true culprit, but that doesn't need to be a negative thought. The computer is like stepping out of that old Lexus and into a Lamborghini. You just have to get used to the speed. Moves are happening so fast that you have no other choice than to adopt a day-trader's mentality. Some of the public hates when we make money and laugh when we lose money, but soon all will realize that the very reasons why day traders exist is that you can't trust a forecast past a week these days. At one point, we even put retirement money in the hands of the professional investment broker like we were told and realized that we have put more money in than it was worth five years later. We could have done better throwing a dart at a dartboard than our broker did. It was time to take back our power, protect our assets, invest with confidence, and trust our instincts. We learned the hard way that there is only one person who cares about your money, and that somebody is you!

The swings of today are turbulent and are only going to get more volatile with the entire world's over-spending fast-paced model. Whether directly or indirectly involved in the markets, you must understand that you are involved whether you like it or not. There is a true need to understand the professionals playing the game. Some of them are using the fastest technology that they can get their hands on to keep up with the pace.

The world market players have their eyes on Forex and this is just the beginning. It's more important than ever to stay educated on the latest strategies and methods for participating in the markets. Next up is an introduction to some of the methods we've used to successfully navigate the market for the past two decades.

In the beginning stages while reading this book we hope that you will give some thought to your current skill level and identify where you are strong and where some work needs to be done. Trading will definitely expose every weakness and even begin to identify some that you didn't even know you had, so it is wise to start being truthful about your current skills and ability to navigate a computer as well as your emotions. Trading seems to throw a pop quiz at you daily. We have put together some questions for you ahead so you can survive and understand the "-ings", three reasons why you may be failing today, and offer solutions using Forex. We aim to show you how leverage can be helpful but teach you about the risks involved by revealing the ability to downsize in turbulent rough patches that you most certainly will face while trading Forex. Follow the money and use the "new edge" that we discuss to help you grow responsibly and become a successful independent trader, thinker, and decision maker.

*Introduction to Today's Forex Market* 5

## ARE YOU READY FOR IT?

Before moving into our strategy we are assuming a few things from you about your willingness to push the buttons yourselves and your ability to navigate through a computer and the software needed to execute the trades. Knowing how to use the equipment is so important that it reminds us of the time we went flying in a single prop plane. The pilot (our friend) gave us the checklist of things to do before take-off. He let us read off each step while he tested all of the key parts on the plane. Yes, this included checking the gas gauge. This guy was a seasoned flyer as he not only knew how to use the equipment but also he understood the importance of testing the equipment before using it. The pilot was able to check what was needed and at the same time he made us feel comfortable before getting into the plane with him as we went through the list successfully together. We don't think anybody—passenger or pilot—would like to fly without checking the equipment or knowing how to fly and land the plane.

We bring up this point and relate it to trading because flying and trading have some similarities. You are the pilot in trading. It is 100 percent on you. No free rides in the passenger seat if you choose to push the buttons yourself. Mistakes in trading won't kill you literally, but financially not knowing how to use the equipment let alone checking the equipment before using it can mean financial suicide. It surprises us so often that traders who come to us for help don't even know how to use the software that well and have been trading and losing real money and quite often big money!! This is equivalent to taking off in a plane, not knowing if the plane works and on top of that not knowing how to fly or better yet land the plane safely. People often think; it's just buying and selling, prices go up and down, how hard can it be, right?

Newcomers are only tuned in to the fortunes they hear are made in trading, and of course in our instant gratification world they want it right now. When we routinely work with clients one on one we screen share with them and begin to teach them not only how to apply a strategy but we especially begin to focus on teaching them how to use the software to implement the plan. We might even out of nowhere throw a curve ball at a student when we are on a practice account. For example, we get the student in the market with a short USDCHF position (U.S. dollar versus the Swiss Franc); a pretty good bet from 2000 to 2011 with low interest rates and debt piling up out of control in the United States (nothing new). We will be humming along and all of a sudden without warning we say the Federal Reserve just raised the interest rate, what are you going to do? Your mind might say the right thing, but as you try and cover the short as prices begin to soar your hands don't know where to turn because you don't know how to do it under pressure.

You might have the best trading strategy in the world in your head, but don't go into the fight without knowing how to use the equipment that is necessary to make it successful. We regularly ask our audience to rate their knowledge and confidence of using the software needed to trade. We have been putting on trades on the computer every day since 2002. Simply put, we have been part of a group of U.S. trading pioneers playing on the field during the shift from open-outcry pit trading to computerized trading. In the beginning we made mistakes and donated unnecessary dollars to the "man" living inside our computer, but our goal was to control the controllable so we could free our minds to think clearly under pressure. There are enough uncontrollable things that can happen in the market, so begin to fix and master what is in your control and do it now while your account and sanity is intact!

So often new traders go on a practice account and try to make money on day one. We understand that this is the overall goal, but in the beginning we feel this is the wrong approach. Start by becoming familiar with each of the buttons on your practice account and how you might be able to use them to your advantage. After you are familiar with the software, then begin to create scenarios and see how quickly and accurately you can act when turbulence hits (i.e., pushing buttons several times and realizing you compounded the problem several times out of nervousness in the moment and in a fully-fledged panic you kicked the cord out of the socket killing the power on your computer and not knowing where the phone number is to call in case of emergency, just to name a few that cost some real thousand-dollar bills). As you become a master at using the software, then implement your strategy to trade with live money. How long this all takes is up to you!

## SURVIVING THE "-INGS" IN TRADING

We thought we would share some of our top computer-related issues that we've faced along the way. They are what we call the *-ing*isms in trading. How about:

1. Lean*ing* on your key-board by mistake, enter*ing* an unwanted position in the market,
2. Spill*ing* that beverage on the keys, and find*ing* your buy button stuck the next day so that all you can do is sell (might not be a bad thing),
3. Forgett*ing* that pend*ing* order or position in your book, and wak*ing* up tomorrow with an unknown position down 100 pips,

Introduction to Today's Forex Market 7

## Important Questions to Consider Before Trading Live

It can be helpful to answer a few questions to see how ready you are to jump into the arena. Rate yourself from 0 to 10, with 10 being the best and 0 being the worst on the following questions.

### Technology Questions:
1. How well do you really know how to use your PC or laptop computer?
2. How well do you know how to use your execution platform and charts?
3. Do you know how to enter/exit the market with the six basic order types; buy market, buy limit, buy stop, sell market, sell limit, and sell stop?
4. Do you know how to attach a profit and stop loss or trailing stop to a position with a one-cancels-other (OCO) order?
5. How good is your Internet connection and do you have a back-up computer or Internet connection?
6. Do you have access to all your account information/statements handy, and a list of phone numbers to call your support desk in case one or all of the above do not work properly?

If you need a platform to practice and tutorials to follow, you can find one to use free at: *www.rdstrader.com/platform*.

### Personal Questions:
1. When you get knocked down can you get back up?
2. How do you act when you lose?
3. How do you act when you win?
4. Do you have patience?
5. Can you execute under control on a moment's notice without panicking?
6. Do you have the will to win?

Bill Cosby once said this: "The difference between a pat on the back or a kick in the butt is about a foot." Don't congratulate yourself too long for a success and don't dwell on a mistake. Get back up and do it better the next time as you are only as good as your last trade in this business. You should strive to have a rating of 10 on every category, but begin to focus on the areas that you rated below a score of 8. Just remember to be truthful with your scores as you are entering a world where you are the judge and jury. When a 10 is not that difficult to achieve, why settle for anything less than perfect?

4. Charts freez*ing* up because your Internet connection just went down, kick*ing* the plug by mistake, shutt*ing* off your computer minutes before an unemployment report,
5. Hav*ing* an untimely message come popp*ing* up on your screen block*ing* you from exit*ing* a winn*ing* trade that turns into a los*ing* trade.
6. Fail*ing* to enter a stop loss while you step out for 1 minute as price action was crawl*ing* at the time, only to find that the market moved 100 pips in the wrong direction by the time you got back.

Remember there are no take backs and cry*ing* in trad*ing*. Nobody cares! It is up to you to do the right things. Control the controllable, there is going to be enough to worry about along the way.

## THREE REASONS FOR FAILURE AND A SIMPLE SOLUTION

We feel that there are three overwhelming reasons for the high failure rate for newcomers: Greed, desire for instant results, and moving too quickly to a professional account. For the first two, get to know yourself and understand when greed and instant gratification are in control. These emotional moods promote volatile results, as they always seem to overrule intellect and it should be the reverse where intellect overrules emotion. You get lured in and want to make that big money, but nobody prepares for a trade to go bad and there is no doubt that not only one trade but many will go bad in your career. We like to say that sanity is always tested at least five times a day when trading. Things don't always go smoothly and building a tolerance for this will be mandatory.

The third reason for a high failure rate is that newcomers start trading with the pros and risking professional dollars on day one. There is no "farm system" like there is in baseball. Most go from practice account to professional account with no intermediate training. Some newcomers can't even put themselves in the game because they are too scared to enter and fear failure. Panic hits when you aren't capable of handling your emotions when initially trading the professional valuations. One of the first questions we ask a new trader is how much money did you make per hour at your old job? We ask not to pry, but to get a feel for what the student is used to earning. One student in particular said that he made $50 per hour and saved enough to open an account. He expressed that it was his dream to make money in the markets. He said that he wanted to trade currency futures. We told him that it's a great market to trade, but you need to learn what can happen because you will face price fluctuations in mere seconds of double the amount of what you are used to making per hour. If you see a $100 disappear out of your pocket in a couple of seconds and you are only used to making $50 per hour, you are in for a rude awakening!

But there are some simple solutions you can employ to avoid more pain and failure. We highly recommended the novice trader start with micro pips at $0.10 and trade Spot Forex. Spot Forex is a market where traders buy and sell the current market value of the currency. Each minimum price movement (pip) per contract can be changed to fit the risk tolerance of the individual from as little as $0.10 up to the standard professional pip value of $10 per contract. Diluting the risk 100x down to $0.10 micro pips (not available in Currency Futures) would teach the student live lessons, and at the same time expose him to 100 times less the professional risk.

There is always uncertainty in the back of every trader's mind in the beginning. We teach newbies to protect their capital in the learning phase not by diversifying as most advisors preach, but by trading professional items at 100 times less than the normal risk. Greed and need starts from the cries of an infant and never stops through adulthood, so when a trader starts for the very first time there is a natural want for a taste of the bigtime. We just don't want you to get chewed up and spit out before you even have a chance to learn. The misfortunes of the majority go unnoticed as the headlines gravitate toward the best, and that is all the newbie can hear.

The money in your account is the life-line, and we want to protect it from what is essentially a kid in the candy store that just got a $50,000 spending limit. Build your skin and move up the ladder. This is the recipe that athletes go through from the farm system to the bigtime, not the other way around, and it should be no different in trading. Needless to say our new friend laughed, walking away saying. "I don't have the time for those kids' games." It showed a lot about his character when he came back to us and told us honestly he was down $50,000. He said, "I wished I would have listened to you in the beginning. I have a lot to learn about myself when I risk live money at those levels."

Things you should know about Mike is that when he began studying economics in college he was learning through the 1987 crash and it forced him to think about defense. Starting from his younger days, he even preferred playing defense in football from fourth grade through college. He just loved to deliver the blows on opponents rather than trying to avoid them on offense. Starting at the bottom of the totem pole in all actuality helped us as well in the beginning of our trading careers. We got a chance to develop a bit in the minor leagues with the low-end starting jobs. Not always pleasant, but when looking back we were thankful for the experience. Before we started trading we were runners and at times we saw the expressions on some of the faces that entered the building with a smile and left with an expression of sheer terror never to see them again. This hit home in a big way. We are our own back-stop and not a bank, so we can't count on a bail-out should things go wrong.

As we became traders, these defensive instincts served us well through the volatility of the first Gulf War in 1992. The base hit and double mentality that we both possess might have limited some of our upside during the expansionary times in 1993 to 1999, but the Tech Bubble and 9/11 at the turn of the century brought back some dark times in our economy. We don't hope for you to start your career in a dark economic cycle but it might not be a bad thing. The housing collapse and credit crunch blow-out at the end of 2007 and beginning of 2008 are constant reminders that things will never completely go smoothly forever. Markets can and will bring you to your knees and kick you in the back of the head if you let them. And just when you think you have seen it all comes the natural disasters with the rampant flooding in the mid-west and raging fires out West coupled with the 2011 Japanese earthquake and nuclear disaster. Don't forget the debt crisis ripping through Europe and the United States coming to a crisis point in August 2011.

If you don't think you need some defense in your game plan, think again. Defense wins championships! Playing solid defense puts you in position to score more often than you think. Playing defense may not be glamorous, but it has kept us controlling our own destiny and we would have it no other way. It may not seem like it today, but it has been said that we vastly overestimate what we can accomplish in a day but dramatically underestimate what we can accomplish in a year. In other words, base hits add up and build a lasting career while homerun hitters throw their back out in a couple of years and the majority that try to swing for the fence fail miserably and have a bad back to boot.

What has kept us around is that we act instinctually and without hesitation. There have been only a handful of eye-popping moments in our opinion in the 1990s but since the turn of the century when the computer era swept into our business we have seen dozens of jaw-dropping moments. Back in 2010 we witnessed the Dow drop 1,000 points and erase 750 of that loss in about 5 minutes during the "flash crash" and the EUR/JPY (Euro/Japanese Yen) basically covering the same distance dollar for dollar.

As volatility seems to increase every year, even base hits get bigger and bigger as volatility doubles, triples, and quadruples. Mike was playing his style and looking for his normal 25 to 50 pips on a trade, but couldn't help it when he made solid contact with a USDCHF August 11, 2011, long position. This was in the immediate days after the 600-point daily drop due to the debt issues and the Federal Reserve response to keep rates locked at historic lows until mid-2013. The violent drop on August 9, 2011, only

*Introduction to Today's Forex Market*

created a 1000-plus point rally in the aftermath over the next couple of weeks. In the chapters to follow, we will teach you how, when, where, and why Mike reversed to the long side in the days that followed.

We have come out on top over the years after being thrown in the professional fire, but the odds are against it should you succumb to greed before you are ready to handle it. Our goal is to move you off of a demo account into trading micro pips and working your way up to the professional ranks with a solid foundation and understanding of the true risks of this business. When Forex came on our radar in 2005 we instantly saw its potential to fit all risk appetites.

To illustrate our point further, we thought it would be helpful to take an in-depth look and compare Forex to other markets to show you its potential in all phases of your career from the beginner to the advanced stages.

# Comparing Forex to Other Markets

So what is the difference between Forex and currency futures? Since both the Chicago Mercantile Exchange (CME) Group and the banks refer to currency trading as Forex, there is plenty of room for confusion out there as both sides of the fence jockey for market share. The CME Group offers the Futures version (sometimes referred to as the Forward) and the Banks offer the cash version (sometimes referred to as the Spot). The products are similar in nature, but we want to briefly mention some of the main differences. Both sides offer an amazing venue for their clients, but to avoid any confusion throughout this book, when referring to Forex we are talking about today's current cash or spot value of the currency. When we are referring to Futures we will refer to them as currency futures.

Let's do our best to compare apples to apples. The *foreign exchange market* known informally as *Forex*, is an over-the-counter (OTC) trading instrument where *today's current cash value of one currency is traded for another*. It is the most traded market in the world, with an average turnover nearing $4 trillion per day. Unlike other financial markets, the Forex market has no central exchange. It operates through an electronic network of banks where corporations and individuals can access and trade one currency for another. The Forex market operates on a 24-hour basis across each of the world's major financial centers every day.

## CURRENCY FUTURES

A *futures contract* is a legally enforceable agreement to make delivery (a short position) or to take delivery (a long position) of a specific quantity and grade of a particular commodity during a designated delivery period (the contract month). Well over 90 percent of all futures positions are liquidated before delivery. If you are long or short you can close out your position or roll it into the next month before the expiration of the contract. Each commodity has different expiration months listed, but the most common is the March, June, September, December quarterly cycle. When we are in the month of December we are speculating on prices three months ahead of time in the March contract, when we are in March we are speculating on prices three months ahead of time in the June contract, and so on. They are both very similar in nature, with the main difference being that Forex traders buy/sell today's prices and Currency Future traders buy/sell prices that reflect what they believe them to be three, six, nine, or twelve months from now.

## FOREX HAS "CARRY INTEREST"

The other difference is that holding a Currency Futures contract overnight doesn't cost anything further or give you interest while holding the position (that is if you don't hold it past delivery upon expiration of the contract). Forex on the other hand has something called carry interest. If you buy the base currency, which is the first currency quoted in the pair, and sell the second currency in the pair (the quote currency), you may receive interest for holding the position past the new day deadline (2 PM PT, 4 PM CT, 5 PM ET) or you may get some taken from you. Banks charge or pay-out interest on Forex trades one time on trades held past the new day deadline normally on Monday, Tuesday, Thursday, Friday, and triple on Wednesdays due to the rollover, as no interest is charged or accrued on Saturday and Sunday.

The rule of thumb is that when you buy the base currency and it carries a higher interest rate than the quote currency you will in most cases receive interest only if you hold the position past the new day deadline. On the flip side if you sell the base currency that carries a lower interest rate than the quote currency, you will most often get charged interest after the new day deadline. The amount of interest received or charged is determined by the amount of leverage used when initiating the trade. Don't overwhelm yourself with carry interest as an individual trader in the beginning. It is important to know about it, if you begin to see yourself holding positions into the new trading day but more importantly you should be paying attention to how your overall position is doing compared to the price where you entered the trade. The rate at which price falls or rises every second while in the trade will create a much larger impact to the value of your account, while the carry interest added or subtracted most generally comes to about a pip per contract but happens only once per day.

*Comparing Forex to Other Markets*

**TABLE 2.1** RDS Trader Top 10 Forex Pairs

| | |
|---|---|
| Euro vs. U.S. Dollar | Australian Dollar vs. U.S. Dollar |
| New Zealand vs. U.S. Dollar | British Pound vs. U.S. Dollar |
| U.S. Dollar vs. Yen | U.S. Dollar vs. Canadian Dollar |
| Euro vs. Yen | Euro vs. Swiss |
| U.S. Dollar vs. Swiss | Euro vs. British Pound |

Overall both Forex and Currency Futures offer you, the investor, unique and important opportunities: Liquidity, leverage and the flexibility of capitalizing on *any* market condition in real time. The popularity of these instruments brings deep liquidity, allowing you to always be able to get in and out of the market in all conditions around the clock. Leverage allows you to participate in an investment of greater value using only a fraction of the cost (think home mortgage). All investments allow you to buy the product first and sell at a higher price, but Forex and currency futures make it easy to sell first without owning and buy back lower at a later time (see Table 2.1).

## UNDERSTANDING LEVERAGE

Forex trading really didn't become mainstream until the turn of the century for the retail trader. As traders and educators it came on our radar in 2005. The main reason we shifted our focus for new clients to start with Forex was because you could move from a demo or practice account to risking live for as little as $0.10 micro pips for each contract and scale up to the standard professional levels of $10 per pip each. We felt this was a great way for a new trader to transition smoothly up to the professional rates as opposed to being thrown into the fire as we were. A pip (in futures referred to as a tick) is the smallest increment prices can climb or fall. The CME Group Currency Futures quadrant does not allow a reduction to micro-pips as low as $0.10. They have tried to capture market share with their e-micro currency contract at $1.25 per tick (pip). Lack of liquidity has yet to make it a viable place to trade. They see thriving liquidity in the standard professional contracts like the EUR ($12.50 per tick per contract) but only seem to have captured about 10 to 15 percent of total volume when compared to Forex.

On average, currency pairs move approximately 100 to 200 pips per day (1 to 2 percent of the total value). On extreme days like in the aftermath of the debt ceiling expansion in the United States in August 2011, we saw some currencies move near 8 percent in one day. A contract or a lot is the term we use for how many we buy or sell (think share of stock). For example, if you bought one contract it would translate in approximately $10 to $20 of risk/reward exposure over a 24-hour span on a $0.10 micro pips setting, but at the standard professional rate at $10 per pip you would face $1,000 to $2,000 of risk/reward exposure on each contract bought or sold.

To understand pricing more fully you need to take a look at leverage. The highly leveraged Forex trading business is what newcomers dismiss. It can take you down in a hurry if you don't respect the fact that you are trading things of much higher value with little money down, but we as professionals love it because we don't have to put that much down to play instruments worth a much greater value. In short, you get a tremendous bang for your buck. After the Dodd-Frank ruling, U.S. Forex traders can trade currency pairs at 50-to-1 leverage. As seasoned traders this ruling was a bit much, but for the overall health and stability (if there is such thing) of the public sector it has made the markets safer. 50-to-1 leverage simply means that for every $50 of risk you need to put up $1 of margin. Margin is basically a side account or good faith money that in laymen's terms you are allowed to write checks (trades) on.

In Forex the standard professional currency pair worth is set at $100,000. This value is sometimes referred to as Unit size. For example if the EURUSD was at perfect parity (where 1 EUR nets 1 USD) the price would be 1.0000. Since each pip increment is 0.0001, this would mean counting backward that there would be 10,000 pips total worth for the pair. A $100,000 unit divided by 10,000 pips equals $10 per pip. With leverage set at 50 to 1 ($1 dollar down for every $50 of worth), this would mean that you would need at least $2,000 of margin (or $100,000 total value ÷ $50 leverage = $2000 margin) in your account. Now we don't live in a perfect world where one currency is equal to another. If the current EURUSD price was trading 1.5000 or 5000 pips above parity (equivalent to an extra $50,000 or units), you would need the $2,000 of margin (based at 1.0000) plus $1000 extra (based on the excess above 1.0000 or 0.5000) for a total of $3000 margin to hold the trade. In this example you would hopefully be maintaining an account balance with more than $3,000 because if you bought the pair and prices started to drop you would get a margin call, or on the computer platforms of today you will automatically be liquidated (forced exit) out of the trade or receive a margin call to offset the imbalance. At the very least

**TABLE 2.2** Forex EURUSD Micro versus EURUSD Currency Futures (assuming 100 pip range)

| Learning Phase | Micro Value | Risk/Reward |
| --- | --- | --- |
| Forex 1 contract | $0.10 to $1 pip | $10 to $100 |
| Futures 1 contract | N/A | N/A |

*Note:* $500 to $5,000 account size recommended

*Comparing Forex to Other Markets* **17**

**TABLE 2.3** Forex EURUSD Mini versus EURUSD E-Micro Currency Futures (assuming 100 pip range)

| Intermediate Phase | Mini-Range | Risk/Reward |
|---|---|---|
| Forex | $1 to $5 pip | $100 to $500 |
| Futures E-Micro | $1.25 tick | $125 to $250 |

*Note:* $5000 to $25,000 account size recommended

**TABLE 2.4** Forex EURUSD Standard versus EURUSD Currency Futures (assuming 100 pip range)

| Professional Phase | Standard Value | Risk/Reward |
|---|---|---|
| Forex | $10 pip | $1000 |
| Futures | $12.50 tick | $1250 |

*Note:* $50,000-plus account size

two times margin is in our opinion the absolute minimum you should carry in your account, but we feel $50,000 when trading professional valuations and $500 when trading micro fits better. This will allow you to trade comfortably up to 10 contracts on each account and give you the bang for your buck that you want. The beauty of Forex is that you can change the currency pair valuation from $100,000 units down to as little as $1,000 units or from $10 pips to $0.10 pips (see Tables 2.2, 2.3, and 2.4).

The goal is to get you to the professional phase valuations that Forex and Currency Futures offer, but Forex does a much better job of allowing you to grow and adjust at your own pace in the beginning and intermediate phases of your career. Even if you are the most seasoned trader, you will at times face a slump and being able to adjust the pip valuations is priceless.

We wouldn't alter the path we initially took to enter this business because all of our experiences were needed for our growth, but as traders and mentors we are here to help deliver what we have learned to help avoid some obstacles that will hinder your growth potential. We would have climbed that mountain a little easier if we had something like Forex at our disposal to guide us through the dollar valuations and price swings in the markets. Fully understanding what we were up against with real-time action but with lower values in the beginning would have knocked our knees fewer times. As we found the new edge for our students, we could help them keep their money intact while they learned. As their potential was revealed we then where able to teach techniques to play conservative when experiencing a slump (losses) and play more aggressively when things were running according to plan.

# CHAPTER 3

# Finding the New Edge

Controlling your ego is a valuable asset for a seasoned trader. You don't bet bigger when you are losing, you bet bigger when you are winning. If you watched the movie *Floored* (a documentary about how pit-trading lost to the computer) you can learn something from one of the featured traders, Greg Reba. Greg said something in the movie that in all actuality is a hidden trading gem when you put aside any of your initial thoughts when listening to Greg; he didn't come across as the most credible source. He simply talked about betting bigger when you are trading well. Most people have it backward and trade conservatively to protect their lead when they are up and trade bigger when they are down to get it back. This logic doesn't make any sense (and cents for that matter) when you think about it. In sports when a player is playing badly, they get benched so they don't take the whole team down. This is hard to do when the emotions of loss are flaring in your head! You just have to learn when to floor it and when to put on the brakes. The feeling in your gut will always give you a foreshadowing sign and if you haven't felt it yet you will at some point, so be on the look out.

Now you don't have to face $31.25-per-tick exposure per contract to get started like Mike did when he began trading 30-year bonds. Trading Futures required no less than $50,000 in a Treasury bill and $50,000 in a trading account to start. $100,000 in and not knowing for sure if you can do it is a huge risk. With Forex, you can put $500 in an account and play with dimes. You play the same game, same price movement as the pros, but now you start risking one hundred times less. Not as big of a gamble in the beginning with how Forex firms structure the playing ground. We have seen people blow through $50,000 or $100,000 and not know what hit them, so we were excited to see micro pips available to help people see how they would react emotionally to market movements with lower dollar values.

So many demo traders and newbie micro pip traders say "I will never risk 50 or 100 percent of my account if I was trading live and risking professional valuations." Our answer is always "Yes, you would!" The most brilliant minds working for top industry firms like AIG, Bear Stearns, and Lehman Brothers risked the farm and lost because they were blinded by greed, so no one is immune. In August 2011 you are seeing generations of ignorance on all our parts as the U.S. government teeters on default. If you voted, the finger points to you and if you didn't vote the finger still points to you. Remember that *emotion overrules intellect*. This doesn't' mean that you can't do it, because the choice always rests in your hands: Buy, sell, or get out.

Trade dimes and see who you are in the beginning. If you start the day with a $500 account and at the end of the day it's worth $250 or $100, it's time to adjust your behavior, and $500 is nothing compared to the value of the lesson you are learning had you been on professional valuations. Don't give your hard-earned dollars unnecessarily to the thing living inside your computer. Since we are all human we know that newbies will get sucked into the emotion in the beginning, so we wanted to teach new traders a lesson in responsibility in their decision making and at the same time learn to respect the dollars in their account. The market is always bigger, meaner, leaner, and in possession of unlimited resources.

Over the years we have seen powerful 6'5" men fold up like lawn chairs under signs of pressure while trading as we watched them hesitate with pure panic in their eyes as $1,000 bills drain from their accounts every blink.

Now we can sit with our students and tell them to be careful with countless warnings about the risks and to be prepared, but most don't really heed the warnings. It's funny how we have to touch the hot stove before realizing. "Show me the money!" they shout. When the panic hits and reality hits, they one day never come back. That doesn't do anybody any good. We truly want to help. Practice accounts do not prepare you for when you step in and start risking live dollars. It's night and day! You will hear time and time again throughout this book to start with lower dollar values and learn expensive lessons and gain experience of the reality of trading while it only costs you dimes. People come to us after spending $10,000 in education from some fly-by-night trading school and down $50,000 in their trading accounts. Often times some of the information given to these students was valid, but what many trading educators lack is the ability to help somebody through the rollercoaster of emotions they will feel. When the money gets too great, the decision-making ability deteriorates and the student quickly self-destructs. They get them starting on the e-mini S&Ps or bonds and throw them right in the big leagues way too soon, when they could have thrown them into a platform that provided the all-in-one ability to adjust to the minor-league valuations up to the big-league valuations. As they climb the ranks successfully they can move to any professional Forex, Futures, or Options market, but if they falter in the lower valuations at least the student has a chance to notice and stop before too much damage can be done with the majority of his or her money intact. Those that falter sometimes even realize that this is just a hobby and continue on low levels with a smile rather than do it in desperation in hopes of getting their $50,000 back.

When the majority of people that start trading wipe out their accounts, you start to scratch your head. As traders and educators we want to slow or stop that cycle completely. We know education is vital and time consuming, but the pressure of "life is short" takes hold, forcing so many to dismiss the learning curve like parking tickets. We had a friend who blew off so many parking tickets that one day he was going to give us a ride home but couldn't because he found the boot on his front tire. It's the same in trading. Don't ignore the short-term pain. Get in there and start learning. There will be a learning curve, but don't donate $100,000 to the market and then decide to get some help. Start with $500 and $0.10 pips to see if this professional game is for you. It is a much more realistic way to learn and grow.

## PRACTICE PATIENCE WITH CONTROLLED RAGE

Of course you can never truly prepare for what is going to happen in such an emotional fear-and-greed game, so being ready for action in our environment is much more like being a policeman or fireman rather than a nine-to-five employee. A policeman or fireman might not have anything to do for a large portion during his or her shift, but all of a sudden there is a call to action and he or she needs to be sharp and ready. How they react in those first crucial moments will be a matter of life and death. In trading we do not deal with life and death, but we do deal with financial life and death on our trades. We don't go starting fires just to participate, but we wait for the action to be set up properly to put ourselves in situations that produce the highest chance of success. In football, they call it controlled rage. Act with a clear mind when the whistle blows and drive your body through your opponent so he doesn't want to try that on you ever again. The only way you can act decisively is to prepare. Why do you think that in every competition, teams and individuals practice? It's so they can act instinctually. As a trade opportunity appears on our radar we act decisively and without hesitation. We hope this book will teach you to do the same.

## FOLLOW THE MONEY

As you get yourself under control and start humming, don't ever let your guard down because shifts appear and the money flow and popularity can and does move from sector to sector. You can't always just pay attention to yourself; you need to be aware of your surroundings, the economy, and your industry. Just when you think you've got it, the rug can get pulled from under your feet. An example of this is when Mike was watching an interview with all-time great wide receiver Jerry Rice about his Hall of Fame NFL career. To sum up he said that he always came into training camp thinking he wasn't the starter. He practiced like he played and studied his opponent and his game day and night. He lived it! You need to do the same in trading. It was funny when Mike heard this because he once told me that he goes into work thinking every day that he has zero dollars in his trading account. If he lost money, he felt that he wouldn't know how to pay it back. This helped him eliminate his fear of getting out of a losing trade as there was no choice, so to speak. He of course would have to answer to me as well. He did however make the mistake of not following the money at one point in his career. One of the best character traits about Mike is that when he makes a mistake he learns from it, etches it into his brain, and does it better the next time he is faced with a similar situation.

For instance, when the economy struggles like it did from 2001 to 2003 and again from 2008 to 2011, investors generally pull out of stocks and flock to secure returns of Treasury Bonds and gold, especially in extreme times. Traders call this *flight to quality*. The backing of the U.S. government Treasury Bonds is thought around the globe as the most secure, well that was before the downgrade in August 2011 from AAA to AA+, but nonetheless pretty secure. Gold holds a strong value in good economies, but especially in bad economies as it is used in many things from jewelry to computers and will always be worth something as it is a rare, hard-to-extract element on earth. As the economy improves the excess built into Treasury and gold prices reverse as investors bring money back to equities. You can see this in currencies as well. The U.S. dollar (USD) typically gets weak in struggling economies as interest rates get low and the dollar gains value as the economy strengthens and interest rates climb. This cycle and pattern has been seen time and time again.

Mike didn't follow the money back in 2001 when the U.S. Treasury Department decided to do something that wasn't expected, which was to discontinue auctioning 30-year bonds. It wasn't a surprise that the world

*Finding the New Edge*

was transitioning to the 10-year note as a standard, but not issuing the long bond was unexpected by all. Open interest shifted away from the 30 year and into the 10-year note and it happened overnight! On that day Mike should have packed his bags and moved to the 10-year pit. What held him back was that he was doing great in the 30 year and the thought that swirled in his head was why fix what isn't broke. What a naïve focus to have. We are here to make money and as a trader you need to have knowledge of this global economy and shift with the times. You don't see Warren Buffett playing only one stock his whole life and buying only one company. Get smart!! You need to be savvy enough to discover and learn what sectors move in tandem with each other and what sectors move opposite. We will cover this in more depth in the fundamental analysis chapter. Being armed with knowledge and confidence allows you to move freely to the hot sector of the time. As an investor, price movement means opportunity and those sectors being talked about bring liquidity which are the two best friends of traders.

## LEARN TO TRADE MORE THAN ONE MARKET

Being knowledgeable across all sectors was now the new breed of trader. Maybe it has always been necessary to know all of the markets, but with so much opportunity flowing on the floor why learn something else, well that is until the computer came along. Mike wasn't going to move slowly this time. So when the computer came along and started to take over our markets, Mike was one of the first rounds of traders to bring a hand-held computer in the 30-year bond pit. Traders around Mike didn't like it, but it was the new reality. As volume on the computer began to take away more than 50 percent of the action in the pits, the writing was on the wall. We began to accept change more readily and prepared ourselves with knowledge and confidence to move anywhere at a moment's notice. This freed our mind to be able to actually hear and see the clues that the world was telling us. When we realized how big Forex was, we listened and didn't hesitate!

Of course consistency didn't come easily here either. There was a new problem, which was shaking old patterns. Mike didn't have a problem picking the most liquid and most popular market, but the old habit of trading just one favorite market all of the time was not an easy pattern to break. Our students ask which was easier; trading in the pit or trading on the screen today. The answer is that there are advantages and disadvantages on both sides. The advantage of the pit was that you could see who wanted to buy and who wanted to sell and get a group consensus. You also could at times get trades from brokers that were selling the bid and buying the offer to gain an edge upon entry. The disadvantage of the pit was that you were always on stage; ridiculed when you made money and laughed at when you lost money. This wasn't a place to be shy when competing against a bunch of adrenalin junkies. It was like trying to grab a piece of pizza in a room full of NFL football linemen after a game. Trying to compete and get ahead of the pack in the pit at times forced you to enter into or take trades you didn't want, which at times turned out to be very costly.

When you trade on the screen you don't see who you are buying or selling to and you always are selling bids and buying offers upon entry. The advantage lies in the fact that you can shop from market to market very easily on the computer and find the best market to trade that is set up according to your strategy. On the screen, you never have to take things you don't want, which is a huge bonus. The problem with focusing all of your attention on just one market like you had to do in the pit is that it was not always set up the way you wanted it to be. Forcing trades on a market that is sending mixed signals becomes a huge problem financially and emotionally. Now you can easily sit in the comfort of your own home or office and turn off the mixed-looking market and tune in to the set-up market. Despite the fact that you have this type of control in today's screen-trading world, we often ask our students this question: Why do you force trades?

## DON'T FORCE TRADES

The answer lies in the fact that we all have been taught from the beginning to go to school, earn a degree, work hard, and don't get lazy. These are all noble gestures, but these thoughts are not always conducive to a trader's success. Sitting around waiting for a trade makes us anxious, because if we aren't trading, we aren't making money and if we aren't making money, we don't earn a living. The pressure builds so much that a forced trade is initiated when you are prepared to only trade your favorite market. Since the typical outcome of a forced entry in the end produces a negative result, we feel that this is burning unnecessary time, effort, and energy. Learn to build and add to your list of favorite markets, because as we have mentioned earlier money flows into and out of sectors freely, so be ready!

This is the exact reason why we began to apply our strategy to other markets. Our favorite Euro/U.S. dollar (EURUSD) may not be set up the way we want it to be today, but as we scan our list the Australian dollar/U.S. dollar (AUDUSD) might look better. Instead of forcing a trade when anxious about money on a market that looks iffy, channel that energy to search for another market first instead of pushing the button on the mixed-looking market. Our current Forex list has 27 pairs on it so we are ready, but we have narrowed the focus to 10 most liquid favorites: EURUSD, U.S. dollar/Japanese Yen (USDJPY), U.S. dollar/Swiss Franc (USDCHF), British Pound/U.S. dollar (GBPUSD), Euro/Japanese Yen (EURJPY), AUDUSD, U.S. dollar/Canadian dollar (USDCAD), New Zealand dollar/U.S. dollar (NZDUSD), Euro/British Pound (EURGBP), and Euro/Swiss Franc (EURCHF). This list wasn't just haphazardly picked as we do have some criteria. Price movement, liquidity, and tight pip spreads (difference between bid/ask) were taken into consideration before a pair moved to the favorites list. Getting into any market is easy, but getting out in any condition—good or bad—is vital. Huge spreads and lack of interest can make things a bit dicey when trying to exit a losing trade that nobody wants to play. After our list was formed we religiously created a game plan each day before trading so we were prepared to move from market to market. When price action revealed a direction (explained in our five core rules), we confidently scanned through our list and took on the market that we felt would give us the highest percentage chance of success according to our strategy.

The edge used to be to trade one market in the pit trading era. We know that there are educators out there today teaching you to just focus on one and get good at one. That might be a good strategy in theory in the beginning, but in reality it will not serve you well as money moves into and out of sectors. Don't get caught without a chair to sit on. In the pit trading era you were able to focus on one market and buy at the price where other buyers wanted to buy and sell where others wanted to sell; the pit edge! As brokers went to the market and bought the sell price or sold at the market to the bid price of locals many times throughout the day, one market was a perfect fit because there were plenty of opportunities each and every day. We paid for the right to have this edge with exorbitant seat ownership or lease fees. Mike at one time was paying more than $5000 per month for the seat lease to trade 30-year bonds. We taught some oil traders at one point that were paying $18,000 per month. It may seem like a hefty price to pay, but it was worth it as the opportunities were plentiful.

Computer trading doesn't come with those high seat and lease costs, but it does come with other costs that don't feel like much at first but when you add them up at the end of the month you will be surprised. Trading only one market on the computer can become a nightmare, because not only is it at times not set up well but also you don't know how many or who is doing the buying and selling at the moment. This begins to create feelings of uncertainty and lack of trust. You also tend to be the one going to the market and buying offers and selling bids like brokers. Giving up the edge carries a spread cost coupled with a commission generally charged on each trade. This all helps us to conclude that it is vital to be knowledgeable about the different sectors and trade more efficiently and effectively by scanning through a list of markets and choose the one that looks the best. The *Computer Trading Edge* is using your execution platform and Internet for what is was designed to do, which is offering you the ability to shop every market from your home or office to find the best deal possible. You don't have to physically travel to all of the stores before making a decision, as you can quickly surf the trading net.

## KNOW YOUR COMPUTER COMPETITION

Our style offers an efficient methodical approach that finds between one and four opportunities per day. The majority of the time we tend to find one solid opportunity when scanning through our list of favorites. Some of you on the other hand might want to trade one market and trade multiple times in high frequency. We are not here to tell you that it is wrong by any means to go this route. Just be sure to weigh the costs with your pocket book. Buying the next great trading software can leave you with continual costs, forcing you to beg with a tin cup outside of your office to meet the rigors of keeping it updated and running like a pure race horse. There are many that find great success in playing the high-frequency game. The idea is to take the educational concepts provided in this book or from your preferred educator and apply them to fit your style. Learning isn't about buying a recipe or a piece of software and thinking that's all you need. Peak performers take the concepts from their mentors and mold them to fit their style. Whether you choose our methodical one-to-four opportunities per day approach or take the high-frequency route, it is important for you to know your competition.

## HIGH-FREQUENCY TRADING

As our culture craves speed, computer trading has bred the high-frequency trader. What is it? It is basically black box or algorithmic trading using computer speed that picks up market discrepancies that a human finger or eye alone cannot catch. This type of trading can manipulate prices so ferociously in a blink and picks pockets leaving some to scratch their heads in disbelief and others in financial ruin. It's not human; it's a program made by a human but implemented by the computer.

Supposedly it costs anywhere from $10,000 to $25,000 minimum per month to have your computer tweaked with cranked-up connectivity piped into the exchange or network of banks that gives you turbo speed. It is being blamed for the Flash Crash in May 2010 which was supposedly started by a huge mutual fund dump that the high-frequency systems picked up on quicker than any trader did and whipsawed the market to take instant profit. It caused the Dow to drop more than 1,000 points and snap back 750 in about five minutes. Price movement at this pace doesn't surprise us these days, which is why we set ourselves up with our fingers on the pulse of the action and real-time access to the markets. High-frequency opportunities look so attractive, but for the times you catch the move there are just as many times that you wish that you could pull the plug on this inhuman type of program. We have heard just as many if not more horror stories about the computer going wild and not shutting off and repeatedly whipsawing many accounts to instant debit. Leaving for work with your program humming with a $50,000 account only to come home with a margin call stating that you owe $20,000, no thanks! We would rather have full discretion about the when and where every day, but use the computer software to help our inadequate speed as humans. We may not catch every move, but we do have solid success and our money intact.

Another issue to face with high-frequency trading is the rate at which technology changes. What you just paid thousands for today may not work tomorrow due to frequent upgrades. It's just like buying a TV; as soon as you go home with a plasma screen, they come out with an LCD flat screen that is just as good for a fraction of the cost. From VHS to DVD to Blue-ray technology, improvements will always plague those that don't have the pocket book to keep up, so just make sure about your overhead when getting started in the high-frequency arena.

The biggest upcoming potential threat to high-frequency trades is industry regulation. The old school, regulated firms are taking notice and fighting back. The industry governing bodies are looking into this type of trading and debating on what should be allowed and what shouldn't. Some of the biggest, best, and oldest market-maker firms are crying very loudly wanting high-frequency trading to be placed under the same scrutiny and ground rules as they are. Firms like Introducing Brokers (IBKR) have to make markets under industry guidelines and are threatening to pull out unless the playing field gets leveled. Under government regulations market makers are required to supply bids and offers across multiple markets to provide liquidity at all times no matter what the conditions. High-frequency traders are not required to make markets across the board, so they can hit and run with lightning speed to produce enormous, quick profits. Since steroid injected computers and greed have no conscience, now not only can a firm be wiped clean, an entire market or economy can be left destroyed. We may not like regulation, but the computer trading arena does need a global referee, if you will.

The high-frequency traders (or should we call them high-frequency programmers) are claiming they are providing more liquidity to the markets. Who to believe? Hardly any of these high-frequency trading firms are willing to comment publicly on their data connections, or anything for that matter. They are super secretive and they can be right now because they are not highly regulated. Believe us, we are not complaining, because we know and understand the risks involved, but we do think the industry needs some regulation in this area. We often debate why competitive advantages are given to some and not to others like we saw initially with the Dodd-Frank ruling. Before the ruling, Forex had a slight advantage and after the ruling Futures seemed to have the advantage. Why not level it for all and let the best product win or let them co-exist side by side?

In our opinion market makers like IBKR are needed to help new and emerging markets grow and become mainstream. This is how great products like the 30-year bonds and the S&P 500 futures markets were built and the reason why they thrive today. A continual bid and ask provided by a market maker in all conditions at all times breeds stability and brings a necessary ingredient for the markets' success: open interest.

Since there is always a buyer and a seller out there, another way to look at high-frequency traders is not as the culprit, but as the ones bringing a new and innovative way to provide healthy competition for the market makers. The problem is that it doesn't seem right to have one team abide by industry regulations and another do whatever they please. It's like the debate about the proper valuation of the Hong Kong Dollar. Some from the United States feel that China artificially pegs its currency and holds it at attractive levels to benefit themselves with no regard to its trading partners around the globe. China argues that the United States does the same. Let the trade wars and the rage of the machines continue.

Big money players are going to have to duke it out and our only real thought about the whole thing is this: We have been in the business since 1989 and we have seen massive trading firms collapse, only to open doors to the next big one. As one collapsed another firm came on, and so on and so on. We have seen (and traded with) the biggest and the best traders in the S&P500 futures and 30-year bond pits only to see them taken over by the next biggest and best traders ever. We have seen the entire way trading has been conducted for more than 100 years be overtaken by computers (the next best thing) causing a mass exodus from the trading floors. Many open-outcry exchanges have closed down and the Chicago Mercantile Exchange (CME) Group is holding on to its floor traders by a thread. So our point is that we are ever changing and evolving in this industry. Some will make it and others will not. High-frequency trading may be the next biggest and best thing, but something else will come along.

Where does all of this leave the individual investor? We wholeheartedly believe that the small investor still can win with a decent computer and an Internet connection. We are here to help you understand who you are

*Finding the New Edge*

playing against and when and how a specific style works best. The markets are large and we must respect that, as we said earlier. Risk management, whether using a high-frequency style or methodical swing approach, is the name of the game and we are grateful that we are disciplined enough to survive and thrive.

## OUR FIRST OBSTACLE WITH FOREX

As traders and educators since 1993 and seeing the success and the collapse of traders and firms alike, we were excited when the Forex industry began opening its doors to the retail trader. The high risks were still there for all, but we saw the benefits for the new trader to transition more smoothly from practice account to live account. Banks began pouring money into Forex in droves in 2004. Maybe it's because they lost their battle to control the Futures markets. They seemed to be in constant battle for domination with the Chicago Board of Trade (CBOT) and CME at the time. Maybe in their boardrooms they said if we can't beat 'em, create something better! We will build our product (the cash market) but make our game bigger along the way. Banks and Forex firms control 80 to 90 percent of all currency trading and the CME Group has captured 10 to 20 percent at best so far. Banks dominate control of the currency markets and they are always trying to move in to the other markets like the equity indexes and metals arena. Banks hold the cash version of these products and call them Contract for Difference (CFDs). Industry regulation to date has kept them out of the U.S. Futures turf but overseas they are freely traded. It will be interesting how it all unfolds, but early lessons learned to follow the money keep us ready to move if necessary and hopefully our story will prepare you to do the same.

Forex was in the cowboy era in 2004, as this was the time it really started getting popular and offered in full force to the retail public. There were some rude awakenings for us early on as we personally got slammed with Refco FX posing as a legitimate registered company when they went bankrupt in 2005. With change comes gut punches. Dust yourself off and get back in the game. It was like when Mike's eighth grade football coach told him to go rub his injured thumb in the mud and get back in the game. Mike finished the game shaking his hand in pain only to find that his thumb was broken when he got it x-rayed later that day. It's okay to make mistakes just as long as your mistakes aren't so damaging that you can't ever come back.

We all felt safe with Refco; they were the biggest Futures and Forex company on the planet at the time. Futures accounts were safe under the Securities and Exchange Commission (SEC) and Commodity Futures Trading Commission (CFTC) protection, but our Forex accounts didn't fall under that same protection. Futures accounts, which were thought to be be the safest in the land are now under fire as well near the end of 2011 with the MF Global collapse. Were we pissed about Refco back in 2005? Hell, yeah!! Did it sting? Absolutely!! But in the end we still knew that Forex was a perfect vehicle for people to learn with micro pips. When Refco went under it carried huge ramifications in our industry, not much different than what happened with AIG, Lehman Brothers, and Bear Stearns in 2008 and of course the U.S. debt crisis that came to a head in August 2011 on a much larger scale. We have survived the craziness to date because we are traders and fully aware of the hazards of this industry. Thankfully we didn't carry all of our eggs in one basket. When you are your own back-stop financially with nobody to turn to if things go bad, you always play respectfully.

We of course welcomed industry regulation over the years since the 2005 Refco debacle. Some of the legislation in 2010 was in our opinion a bit harsh as we have stated for experienced traders, but it's hard to blame politicians for passing the Dodd-Frank Reform Act across all markets. It actually does promote more safety and accountability, which is a good thing.

Not only did we have the experience of seeing firms fall, being caught in the middle of one, but at one time Mike saw a trader try and take somebody's spot in the pit one day and physically get launched out of it. He got thrown off the top step pretty hard. He never came back! Change can be painful, but in reality it is just nature's way of telling you that you are growing. It's funny sitting in a comfortable office these days watching computer monitors when I think of when Mike used to come home with stories of how he was so jammed in the old bond pit; bodies were pressed so tightly together that it was enough to lift his feet off the ground. It was so ridiculous at times that you just had to laugh. We apologize in advance for the over share here but if somebody just so happened to be gassy that day, you could actually feel it on your body.

Why subject yourself to this? High stakes adrenalin all having to do with money was the answer. We got caught up in it but never lost our head. Do we miss the pit? At times we do, but the comforts of our office and playing different markets is the new fun.

The office is now quiet and you watch numbers and charts more intensely, but the emotions mentally and physically remain the same. We at times laugh when we find that we are sweating and haven't moved off of our chairs. Our survival recipe was to be the Tony Gwynn of trading: base hits and doubles. Refco just gave us a little wake-up reminder along the way. As we said to our pit trading students back in the day and what we continue to preach to our screen trading students today; "Learn to play defense; It's not how much you make; It's how much you don't lose." The closing message at the end of our e-mails and classes is always: "Trade strong, trade smart but always have enough to come back and trade tomorrow!!

## GROW RESPONSIBLY WITH FOREX

After knowing a bit more about our background and move to Forex we thought we would bring up one further point about the beauty of being able to adjust the valuations of the pip. Student always ask; How do I grow trading Forex when I start with dimes in the beginning? Students always want the bigtime immediately. We don't blame them! The first reason we got involved in this business is to make a ton of money. The sky is the limit and better yet, you as the individual control your own destiny; you are your own boss!! The words of Les Brown ring in our ears when he says that he would rather "go out climbing a hill rather than sliding down a hill." Don't expect to get a helicopter lift to the top of the hill when you start. In other words start dreaming big, but get climbing. With no guarantees of success on any journey the flip side of the coin is that we know the sky can come crashing down. To hedge ourselves we must move at a pace that is within our grasp and at the same time tests our edge and willingness to grow. How can we treat the markets and our money respectively and still grow?

There are three main reasons for us to get you off of the one-lot and $0.10-pip mentality and get you as soon as possible thinking bigger. First as you know, the minimum amount that you can buy or sell is one lot or contract. A one lot isn't going to do it because it is an all-in, all-out mentality and it breeds limited upside potential. When there is plenty of volume for you to trade more than one, you need to take advantage of the upside possibilities and match it with the potential that is within your grasp.

The second reason is that the financial market is a very dynamic animal. It ebbs and flows as well with public sentiment (fear and greed), interest rate movement, geo-political events, natural disasters, and so on. We can never fully predict what will happen. In 2008 nobody was predicting that Lehman Brothers and Bear Stearns were going to be extinct or in 2011 Democrats and Republicans alike would almost bring our nation to the brink of default. Or that Greece and Spain were going to be rated as junk. All of the uncertainty means that you are not going to be right every time. You may need to get out and start over or momentarily take some profit and let some contracts run in order to manage your risk along the way. The one lot is extremely inflexible and very limiting in an unknown environment. You are either all in or all out. Did you ever get into a trade with a one lot and take a small profit, because you were waiting for hours and got frustrated as it came up short of your desired objective? Yeah, and as soon as you took profit, the market raced to its intended target, leaving you kicking and screaming. How about this one: You got in with a one lot and the market just missed your objective and it turned around and stopped you out for a loss. Teeth are clenching just thinking about it!!

The third reason is that you can trade more contracts with Forex and at the same time not risk the farm in the learning phase. As we have mentioned earlier, you have the ability to alter the pip-per-contract value from $0.10 to $10. This is 100 times less the standard professional rate. Most educators and firms get you trading 1 standard professional contract to start. We get you to build your tolerance up to 100 contracts at $0.10 per pip or the equivalent of 1 standard professional lot (100 contracts × $0.10 = $10 per pip). If something happens that shifts prices temporarily in the wrong direction with the 100 lot, you can take off a portion or half to minimize risk and as things turn back favorably simply add contracts back to the idea.

This approach helps you in two ways: It increases your flexibility and profitability during the learning curve and at the same time begins to prepare you to trade and handle 100-lot increments. Once you know how to handle this amount of contracts you in a sense are teaching yourself ahead of time how to handle 100 lots when you eventually move to the professional $10-per-pip rate. If you initially start with $10-per-pip valuations and can only handle one at a time, you are not teaching yourself how to be flexible or ready when the time is right to move forward and think big. Thinking with foresight and trading 100 micro contracts will give you a head start to achieving your goals and becoming financially independent.

## BECOME AN INDEPENDENT THINKER AND DECISION MAKER

Before getting into our strategy, we want to make one final point on the need for you to become an independent thinker and decision maker. We all need a mentor in the beginning, but many rely on their mentors like a drug. That doesn't serve anybody's interest in the long run. You must be prepared for anything and everything as you can get picked clean in these markets! You had to have some thick skin in the pit-trading era and it hasn't changed much in the computer trading era we face today. Price action still goes up or down, but price flow is amped up with computer speed. We just don't stand for a living anymore; we watch the action from monitors and enter trades via software that pipes into exchanges and banks around the globe.

It often surprises us that most prospective traders come with an unbalanced approach. Some come with a trading plan but don't know how to use the software to implement the strategy. Some know how to use the software but don't have a plan of how to attack the markets. Some need training with both. There is one common thread that binds us all, which is the desire to push the buttons ourselves.

In 1993, as expected Mike was pretty green in the beginning and relied heavily on the support and resistance numbers offered by another analyst on the trading floor. He had a huge following. The analyst didn't teach us; he just gave his target points for the session. Mike was doing his own analysis at the time but just wasn't confident enough yet to use it as his primary source for live buy/sell decisions. One day the analyst didn't show up for work. He went on vacation and didn't make arrangements to deliver his report while he was gone. Uh, oh. Mike was left blind and had to make his own calls. A strong sense of unease swept over his body. It felt like the teacher just slammed a pop quiz and he didn't do the homework. Never again would he put himself in that situation. Mike has been thrown into the fire in other areas of his life before and has come out on top each and every time and this was not going to be any different. The feeling of unease is in actuality one of life's precious gifts. You just need to get over the fear. It's funny how life puts you in situations and tells you specifically what you need to do. This was one of those times. Mike has done his own homework ever since that day and hasn't missed a day since.

This book aims to deliver that knowledge and create a bridge for you to walk across the volatile currency markets to success. We look to create independent thinkers and decision makers that can act with precision and without hesitation. Computerized markets move at lightning speed, so having a pre-planned routine with a discretionary approach will make the difference between winning and losing. We will present you with a unique trading methodology called the Rotating Directional System (RDS).

RDS is a rule-based discretionary trading methodology that establishes risk management first. Our style offers the trader a trend-side philosophy that predicts time and price objectives using counter-trend reversals as a guide for entries, exits, and overall worth of the trade. As prices reach a specific zone objective, new rotation significance is placed on this area. As you learn how we combine a fundamental approach with the technical timing zones, you will find it gives you (the trader) an overall updated directional sense of what can be expected for upcoming price action. Foresight not hindsight! It should be noted that we have successfully applied this approach to treasuries, equity indexes, grains, metals, energies, and now currencies.

This approach combines both technical and fundamental concepts to help you not only have the confidence to buy or sell but also provide you with the fuel and expertise to time the idea with precision and accuracy. We will sum up our approach with what gives us the conviction to buy or sell with Fundamental Analysis, time the idea with a homework rule coupled with four intra-day technical swing timing rules and put all of the pieces of the RDS strategy together. No strategy has any merit unless you review, so at the end of the book we will offer performance evaluation and peak performance tips to help create the longevity and consistency you seek in the markets today, tomorrow, and for a lifetime to come.

# CHAPTER 4

# The Long and Short of Fundamental Analysis

Mom always said to look both ways before crossing the street. This advice still holds true, even in the financial markets. There are two prime schools of thought when studying the art of trading Forex: *Fundamental Analysis* and *Technical Analysis*. This chapter will focus on the fundamental side of trading or what we consider the side that strengthens our opinion to go long or short. As we get into the technical side in the later chapters we will focus on what technical indicators do best, which is to help timing.

Fundamental analysts use economic data, government policy, and more importantly Federal Reserve Policy when trying to forecast future price movements in a specific currency pair. There are many important fundamental events each month, but the two most important that receive the most attention and press are the key Federal Open Market Committee (FOMC) interest-rate policy-decision meetings that occur eight times per year and the employment data that is released the first Friday of every month. These reports create bulls and bears to react on the strength or weakness of the report as each currency pair adjusts to where the data suggests prices will land. Typically most of the Forex software used to enter and exit trades provides a real-time news feed that alerts you with the figures at the key times these reports are released. Watching market news networks like CNN, CNBC, or the Bloomberg channel to name a few will provide you with additional insights on economic conditions. We have put together our fundamental approach to economic events in the following pages, which have proven to be very effective in our trading.

## PUT YOUR MONEY WHERE YOUR MOUTH IS

We have placed our approach successfully on many markets over the years, treasuries, equities, metals, energies, and grains and we felt why should this be any different with Forex? Well, it wasn't. Simply speaking price can do one of two things in any market, go up or go down. The emotions of the traders in all markets are the same; the only adjustment to make is to get familiar with the different speeds and pip values, as they often vary from market to market. Until the powers that be change the up and down only rhythm of price and the world population shifts into a different range of emotions to something other than the fear and greed spectrum, we will attack the markets in the same manner as we did from day one. The only real shift made over the years is to the computer. A computer is now a necessity, not a luxury.

You will need to learn and digest what each report means to ensure that you act instinctually through employing some simple preparation techniques. As a report nears its actual release, we get bombarded by all the news sources' and analysts' opinions about the upcoming release. When the releases hit, prices are going to fluctuate one way or another and sometimes even violently. Theory is only part of fundamental analysis. What people most often forget is the fact that those textbooks they read are only one dimension. We are emotional human beings buying and selling. This forced us to recognize that understanding theory is important, but equally important is to know something about the economic policy decision makers. As the decision makers speak or act they truly can bring chaos to the market in moments. The new computer trader of today sometimes doesn't understand the anxiety that these reports bring. We watched so many traders get so revved up before these reports that you could see and at times smell the tension in the air. If you run marathons, think of the start of the race. We always used to joke that it's only a minute out of our lives. The problem is that the minute can create fortunes or financial ruin.

## KNOW YOUR ECONOMIC CALENDAR

Many ask us how to minimize the internal tension felt before these reports. First, it is mandatory to thoroughly prepare for events prior to their release so that no matter what happens you will be able to act instinctually rather than fumble through, wasting valuable time. The biggest difference between 1989 and today is that all markets are bigger, faster, and on steroids (the computer). We light-heartedly refer to the lessons taught along the way as our doctoral dissertation from Hard Knocks University. We had the market's best teacher, Professor Losing Real Money.

The time of each report is posted well in advance, so it is important to build the habit of checking the economic calendar every day. You can find a list of these reports at our web site, complete with links to the definitions of each and why investors care about these events (www.rdstrader.com/reports). We have inserted tables to help you prepare and learn them all or brush up on the ones that you don't know. All reports are important in the end, but as we have said the two most widely anticipated reports that we will focus on in this chapter are the FOMC Meetings and the Employment Report. See Table 4.1.

It is also vital that you know the players as they sometimes make surprise appearances throughout each month. Be sure you are aware of the players on the Federal Reserve Board and know the names of each Federal Reserve Bank President (Table 4.2).

Don't forget about government officials, as they can rock the markets on a moment's notice. Obviously the President is the important member here, but one that quite often creates volatility in the financial markets is the Treasury Secretary (Table 4.3).

We mention all these key events and players because when you are fortunate to have been around in the markets as long as we have you will find preparing and knowing who, when, where, and why will help alleviate some of the anxiety faced while trading so you can focus and concentrate on the opportunity at hand.

Whenever a government official or Federal Reserve Member pops up in the news wires or appears on TV, pay attention! If it just so happens that you find it was simply a dedication of new flowers in the Rose Garden, go back about your business, but don't ever initially dismiss their appearance.

What makes the timing of getting to know events and policy makers sooner rather than later is the fact that you can study the effects of some of the most monumental policy decisions from 2008 to 2011 that we have ever seen in our history. We are quite sure this time period has dropped the jaws of economic professors around the globe and may begin to rewrite a few text books. The U.S. government and the Federal Reserve's actions were due to the economic collapse that is rivaling the Great Depression in the 1930s. The taste for over-spending as a country and around the world came to a boiling point during this stretch. The housing collapse and credit crunch in 2008 kicked it off in the United States and abroad.

Before we breakdown what direction this generally drives currency pairs, let's first outline the pivotal moments. From reading the Federal Reserve policy statements (released eight times per year) you will find that they started their Quantitative Easing Package in response to the economic turmoil that boiled over at the onset of 2008. The earlier round of

**TABLE 4.1** Key Economic Report Times (Central)

| | |
|---|---|
| ADP Employment 7:15 AM CT | Housing Starts 9:00 AM CT |
| Beige Book 1:00 PM CT | Import and Export 7:30 AM CT |
| Chicago PMI 9:00 AM CT | Industrial Production 8:15 AM CT |
| Construction Spending 9:00 AM CT | International Trade 7:30 AM CT |
| Consumer Confidence 9:00 AM CT | ISM Mfg. Index 9:00 AM CT |
| Consumer Price Index 7:30 AM CT | ISM Non-Mfg. Index 9:00 AM CT |
| Consumer Sentiment 8:55 AM CT | Jobless Claims 7:30 AM CT |
| Durable Goods Orders 7:30 AM CT | Motor Vehicle Sales—varies |
| EIA Petroleum Status 9:30AM PM CT | New Home Sales 9:00a AM CT |
| Empire State Mfg. Surv. 7:30 AM CT | Pending Home Sales Index 9:00 AM CT |
| Employment Cost Index 7:30 AM CT | Pers. Inc. and Outlays 7:30 AM CT |
| **Employment Situation 7:30 AM CT** | Philadelphia Fed Survey 9:00 AM CT |
| Existing Home Sales 9:00 AM CT | Producer Price Index 7:30 AM CT |
| Factory Orders 9:00 AM CT | Productivity and Costs 7:30 AM CT |
| **FOMC Meeting 1:15 PM CT** | Retail Sales 7:30 AM CT |
| FOMC Minutes 1:00 PM CT | S&P Case Shiller HPI 8:00 AM CT |
| GDP 7:30 AM CT | Treasury Budget 1:00 PM ET |
| Housing Market Index 9:00 AM CT | Treasury Interntl. Capital 8:00 AM CT |
| Chain Store Sales—varies | Leading Indicators 9:00 AM CT |
| Challenger Job-Cut 6:30 AM CT | MBA Purchase Apps. 6:00AM CT |
| Chicago Fed Ntl. Actvy. 7:30 AM CT | Money Supply 3:30 PM CT |
| Consumer Credit 2:00 PM CT | Monster Employment 5:00 AM CT |
| Corporate Profits 7:30 AM CT | NFIB Bus. Optimism 6:30 AM CT |
| Current Account 7:30 AM CT | Quarterly Services Survey 9:00 AM CT |
| E-commerce Retails Sales 9:00 AM CT | Rebook 8:00 AM CT |
| EIA Natural Gas 9:30 AM CT | Richmond Fed Mfg. 9:00 AM CT |
| Farm Prices 2:00 PM CT | State Street Confidence 9:00 AM CT |
| Fed Balance Sheet 3:30 PM CT | Treas. Bill, Note-Yr. Auc. noon CT |
| FHFA House Price Index 9:00 AM CT | Treasury Refunding 8:00 AM CT |
| FOMC Meeting Begins1:15PM CT | Treasury STRIPS 2:00 PM CT |
| ICSC - Goldman Store Sales 6:45AM CT | Wholesale Trade 9:00 AM CT |

*Source:* www.econoday.com

quantitative easing is generally referred to as QE1. Between December 2008 and March 2010, the U.S. Federal Reserve purchased $300 billion of longer-term Treasury securities, $175 billion in housing-related agency (Fannie Mae and Freddie Mac) debt, and $1250 billion of agency-guaranteed mortgage-backed securities. In the statement released after its November meeting, the Federal Reserve announced a buy-back program of $600 billion of longer-term Treasury securities by the end of the second quarter of 2011, in what is known as another round of Quantitative Easing (QE2).

## The Long and Short of Fundamental Analysis

**TABLE 4.2** Federal Reserve Board Members and Bank Presidents 2011

| Federal Reserve Board | Federal Reserve Bank Presidents |
|---|---|
| Chairman: Ben S. Bernanke | New York: William C. Dudley |
| Vice Chair: Janet L. Yellin | Philadelphia: Charles I. Plosser |
| Kevin M. Warsh | Cleveland: Sandra Pianalto |
| Elizabeth A. Duke | Richmond: Jeffrey M. Lacker |
| Daniel K. Tarullo | Atlanta: Dennis Lockhart |
| Sarah Bloom Raskin | Chicago: Charles L. Evans |
| **Federal Reserve Bank Presidents** | St. Louis: James Bullard |
| Dallas: Richard W. Fisher | Minn.: Narayana Kocherlakota |
| San Francisco: John C. Williams | Kansas City: Thomas Hoenig |

*Source:* www.federalreserve.gov

**TABLE 4.3** U.S. Government Officials 2011

| U.S. Cabinet Members | U.S. Cabinet Members |
|---|---|
| President Barack Obama | Housing Secretary: Shaun L.S. Donovan |
| Vice President: Joseph R. Biden | Transportation Secretary: Ray LaHood |
| Secretary of State: Hillary Rodham Clinton | Energy Secretary: Steven Chu |
| Treasury Secretary: Timothy F. Geithner | Education Secretary: Anne Duncan |
| Defense Secretary: Robert M. Gates | Veterans Affairs Secretary: Eric Shinseki |
| Justice: Eric. H. Holder Jr. | Security: Janet A. Napolitano |
| Interior Secretary: Kenneth L. Salazar | Chief of Staff: Bill Daley |
| Agriculture Secretary: Thomas J. Vilsack | EPA: Lisa P. Jackson |
| Commerce Secretary: Gary F. Locke | Management/Budget: Jacob J. Lew |
| Labor Secretary: Hilda L. Solis | UN Ambassador: Susan Rice |
| Health/Human Services Secretary: Kathleen Sebelius | Economic Advisor: Austan Gollsbee |

*Source:* www.whitehouse.gov

We also saw a fierce, dragged-to-the wire debate on Capitol Hill between Democrats and Republicans to implement a debt-ceiling increase coupled with a much-needed debt-reduction package. An oxymoron but that is what was on the table. August 2, 2011 a package was finally agreed upon by Congress and the Senate but it came up way short on spending reduction in the years to come according to Standard and Poor's rating service. They dropped our perfect AAA status to AA+. When we hit August 9, 2011, the Federal Reserve released a statement calling for a cap in interest rates until mid-2013. This leaves interest rates locked at historic lows of 0.25 to 0 percent. A first-of-its-kind statement locking down rates for two years essentially makes the two-year note a fixed T-bill.

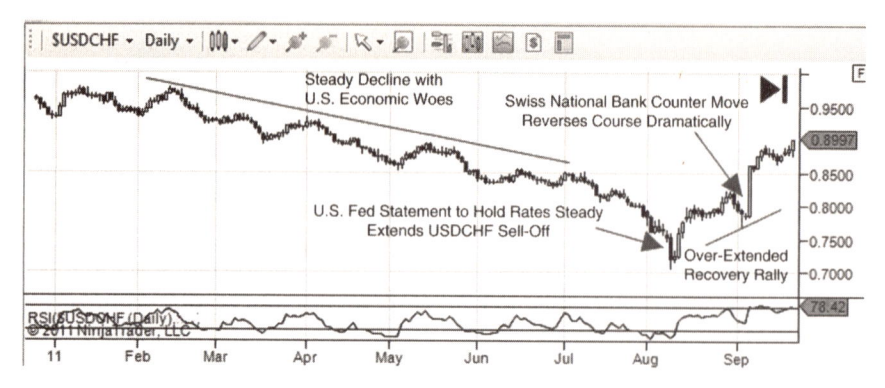

**FIGURE 4.1** USDCHF 2011

With big events come big decisions, and these decisions are creating historic volatility. As our policy makers inject money into our system, whether indirectly by lowering interest rates or directly with its Quantitative Easing Packages, it creates a weaker U.S. dollar (USD) outlook. When something is abundantly made available (USD) it makes common sense that it drops in value or price. Simple supply side economics: Abundant supply creates low prices and diminished supply boosts prices. Leading up to August 2011, a devaluing of the greenback was widely apparent. As far as volatility is concerned, after the decision to keep rates capped at historic lows by the Federal Reserve on August 9, 2011, we witnessed a 600-point drop with the U.S. dollar/Swiss Franc (USDCHF) (see Figure 4.1). The Swiss Franc (CHF) was the safe-haven play up to this point before the Swiss National Bank (SNB) stepped in weeks later with their own move to devalue the CHF to shake off the attraction to their currency.

## DECISION FALL-OUT

What does all of this mean for the U.S. dollar in the coming years? Now we can get into a fundamental debate with you or give you the traditional Democrat or Republican response and express all the things we feel are right and wrong with the debt decision, but there is too much talk. Some on one side of the fence feel the Fed QE1, QE2, and any further QE stimulation along with the U.S. government's appetite for borrowing are to blame, while others feel Europe, along with many other global leaders', excessive spending and borrowing are the culprit. You will even find some saying China is to blame for artificially pegging its currency to attract consumption of Chinese products. As people express their opinions, they always seem to finger point, as it turns into a he said/she said argument. We have heard politicians say what they believe and of course what they say, if implemented, will benefit their ideals. Debate is necessary in order to make a decision but the drama that the media fills our head with is enough to make it spin off. In the end, opinion—whether coming from an economist or the various media outlets—doesn't really make an impression on us. What has always been important is when the decision makers finally make a decision.

We have been saying for years that we have never met an investor that gets involved in the market with hopes of losing money, so recent price action is pretty revealing to help with upcoming buy/sell decisions of your own based upon what you know. When price moves, somebody bought and somebody sold; a decision has been made! Right or wrong becomes the only outcome when the game is on. What we get post entry is a big dose of reality.

In the aftermath, the bulls and the bears that react and make decisions to buy or sell from us is much like pitting Jordan's Bulls against Ditka's Bears. Sounds like a Saturday Night Live (SNL) skit: Farley choking on a steak bone having one of five heart attacks and Jordan's guest appearance dancing in a hula skirt. Ditka and "Da Bears" always seemed to win on that skit, but as we bring our light-hearted analogy to currencies there may be a silver lining to USD bulls. We don't mean to make it sound, but it looked a bit child-like to hear all of the political chest beating by both sides during the debate.

We think investors might be seeing a bright spot on the horizon for the bulls to shine as the USD seems to be on a bit of a comeback immediately following the debt ceiling drama (and yes, even a bit against the CHF). Higher deficits do not bode well for USD strength, but if spending and taxation get under control, a reversal may be in order in the years to come and it may be what side-lined and battered USD bulls have been waiting for. The typical response is that after all of the bad news is out in the open, the healing begins and reversals in trend are generally in order. Since we personally can't move the market ourselves, we have to rely on the market movers (governments, Federal Reserve, banks, and hedge funds) to help move prices to our desired spot. They can move the markets and it is up to us as individuals to decide which team we want to join (see Figures 4.2, 4.3, and 4.4).

Now don't take our word for it about a possible bull USD run; take a look at how price was reacting leading up to the debt ceiling decision (July) and the days after the decision was made (early August). See Figures 4.5, 4.6, and 4.7.

Yes, this of course can be just a small mini-run as the reality was that in the first days after the decision, the USD run was due in large part to

**FIGURE 4.2** Australian Dollar/U.S. Dollar (AUDUSD) Pre-Debt January to July 2011

**FIGURE 4.3** Euro/U.S. Dollar (EURUSD) Pre-Debt January to July 2011

**FIGURE 4.4** U.S. Dollar/Japanese Yen (USDJPY) Pre-Debt January to July 2011

*The Long and Short of Fundamental Analysis*      **43**

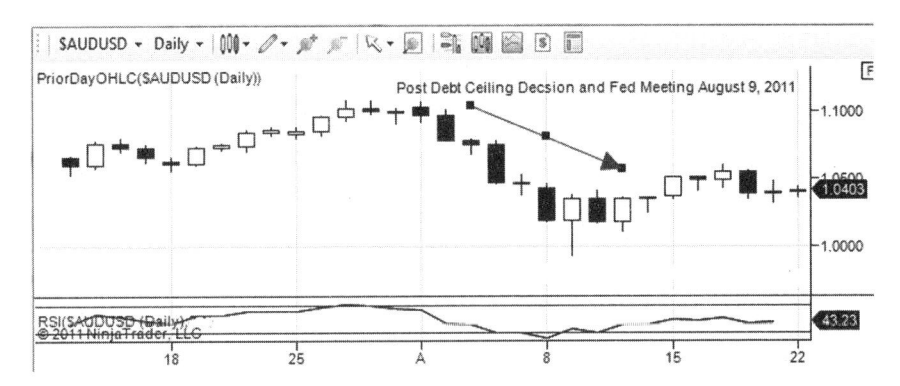

**FIGURE 4.5** AUDUSD Post Debt/Fed August 2011

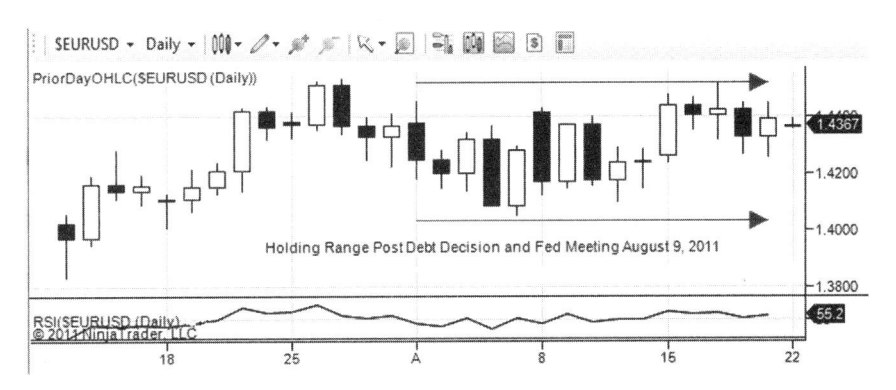

**FIGURE 4.6** EURUSD Post Debt/Fed August 2011

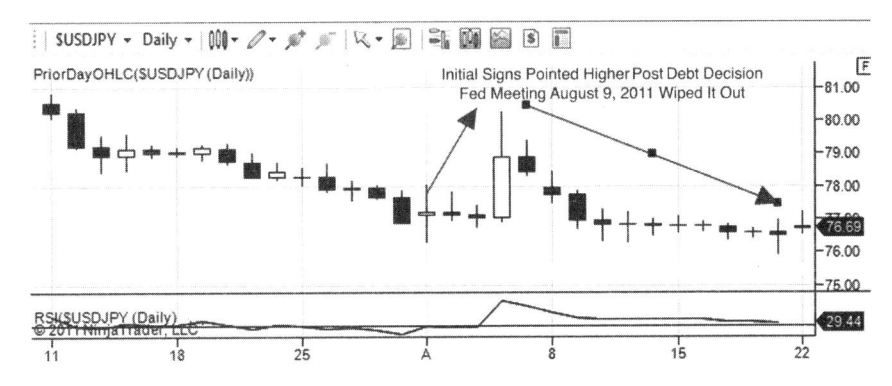

**FIGURE 4.7** USDJPY Post Debt/Fed August 2011

the Swiss National Bank's (SNB) rate cut and the Bank of Japan's (BOJ) intervention to try and stunt the strength of their respective currencies. The USD has moved back to new lows in the latter half of August against the JPY as markets maybe eyeing Japan's next move and any further QE packages that the U.S. Federal Reserve may offer.

Along with a staggering gold run over $1900, the currencies that seem to love the U.S. debt woes have been the JPY and CHF. Both pairs along with gold and treasuries have been sought after as safe-haven plays during the first eight months of 2011. When comparing the two currency pairs against each other (CHFJPY), it seems the CHF strength signals the globe has been tagging it as supreme. There is always a ripple effect. The SNB acts, the U.S. government deals with debt, and then the BOJ steps in with a move and the cycle continues. We will teach you to watch for clues in price to signal a direction and when the news confirms it, just react! See Figure 4.8.

As market movers act we need to pay attention. It also shouldn't surprise you that an investor like Warren Buffett didn't step in with a big play until he heard that the Federal Reserve was going to keep rates locked until mid-2013. He saw an opportunity to buy deep into Bank of America with a mere $5 billion investment. He of course understands that he can lose, but he took a high percentage bet in a fearful time with a bank he likes at bargain prices.

As an individual trader we have to step on the backs of the market movers and go for the ride when we enter the market. We need them to move prices to where we desire. Who is winning becomes the real question. Timing is of course important and making a timely decision according to your time tolerance is equally important. Experience over the years with

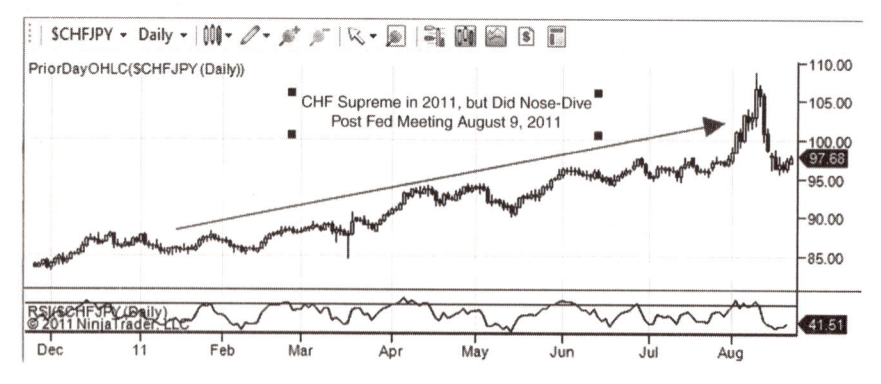

**FIGURE 4.8** CHFJPY Supreme in 2011

*The Long and Short of Fundamental Analysis* **45**

Gulf wars, tech boom/ bubbles, 9/11, housing collapse, credit crunch, and debt ceiling drama tell us to take things into consideration week by week when trading Forex or Commodity Futures. In the following chapters you will see how our model has adjusted to a time frame that fits our tolerance in accordance with our instant-gratification world. It has kept us in the game for the last 20 years.

If jobs data tumble in the United States, investors will continue to seek the CHF and the JPY for safety. If the United States gets its house in order and jobs become available, a USD bull run is in the cards. **Now we have decided long ago to play the markets in mostly one- to two-hour time frames and occasionally inside a week,** so you won't find us attempting to give any lengthy predictions. How can you trust any lengthy predictions anyway with the extreme moves in Currencies and Commodity Futures with the advent of the computer into the trading world? Moves that are correct in moments in today's climate were not in the weeks and months it took before the computer era. Mike immediately cringes when calling a currency supreme like the CHF. Two days after the 600-pip drop in the USDCHF, prices rallied back and wiped out all of those August 9, 2011, losses post Fed decision to keep rates locked until mid-2013. He took a successful long trade on August 11, 2011, on a huge upside reversal day. As you get to know our strategy in the next chapters you will discover how he did it and how you can take advantage of the swings as well (see Figure 4.9).

The beauty of settling the debate in the markets is that when you get some lengthy predictions from somebody, they generally aren't from traders. They know that as soon as you think you have it pegged, you get slapped with something that wipes it out flat. The only people who should be making long-term forecasts are the markets movers like the Federal Reserve Banks around the globe and each respective government. They along with the International Monetary Fund (IMF) are the only ones that hold all of the cards. They are the global referee if you will. Our financial

| Instrument | Quantity | B/S | Open Date Time | Open Rate | Entry - Close Date/Time | Close Rate | Pips |
|---|---|---|---|---|---|---|---|
| USD/CHF | 1 | B | 08/11/2011 09:52 | 0.7606 | 08/11/2011 10:03 | 0.7658 | 52 |
| USD/CHF | 1 | B | 08/11/2011 10:10 | 0.7630 | 08/11/2011 10:19 | 0.7645 | 15 |
| USD/CHF | 1 | B | 08/11/2011 10:11 | 0.7611 | 08/11/2011 10:35 | 0.7641 | 30 |
| USD/CHF | 1 | B | 08/11/2011 10:47 | 0.7605 | 08/11/2011 11:00 | 0.7615 | 10 |
| USD/CHF | 1 | B | 08/11/2011 11:17 | 0.7595 | 08/11/2011 11:25 | 0.7605 | 10 |
| USD/CHF | 2 | B | 08/11/2011 10:59 | 0.7622 | 08/11/2011 14:12 | 0.7640 | 18 |
| USD/CHF | 1 | B | 08/11/2011 12:24 | 0.7550 | 08/11/2011 14:17 | 0.7635 | 85 |
| USD/CHF | 3 | B | 08/11/2011 11:01 | 0.7594 | 08/11/2011 14:21 | 0.7625 | 31 |
| | | | | | | | 251 |

**FIGURE 4.9** USDCHF Reversal Long August 11, 2011, Statement Snapshot

referees hose down and brush off some of the chosen companies as they fill up their piggy banks and shove them back into the game. We aren't complaining just as you shouldn't, if you feel so inclined, because we chose the markets, they didn't choose us. Always keep yourself tuned into what they are saying and doing, as it will help you adjust along the way. You will hear us say it time and time again: Since a weatherman doesn't forecast past a week, why should we? So we will continue to adjust on a weekly basis and ride the backs of the market movers as the news and price shifts.

# CHAPTER 5

# Price Never Lies

Imagine a gunman demanded an answer to a question, and you could ask only one question in return before answering.

Gunman: "Would you buy or sell the USDJPY right now!?"
You: "What is the current price?"
Gunman: "76.03"
You: "Sell it!"

Clearly, there was no time to consider an in-depth technical and fundamental study in this scenario. What becomes important in a hypothetical moment like this (to make a point) is to know the basic information and be decisive. The point you need to realize is that we did not choose to sell the U.S. dollar/Japanese Yen (USDJPY) as a random 50-50 coin flip guess. We chose to ask about where price was currently to help us choose a side (buy or sell). Since the USDJPY price was below the equality line, or what we call the parity line at 100.00, we opted for the side that was winning, which was in this case to sell. Society is attracted to valuable things, plain and simple. Once you know your risk on the idea and you have an opinion, get after it! Don't sit on your thumbs.

Now it's not always that easy to just consider price, as we do have other factors but you would be surprised at how far this idea can take you. You might ask why you would look to price under that type of pressure and be so certain with your conviction. It's simple. The overwhelming majority of people will follow winners and you can be assured that their intentions upon entry (long or short) were to make money and not lose it. You must come to grips with the reality that we live in a society where winning isn't the only thing, it's the everything mentality. With this notion in mind, we can use price to give us a clue to current market sentiment (bullish or bearish). If price on the Euro/U.S. dollar (EURUSD) was 1.4041, that means that for every 1 Euro you would get 1.4041 U.S. in exchange. This is telling you that the Euro is more valuable than the U.S. dollar and confirming that buyers are winning more often when looking to this pair.

Now you can make arguments up and down the street about how you believe the opposite to be true, but we always say "then why isn't the rest of the world feeling the same way?" Price on the EURUSD would be below the 1.0000 parity line if the USD was stronger. Eventually you may win this battle, that is, if you haven't gone broke a thousand times over trying. We recall reading back in May 2010 that the Euro was going to fall through and test 1.0000, but it stopped short in the 1.1900 area in June 2010 and proceeded to climb near 1.5000 one year later in June 2011. If you just so happened to hop on the forecasters advice and sold at 1.1900, price action would have gotten as bad as $31,000 against each contract at the standard professional rate. You would have recovered a bit in July 2011 and only been down about $20,000 per contract on a short play from 1.1900. That's a lot of pressure to overcome in terms of money and time to be fighting the wrong side of the market for more than 12 months. Did you ever hear the phrase "The trend is you friend"? While not foolproof, it can bail you out of most difficult situations.

If you are not a believer in this notion, just begin to take a closer look as to what dominates the news in business, sports, and everyday life. Love 'em or hate 'em, the Yankees have won more World Series titles than any other pro baseball team and we are sure when you look at your favorite team in the current standings that you take a glance and see how the Bronx Bombers are doing. It shouldn't surprise you then that they have one of league's biggest payrolls as well. The best are drawn to the best, and the teams that pay the most get the best; it's as simple as that. Even in business a person like Warren Buffett dominates the headlines, so it shouldn't surprise you that he makes the most, and in turn that drives people to invest alongside and with his companies. It's exactly the same in trading the Forex markets. People follow winners!

## PARITY: TRADE WITH THE WINNERS

As we have mentioned, currencies make it simple with the parity line for starters. In an equal world the EUR/USD would be 1.000 where one Euro would be equal to one U.S. dollar. Since prices were at 1.4041 in our earlier example and throughout the life of the currency to date, buyers have been doing better in the long run than sellers. If forced to make a choice under the gunman's directive, choose the side that is winning. Let's face it,

*Price Never Lies* **49**

**FIGURE 5.1** EURUSD Parity Examples 2011

money not being an object, would you desire to drive a Yugo (no offense) or a Mercedes? Remember that the trading business and any business for that matter focus on profit, and nobody is immune to the attraction of the almighty dollar. You don't see people giving away Yugos as top prizes because they generally will not generate a buzz, but when you see a Mercedes as the top prize you might consider entering the contest.

Every time prices move up one pip or fall one pip with the EUR/USD at 1.4041, somebody on both sides put money and their idea on the line. The traders that get involved are not armchair quarterbacks anymore. Since making money is the driving force, the sellers of the EURUSD in the long run may eventually be forced to join the buyer's party to cover their loss, fueling further upside momentum for the winning side. Buyers will continue filling their greed gas tanks and at times even add to their position, keeping the upside momentum intact. Following the herd mentality might not be a bad word, when you look to the charts from the start of each year like January 2011. See Figures 5.1 and 5.2.

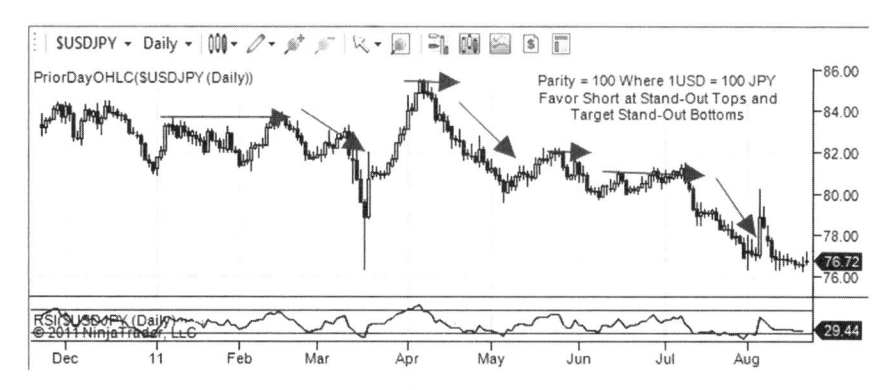

**FIGURE 5.2** USDJPY Parity Examples 2011

## TUNING IN TO YOUR CIRCLE OF INFLUENCE

Now that you can at least begin to take a side (long or short), let's begin to build confidence in the idea of using your inherent knowledge. You don't always just want to take a side boasting with confidence that your idea is infallible and indestructible. All good times seem to end and bad times never last forever. Kenny Rogers says in his famous song—not speaking to traders but we feel it is appropriate—"Know when to hold 'em and know when to fold 'em, know when to walk away and know when to run, never count your money when you're sitting at the table, there'll be time enough for counting when the dealing's done."

Problems occur when prices get over inflated during the trend as greed consumes us all. If you don't pay attention to when the market pauses and retreats at the end of bull or bear runs, you can get left without a chair to sit in. Later in this chapter we will demonstrate the ebb and flow of prices to reveal when to get on and off of the trend with what we call the Window of Opportunity Rule. In the aftermath of a run the pieces will get picked up and the process will start all over again just as day turns to night and night turns to day.

To help gauge the timing on your next great trade idea, just begin to tune to the current climate. The tools are there and the circle of influence that currently surrounds you most times offers plenty of clues to build your confidence to act. Let's take a circle of friends for example, which is not made up of all traders. As you get to know them you will find specific clues to market direction naturally. For example, we have a friend who builds the sets for a huge, well-known retail clothing store. The commercial that is going to be filmed is all done on a stage that he and his team construct. In 2008 and 2009, jobs were scarce for him. The store cut way back on their advertising budget because the market was doing poorly and people weren't out spending as much on clothes. That news alone told us, hey if the big stores aren't spending advertising dollars yet, they still foresee tough times ahead. If they aren't spending on advertising they surely aren't hiring yet. This confirmed to us to speculate further for continued weak jobs data, low interest rates, and a weak overall USD. In other words, keep shorting the USD.

When we entered 2010 our friend began to get solid work again, which told us things are shifting. The climate was starting to point in a positive direction. The news we heard on TV was getting more positive and jobs were starting to pick up. As long as there are no setbacks, such as threats to stability in the Middle East and no natural disasters happening, maybe a shift in sentiment and a stronger dollar is on the horizon. Just the act of tuning into the news and your surroundings will help you on your path. Sometimes we see students come to us and tell us they are paying thousands of dollars for news that they have right in front of their faces, free of charge. We are business owners just like you, and our financial resources and natural resources are important. What you decide to pay for services should never be done haphazardly, especially if you get an equal result from just applying some street smarts when it comes to trading.

Here is another example of market timing in action, all by paying attention to the clues that our friends and neighbors gave us. When we decided to buy a town house in 2003, the Fed was dropping interest rates like crazy during the 2001 to 2003 period—a record 13 consecutive cuts. The refinancing frenzy was here. Not just one of our friends was buying a home, many started. If existing homeowners weren't selling their homes, they were refinancing. We had a five-year time horizon, not knowing for sure, but we felt the place wasn't going to be something that we would stay in forever. We also knew that many homeowners were loading on the five-year Adjustable Rate Mortgage (ARM) freight trains as well, and all of those would start coming due in 2008. As the economy was recovering and gaining strength through the 2003 to 2007 period, the Fed started raising interest rates and all of those five-year ARMs coming due would be subject to paying higher interest rates when their terms were up.

We of course didn't know the gravity of how big firms like AIG, Lehman Brothers, and Bear Stearns were abusing the loans they offered, but knowing the overload building and the greed oozing out of everybody's pores, we felt a market top coming in 2007 or 2008. It's not only having the great idea to enter into an investment, it's equally important to know when to get out. Remember what Warren Buffett teaches us: "Be greedy in fearful times and be fearful in greedy times."

Lifestyle issues were playing on our psyche at the time as well. When 2007 hit and we were trading from home on the screen, we got fed up with the Chicago winters and the gray skies and headed for a warmer climate in California. As we grew tired of exercising indoors six to eight months out of the year, we felt the current economic landscape and gray skies fueled the perfect time for a move. Just learn to listen to your internal clues, tune into your circle of friends, make a decision, and act. After the move to Los Angeles, we rented for a year in 2008 and as things seemed to stabilize we bought again in Hollywood in 2009 as we heard and witnessed money pouring in to revitalize the area.

Here is a tip we follow: Start counting the construction rigs lining your sky-line view. Do you see any? And, if you do, are the workers actually showing up each day and working? We asked our real estate agent about future developments that she may have heard about in the area. She said that they were putting in a new Trader Joe's, a "W" Hotel, and luxury condominiums, as well as building another row of condos in the vacant area a half block from where we were going to buy. The view may not look too pretty when you move in, but since the completion of all mentioned, it looks pretty good so far. In the end you don't know what will happen, but we would rather have done all that we could before making a decision to buy, sell, or do nothing.

## ASKING THE RIGHT QUESTIONS

Thankfully you don't have a gun to your head when making a decision, so you can look at some of the other clues that are available with complete clarity. Let's consider a 24-hour day chart. Forex markets are open 24 hours a day, 6 days a week (Sunday through Friday). A new day in Forex starts for us on the west coast at 2 PM PT/4 PM CT/5 PM ET. On every chart there are four key components a trader considers: the open (start of the day 2 PM PT), the high (highest traded price over the next 24 hours), the low (lowest traded price over the next 24 hours), and the close (finish at 2 PM PT the next day).

Once you have the parity line concept in place and commit to a direction (long or short), you can begin to use the four key points to help you adjust to what everybody else is thinking along the way. As information about price is revealed, two important questions emerge:

1. When does the market mover (Federal Reserve Banks, governments, and hedge funds) eat?
2. When does the market mover sleep?

Since the market is bigger than all of us and we need market movers to take our trades in the proper direction, it is important to respect what they tell us about the direction of price, to time the idea we see at the end of the session areas where the buyers got tired of buying (the high) and sellers got tired of selling (the lows). These are two important points about price to remember. Taking it a step further, the chart will eventually reveal highs/lows that stand the test of time. We refer to these significant market tops and bottoms in honor of the great Charlie D, a legendary bond trader, in very simple yet understandable terms and call them the *Big Dog* areas. In the pit Mike used to be able to see and trade with the real Big Dog himself,

*Price Never Lies*

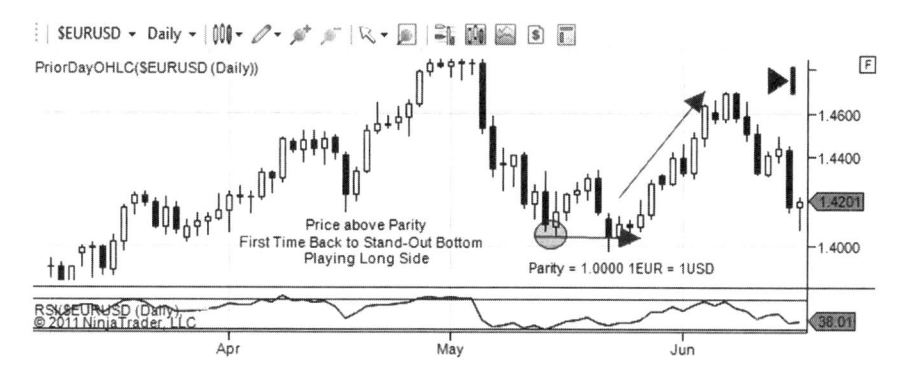

**FIGURE 5.3** EURUSD Stand-Out Trend Lows 2011

but now since the advent of computer trading the Big Dog on the computer is price and the Big Dog eats along the way and goes to sleep at the tops and bottoms of a session. It is vital to remember these areas to guide your long or short.

You know the cliché "Buy low, sell high." Let's put that in conjunction with prices trading above parity when looking at the EURUSD in 2011 (Figure 5.3). We would prefer to play the long side as prices retest a daily big dog low for the first time when the parity line is the same or further below this line in the sand. On the flip side, we would favor to sell as prices retest a big dog top for the first time when the parity line is above. We lose trust in selling a top when the parity line is below our feet so to speak, and lose trust in buying a bottom when the parity line is still above our head. We favor teaming with the side of value or what traders call the momentum side. As we look to the USDJPY (Figure 5.4) or the USDCHF

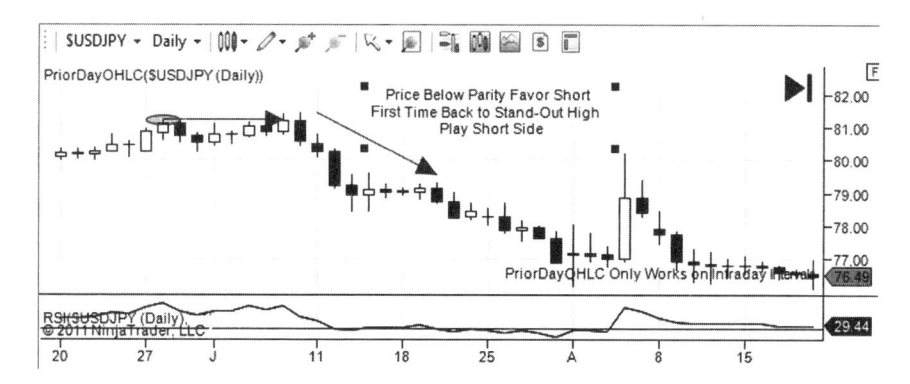

**FIGURE 5.4** USDJPY Stand-Out Trend Highs 2011

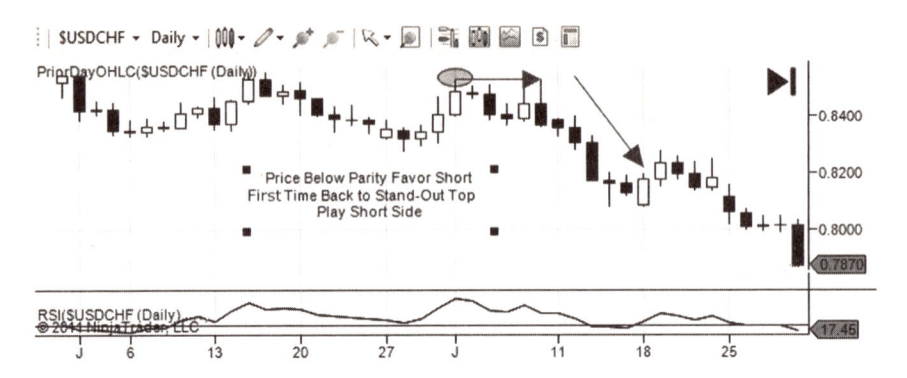

**FIGURE 5.5** USDCHF Stand-Out Trend Highs 2011

(Figure 5.5)—both trading below parity in 2011—we would favor the short side, so as we reach stand-out highs the opportunity for successful sell trades have been apparent.

## WHERE DOES THE BIG DOG EAT DAY TO DAY?

Since the thought of the Big Dog in actuality came from legendary bond trader named Charlie D, it reminds Mike of the time when he saw him speak. At one of his presentations he began referring to himself (not bragging) as the Big Dog. He would say don't take on or confront the Big Dog when I have both of my arms waving in the air and I am buying everything in sight. When both arms were up, it signaled that the trader was willing to trade 10 or more contracts, but Charlie D would frequently trade thousands at a time and everybody knew it when it was happening. Somebody in the audience wryly asked, "When will we know that you are done?" Charlie D's personality truly came through here when he candidly replied, "When I put my arms down!"

You may as well start to come to grips with that fact while you still have your wits and resources intact. Playing in the teeth against a stronger opponent (a.k.a., the big dog) is a losing battle. We don't know who the big dog is on the computer since all we see are numbers these days and not the faces. When referencing the big dog from here forward, we are referring to price.

When price action is going against your intended path, you are not going to stop it. To take the visual up a notch, we at times refer to the size of the market as equivalent to trying to make a lay-up in the paint against

Shaquille O'Neal. He's 7'1". It's not going to happen. If you are 7'1" and a professional basketball player, please insert something better like Superman. Either way it's not going to happen. However, to borrow from the popular TV show *Survivor*, you can outwit, outlast, survive, and thrive. You just have to know how to play a stronger opponent. When in a David-and-Goliath setting, you need to begin to play your opponent when he is tired and jump back on the trend when Goliath re-ignites.

Because you can watch price action without participating, something David couldn't do in his situation, you will begin to discover when your opponent is tired and when it's time for you to act. Hedge funds or other market movers on bearish fundamental events sometimes see it as an opportunity to unload large short positions to offset some of their load with buying to take profit as they are certain to find many sellers in those conditions. The opposite-than-expected price action that you see can be and at times is very confusing to new traders. They read the news and say the textbooks told me to sell and I did but prices went up and stopped me out. Only in the aftermath when the big fund is done buying do prices resume on their intended path. Mike always remembers what Charlie D was trying to tell the audience that day. Wait until he is finished and has put his hands down, you will be a happier and more profitable trader.

It's like when you see a new housing development being built in a run-down area. Your real-estate broker tells you that it's going to be the next big thing and you jump in on the deal. You soon realize that many times it takes years for it to pay dividends. Being the first one into the new development can most times be a painful financial journey. It may be the right play, but it's too soon.

## WHERE DOES THE BIG DOG EAT THE MOST?

With this thought in mind we simply began favoring long when prices are above parity and favoring short when prices are below parity. We just added to the equation and put to memory the stand-out highs and the stand-out lows on a daily chart to help our timing. Traders will refer to these significant areas as swing tops and bottoms but we of course refer to them as *big dog tops* and *big dog bottoms*. When getting an overview of the action, we began to see where we could take advantage of the market in transition. Confirmation of a top or bottom became prevalent as prices shifted in trend or in other words as uptrends (higher daily highs and lows) flipped to downtrends (lower daily lows and highs) and vice-versa. See Figure 5.6.

**56**                                           THE RDS FOREX SYSTEM

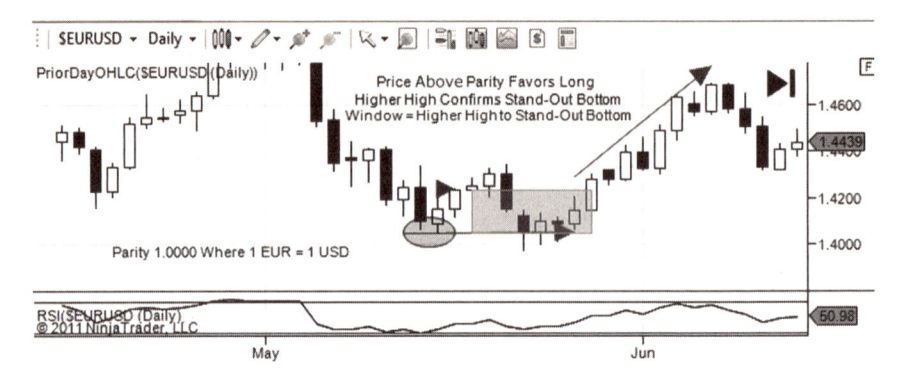

**FIGURE 5.6** Entry/Exit Using Parity, Swing Bottoms, and Trend Flips (mark point where you see higher highs) EURUSD

As prices fall into a downtrend moving counter to the parity-favored direction, we will back off or cover (exit) long plays. As prices shift back to an uptrend the confidence to jump in long re-ignites as the example shows. You can work the long side of the market from the spot where you first witnessed higher highs to where the stand-out low appeared. As we explain our five core rules in depth, this area will be referred to as the Window of Opportunity. See Figure 5.7.

As prices shift to a lower low with parity above the stand-out high, confidence to go short builds. Most times you will even get a chance to sell that top as the market often revisits the areas. We feel confident to take on a short position as prices revisit the top the very first time. If the direction turns counter into an uptrend, we of course will back of the short-side bias.

As these tops or bottoms reveal themselves we begin to see specifically the when and where. We also begin to see the areas to avoid. When prices

**FIGURE 5.7** Entry/Exit Using Parity, Swing Tops, and Trend Flips (mark point where you see higher highs) EURUSD

Price Never Lies 57

are trading in between the stand-out high and low, the momentum is there but if you miss the chance half way through the frenzy, it can leave you in the meat grinder. It's like deciding to cross a busy intersection when the "don't walk" signal is flashing. You know you have a few seconds but you don't want to get caught in the middle of the street if the light turns, leaving you vulnerable to getting run over.

Early on in our career we knew that a sound strategy needed more than just one source to guide buy-and-sell decisions. We found using the parity concept only as a gauge didn't help a short play for such markets like the New Zealand dollar/U.S. dollar (NZDUSD). The New Zealand dollar (the kiwi) has been on a pretty good run higher in 2011 despite the fact that it is trading below parity.

A way to help trade a market that is on the mend is to take notice of its annual reset button. We realized that just as all of us as individuals have an annual reset button every year with our birthdays and collectively we have one at the end of each year with a New Year's resolution, the markets do as well. It's called the year-end closing price. "Every dog has its day," as the saying goes, so don't be stubborn when the writing is on the wall. *We learned to map the closing price on the last trading day of each year as a way to tweak the parity marker and combine the adjustment with the stand-out high/low concept to help keep us current.* Since life is about change and change can happen in an instant, we must keep up with what's on traders' minds today. What happened years ago may not be what is influencing today's price. Just because a currency isn't above parity with the USD doesn't mean that it can't rise, especially in times like we witnessed in first half of 2011. Times like these have taught us to hold the previous year's closing price as the annual parity line to help keep our bullish/bearish bias in check and up to date. See Figure 5.8.

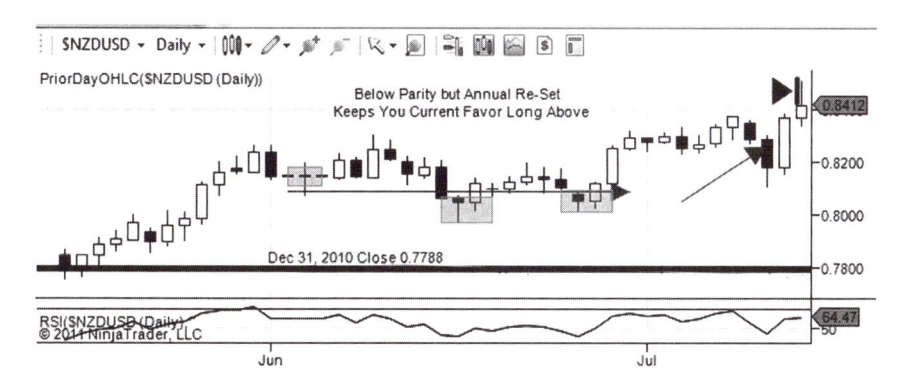

**FIGURE 5.8** Entry/Exit Using Last Year's Close, Swing Tops, and Swing Bottoms NZDUSD

As we get to our five rules, you will see how we adjust using some of the same concepts to help us day to day.

## WHAT TIME DOES THE BIG DOG EAT?

We of course hope you are gaining confidence as to where the big dog eats the most by considering the parity line/prior year close and waiting for flips back on the trend side before entering into an idea long or short. Another factor you will want to consider is what time the big dog eats. We know that you want to become rich yesterday but the thought of preparing for time is going to directly correlate to your energy. The mental energy used during trading is not to be taken lightly. The longer you watch the more impatient you can get. You might have already heard yourself many times shouting at your screen like it can hear you "Alright already, just go where you are supposed to!" These thoughts can take you down. You can't control when and you can't control how long. What you can do is look to recent action in order to develop a feel for when and how long. If you can get a handle on these two trade stoppers and can control yourself to wait for the "when" (your price) and prepare for the "how long" you will be a step ahead of most and on the right path to becoming a successful trader.

The most overwhelming stumbling block for traders is that they hold on to losers longer and exit winners too quickly. Part of the problem many traders face is the fact that they don't prepare for how long they may have to wait before entry and how long a trade may take to reach its destination. *When you look at charts and see significant periods of times all rolled up nice and tidy into an open, high, low, and close, begin to study the length of time price moves generally take to run specific distances (profit/loss targets) rather than only how well your strategy would have worked.*

When you put a timer on the trade and price begins to move in your favor, breathe through it. You might even uncover that you have been in the trade for only five minutes and have an urge to exit and take the small profit, but you have earlier prepared for the trade to take days. Breathe! David Harp wrote a nice book called *The Three Minute Meditator*. He didn't write the book for traders, but we used it for the specific purpose of teaching us to relax through winners and shoot for price in conjunction with time. On the flip side, if a trade isn't working and prices should have reached your profit target during the time allotment you gave it, cut the cord.

Relaxing our breathing can help the situation, but it is hard to break natural rhythms your body feels. We personally struggled with long-term trades because what happened if you held an idea for three or more days and the trade didn't work out? This plays on your psyche: 36 hours of work on one idea and down money, ouch! The uncertainty of tomorrow let alone in a week is overpowering in today's financial markets. You just don't know. You might think you know but then comes an early resignation by a key official, an earthquake, a flood, a terrorist attack, a treasury department policy shift, a bankruptcy, and so on. We personally began to focus on ideas that were a little more predictable and not force our bodies to hang with something it naturally didn't want to do. The time tolerance that internally worked for us and matched the rhythm of the markets fit with ideas that spanned a couple of hours to a couple of days at most.

Traders that come to us don't seem to put a value on their time, especially when the idea starts to turn bad. This is a big mistake. *Don't hang with a bad idea just because you can afford it.* If price action should have reached your target by now and it hasn't, it most often signals that it will not. If you can get a handle on the thought that every idea is not going to work and you begin to take action to exit trades that haven't responded over time as predicted, you will notice that your imbalanced win/loss ratio will improve. Preparing for time will naturally build your skills to hang with winners as well, when you look at the clock and realize you have only been in the trade for a fraction of the time you predicted. There is no greater pain in trading than hanging with a loser to your stop price when you knew it didn't feel right much earlier due to the time invested and on the flip side taking that profit way too early only to see it reach your target as predicted. *The biggest demon to contend with as a trader is instant gratification.*

With the ease of entry on today's trading platforms, it often times leaves the beginner pushing the buttons haphazardly and sometimes spending countless hours mesmerized in front of the computer screen. You must begin to break this habit. Society drummed in our heads to study hard, work hard, and you will get ahead. Trading is not a normal nine-to-five job. You must learn to wait for your moments. In the pit trading environment it was a no brainer; all the action took place in the pit during normal working hours. The computer coupled with a globalized economy now allows for a 24-hour trading day. If we sit in front of the screen we naturally want to push the buttons and make money. The problem with this behavior is that action is not always set up in the best location and if an impatient trader is at the wheel the likely outcome is loss.

The beauty of trading software is that you thankfully have a built in employee that you can pre-set with entry and exit orders in case prices make a move to an area that you like during your sleeping hours. You can set buy/sell limit orders and attach one-cancels-other (OCO) profit targets and stop losses before you go to bed at night to hedge if the move happens while you are asleep.

Using the software to help should give you peace of mind so you can rest and recover normally and be fresh the next day, rather than sitting mesmerized in front of your computer screen for 24 hours straight. Becoming efficient with your time and placing a value on it will be equally as important as it is to making money.

# CHAPTER 6

# Play at Peak Times

Since we all seem to be trending toward instant gratification, we just learned not to suppress that emotion but rather embrace it. Once we aligned our most productive hours with the time market prices tended to move the best, this solved the instant-gratification problem we internally faced. *A trader's friend is volatility not its enemy.* When price moves there is opportunity and when there is opportunity we need to be sharp and focused. You will eventually need and want to structure your focus around these volatile hours because it will solve your patience issues as prices will move enough to captivate your interest.

So what are the peak times around the global clock? The most vibrant economic reports are released at the start of the day session, so this is an obvious time to expect volatility. Since the world seems to be on a two-hour parking meter attention span, the first couple of hours of the day session are the most active. We witnessed this attitude and emotional frenzy routinely every morning on the trading floors. Traders were hyped up with a fresh pile of money to start their day and when the bell rang to begin, it was like a kick-off in a football game or the gun starting a track meet.

With that in mind it's not surprising to conclude that we need to be on the top of our game and be most productive during the first couple hours of the day. Understanding the global time clock will help you to use your financial and physical energy wisely. When price action has energy, be focused and decisive. When price action is quiet, don't press for action; take a break. If you adhere to this advice during the time you watch the markets on your computer you will begin to use the instant-gratification emotion to your advantage. Price moves happen much faster in today's world. If the big dog is on steroids at the start of the day you can hit trades farther, harder, and faster. You should note that this can work for you or against you, so always be prepared and balance market time with your internal patience and risk/reward tolerance. Understanding how long moves generally take (High − Low = Range) will take you a long way. We will study this simple formula in great detail as we move deeper into our strategy.

Table 6.1 depicts the hot times when price action is most volatile and meets all of our instant gratification needs. We are sure it will for you as well.

You can search through all of the studies and back-test as many strategies as possible, but don't ignore your personal time tolerance. You will most times be surprised at how we vastly underestimate what we can accomplish in a year and vastly overestimate what we can accomplish in a day. We once started helping a struggling trader who came to us in frenzy and angry at the world, especially trading educators. He was following a widely respected market newsletter. This particular newsletter gave insights on longer-term trades that sometimes took months to develop. We said, "That's great Joe! But can we ask how long you personally hold on to trades?" He paused and said, "Well about five minutes. I have to get out when I am down $50." Do you see the problem here?

Tip: Before you invest in a mentor be sure to have a handle on your time tolerance (1) and risk appetite (2).

**TABLE 6.1** Hot Currencies by Region 24 Hour Clock

| Country | Prime Hours | Currency Focus |
|---|---|---|
| Japan, Australia, New Zealand | 4 PM PT/6 PM CT/7 PM ET to 7 PM PT/9 PM CT/10 PM ET | U.S. dollar/Japanese Yen (USDJPY), Australian dollar/U.S. dollar (AUDUSD), New Zealand dollar/U.S. dollar (NZDUSD), Euro/Japanese Yen (EURJPY) |
| London/Europe | 10 PM PT/12 AM CT/1 AM ET to 1 AM PT/3 AM CT/4 AM ET | Euro/U.S. dollar (EURUSD), British Pound/U.S. dollar (GBPUSD), Euro/British Pound (EURGBP), Euro/Swiss Franc (EURCHF), U.S. dollar/Swiss Franc (USDCHF), Euro/Japanese Yen (EURJPY) |
| United States/Canada | 530 AM PT/730 AM CT/830 AM ET to 830 AM PT/1030 AM CT/1130 AM ET | EURUSD, USDJPY, USDCHF, GBPUSD, NZDUSD, AUDUSD, U.S. dollar/Canadian dollar (USDCAD) |

*Play at Peak Times*

1. Start getting your information from someone who fits your time tolerance. Get a feel for how long your mentor holds on to their trades before subscribing.
2. Understand that $50 is five pips in Forex and price moves of five pips occur in seconds. The solution for this trader was smaller pip sizes of mini ($1 pips or 50 pips equals $50) to micro ($0.10 pips or 500 pips equals $50). A micro-pip solution put him in alignment with his analyst's forecasts. This also allowed him to be more relaxed so he wouldn't force a money tolerance issue before an idea had a chance to show its success.

Once you have a feel for your tolerance you can then seek the best help for your style. If you are struggling and don't quite yet realize how long to hang on with trade ideas, begin to first look at how long you can generally handle things in your outside life to give you clues. For you traders out there who think you have a handle on this, most times you will discover that what you think and what you actually do in the moment most times fall on opposite side of the spectrum.

## TEST YOUR PERSONAL TIME TOLERANCE

We always present new and experienced traders that seek our help with this scenario; let's say we are going to meet for dinner. We choose the place and set the time for 7 PM. It's now 7 PM and you arrive on time at the restaurant (in trading it's equivalent to entering the trade) and see that we are not there yet. You sit down and order a beverage while you wait (price action slightly turning against you). You look at your watch and its now 7:15 PM. Most times people in this setting will say things like they must be hitting traffic (I can handle the amount I am down on the trade). You begin to look at the menu (you still love the trade entry idea). It's now 7:30 PM. We still haven't arrived, leaving you waiting (crossroads on the trade, you start to doubt). You might say things like "Am I in the right place?" "They did say 7 PM?" You check your phone calendar and confirm that the time was 7 PM. You are now getting the sense that we might not show and are getting agitated. Its 7:45 PM (emotions are taking over). Its #@$%$# 8 PM now! Never again! Trading is so similar to waiting for somebody at a restaurant. You might even begin to get a little self-conscious sitting there by yourself. At times you will feel you are all alone on an island while in the market as well. If prices haven't shown you something good in the first 15 to 30 minutes, most times you are in for a long rough road ahead. *Begin to trust your intuition no matter what.* It will be the first steps to learning how to handle the ebb and flow of emotion along with profit and loss. When you aren't feeling it, and price isn't showing you something great, get out, especially if your instincts are telling you. Learn to hang with the positive trades better when your intuition is working in tandem with price.

Let's take it a step further and reverse the situation where you arrive late. You join friends at dinner or at a bar and find they have already eaten and have been drinking. You on the other hand arrive perfectly sober. It's hard to get in the groove of the conversation and you're pissed that you couldn't get there on time (equivalent to missing the entry opportunity in a trade that would be working). You start to feel that you missed all of the laughter and might even find what your friends are laughing about not that funny. Relating this analogy to trading, it's like thinking the market is going to climb 100 pips and you watch it rise 99 and then you finally get the courage to enter. You buy it only to find prices fall back hard in your face. You missed the party! Sit this party out and wait for the next one. *There are approximately 220 trading games a year, there will always be another opportunity.*

Mike remembers a time in the beginning of his career. He got to work early and settled into his one square foot space in the 30-year bond pit. The bell rang at 7:20 AM CT and he stood there and couldn't find the courage to get involved before 8:30 AM CT. Price action just moved a bit too quickly the first hour for him after the prime economic reports were released. There was a lot to lose in those moments. This of course left him unsettled as he realized that he was missing prime opportunities. He tackled this problem by setting a goal to not trade prior to the report but to begin minutes after the release if the opportunity was ripe. Do you know how he overcame this fear? He just started to prepare for how far prices tended to travel in those volatile moments and calculated the worst-case scenario (buying the top or selling the bottom). Remember, high minus low equals range. When he realized that he would still have a pulse and a heartbeat, if the worst became reality, the tension eased in his body. He also took a few tips from David Harp's book we mentioned earlier. Preparing ahead of time calmed his fears while in the moment. Another nice book to help with this is to read Susan Jeffers' book *Feel the Fear and Do it Anyway.*

We just can't stress enough that the majority of what you need to realize about yourself as a trader is right in front of your nose. You will soon discover how to manage your trades alongside your personality just by simply thinking of the moments when you are out with your friends. If you are like us most times when you hang with friends you will know in the first 15 or 30 minutes if it's going to be fun or not. This is no different in trading. Prices will tell you much of what you need to know (good or bad) in that first 15 to 30 minutes.

*Play at Peak Times*

If our dinner scenario resonates with you as it does for most when we ask, you will understand our shift to a 15-minute chart, applying the same concepts of stand-out highs/lows, but on a shorter time scale from daily to 15 minute. This began to balance our thoughts better with the majority of the players we face on the computer. After you get good at taking the first 15 to 30 minutes into consideration don't forget about duration of the trade. Remember the time clock we mentioned earlier? Take a break and stretch your legs after a couple hours on your trade ideas. That's generally how long the party lasts. Like it or not we are conditioned to have about a two-hour internal time tolerance. We most often lose interest or focus as we surpass two-plus hour flights, two-plus hour dinners, two-plus hour movies, two-plus hour car rides, two-plus hour meetings, or two-plus hour classes. We loved James Cameron's movie *Titanic*, but three-plus hours left us squirming in our seats to get the blood circulating. It is no different in price potential of your favorite markets. Even if you missed the start of the party on the trade another will come along within the next two hours. Keep your cool!

## MAP YOUR TOLERANCE TO THE MARKET

We found a way to help prepare you for time issues that will certainly come up. Since you may not know what type of trader you are yet, such as one who waits and plays using longer-term stand-out swings or intraday swings. A method to help is to first look at a daily chart. Look back in time at a stand-out top and bottom on the chart and visualize the direction that you would have wanted to play it based on the parity/prior-year close concept. Count how many days it took to get to the area you wanted (the entry) and count how many days it took to move to your target (the exit). See Figure 6.1.

Really begin to consider if you can handle that length of time with money on the line. If you saw the movie *Secretariat*, there was a scene when John Malkovich's character didn't want to watch to see if Big Red would achieve the Triple Crown. Diane Lane's character forced him to watch alongside her as the horse eventually achieved its goal. You may think you can hang with the trade and watch, but only you can answer this question. Prices generally don't run in a smooth direction and remember that a daily chart may look pretty at the day's end but it could have traveled up and down its range multiple times in a 24-hour span leaving you with anxiety and doubt along the ride. You will also have to contend with holding on to a trade that doesn't turn out after multiple days of holding it. This can of course drain your physical energy as well, so take this into consideration very carefully when you look into longer-term swing patterns.

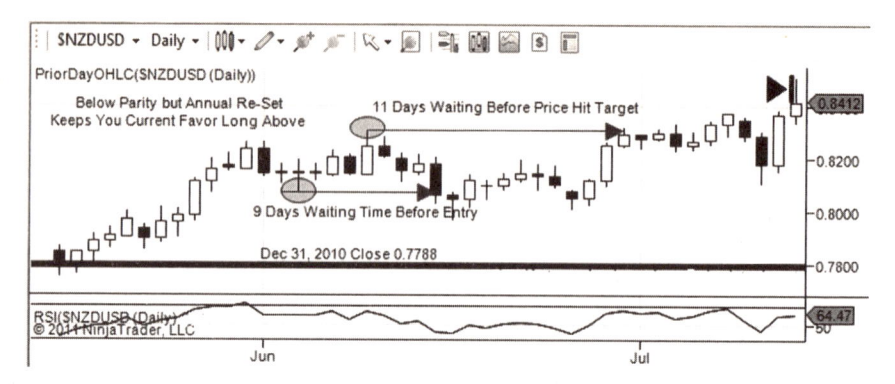

**FIGURE 6.1** Counting Days to Entry and Exit

There are not that many chances for longer-term plays each month and, if you need more action as we found we do, you can simply apply the same concepts outlined so far to tighter time frames. You will learn that we favor a 15-minute chart as we found it to balance our instant gratification concerns with the overall uncertainty the computer and financial markets bring from week to week.

## YOU DON'T NEED AN ECONOMICS DEGREE

As we map our time tolerance to the parity/previous year close, stand-out high/low concepts discussed so far, we now can apply some fundamental preparation concepts to build our confidence on direction. The biggest point we want to express is that you can gain a sense of direction from the fundamental news, but begin to couple our price concepts to help paint a truthful picture without having to do years of research before you enter your first trade. *We have had students come to us that spend more time than necessary back testing and wearing the student cap as a shield to hide themselves from their true internal fear of trading.* You will not know until you enter a trade, so do it with a dime and get off of the demo. You have to start risking sometime and you will never know unless you start risking live.

In order to get really good at trading, you will need to get a bit more sophisticated with fundamental analysis as we don't want to make any blind guesses. When Mike received his degree in economics at Lake Forest College back in 1989 he told me about some extremely dry courses. His economic professors were also looking pretty pale and desperate for some sunshine on their faces, and their personalities as well. We do want to touch on some of the key elements of theory they discussed, but apply them with practical insights we have discovered in the real markets that so many professors fail to teach.

What college professors do not teach is strategy. *Our culture has in actuality prepared you to be a trader from the start; you just might not know it yet.* We just will help you tap into the strategy aspect that your teachers have failed to deliver. You can't teach a person how to tackle on a football field using a chalk board, let alone buy and sell in the markets with a manual.

In trading there are two teams: bulls (buyers) and bears (sellers). Sports and competitions are divided in the same way. For that matter so is Washington, D.C., with Democrats and Republicans. Step into a courtroom and there is a plaintiff and a defendant. Walk into a grammar school during recess and see the kids divided into two groups playing dodge ball or kick ball. In childhood or adulthood life is a series of competitions whether playful or serious. We all need something to do when we grow up, so for the time being we are grateful that the supposed smartest people in the world (our U.S. government) came to their senses and didn't screw up (at least not totally yet) one of the greatest adult games on the planet: our economy! With the drop to AA+ by the ratings agencies, our government and policy makers need to be doing more in terms of controlling spending and borrowing more commensurate with the rate income flows back into Washington.

If we don't have an economy, what would we grownups have to do? Maybe we could act in kind as it seems they have and decide who wins with a good game of dodge ball with winner take all! We don't mean to make this sound so trivial, but we are actually a bit in awe at how immaturely our government on both sides played politics down to the wire before the debt-ceiling decision in early August 2011. Nothing like a nice global adrenalin rush to get the party started! We realize they are in their position to make tough decisions that affect billions around the globe. Tough debate is necessary as both sides have a point, but with the world watching the U.S. government throw up a last minute desperation shot with seconds to spare, come on!! One thing is for certain, volatility is here to stay and that should provide ample opportunities for those that look to trade the markets, especially the Forex markets.

## FEAR AND GREED HAVE NO BOUNDARIES

No matter if you agree with current location of price or not, it is there for a reason. When prices move somebody bought and somebody sold and as we have said earlier *we have not met a trader or an investor yet that got involved long or short in the market with the intention of losing money.* When we first understood that price is the truest measure of market sentiment, success and consistency began to soar.

As an individual investor we do not have the resources like the U.S. government or large investment firms like J.P. Morgan or Goldman Sachs. They have the ability to hire 50,000 interns in a blink to do the research. As an individual you have to keep things in real terms financially on this endeavor. You can however use what they are doing to help. Remember that they put their pants on the same way you do, they just do it on a bigger scale. You just need to know when to jump on and off the wagon. Begin to understand two things:

1. World governments and large financial firms can push the market around, so respect is in order.
2. Fear and greed infiltrates all walks of life the same, no matter if you fall in the haves or have-nots category.

The haves will move to join what works and abandon what doesn't in a heartbeat. It's Darwinism at its finest for survival of the fittest. What we have seen in the financial community with AIG, Lehman Brothers, and Bear Stearns we have also witnessed with the have-nots. Mike once saw two homeless men that he at one time or another gave both some money to. One day when running by he witnessed the two in an argument. They happened to be fighting over a prime spot under the viaduct. One said he was first and should keep the spot but the other said his belongings were there so it's his. The police in the end had to break it up. Fear and greed have no boundaries! Price and location don't lie! Parity/previous yearly close and flips back on trend are the building blocks that will carry you a long way.

## ACT NOW AND ASK WHY LATER

Once we began trading back in 1993 we learned some hard facts and core lessons that hold true today with Forex. We know how prices should respond theoretically but we also know that sometimes when the economic or geo-political event is unleashed on the marketplace, price action does the opposite of what theory taught us. We scratch our heads and wonder why. We have learned that market participants may already be loaded up too much in that theoretical direction. The report result wasn't significant enough to get more people to join the wave, causing prices to turn opposite to what was expected.

*The natural course a trader takes is to wait for the news and take their eye off price, see the result, and then act. Our goal is for you to shift that instinct.* We came to the realization that when prices move sharply,

*Play at Peak Times*

they are moving for a reason. Watching the speed and direction of price is the signal. As you watch price action enough times, you will begin to see normal rhythms and abnormal spikes. Normally these jumps or spikes have a reason to them that directly correlates to a piece of news that just hit the markets. While in a position (long or short) the reason at the moment becomes insignificant. If you need to adjust, then adjust. Look for who, what, where, when, and why after the fact. The problem we identified in ourselves and our students is that we all have hesitated when price action moves in an unfavorable direction. Isn't it ironic how you easily just take the winner but get all flustered and agitated when losing? Now of course you need to know something about why price moves north and south, but all of this will become pre-market homework and should be instinctual when in the moment.

## SURPRISE FUNDAMENTAL OR GEO-POLITICAL EVENTS

Some of those early lessons and what Charlie D was trying to teach us weren't fully understood in the beginning as we had little experience, but one day when Treasury Secretary Robert Rubin resigned from office mid-morning in 1999 it hit Mike right in the gut. It didn't seem like a big deal to him at the time, but was he wrong. Textbooks and classrooms did not prepare him for what he was about to experience.

He was long bonds at the time, and market price action began to shift and move more quickly than usual, especially for mid-morning trade. Shortly after price action soon started to get whippy (volumes thinned out on the bid /ask and prices began moving rapidly). Soon after the whip, price action took on an overall negative tone and started to drop dramatically. This all happened inside of a minute. Mike's first instinct was to elbow the trader next to him. "Hey, what's going on (first mistake)?" His colleague didn't know. Mike held tight (second mistake) and looked at the news wires and finally it came across that the Treasury secretary resigned (rhird mistake). He didn't know if that was bearish or bullish at the time, but the way prices were dropping it started to tell him that it was bearish. Rubin actually leaving wasn't necessarily bearish, but the news fueled thoughts that interest rates may increase with new blood in the seat. *"Hawkish" or negative tones most often prevail for incumbents as they need to show the markets that a new sheriff is in town.*

Mike wasn't experienced enough with strategy about this at the time; he just knew he was losing money and fast. Long the market obviously was not a good thing for his trading account, so he then exited the trade at a loss of $1000. Thankfully, Mike maintains the discipline to cover bad ideas before a loss gets too overwhelming, because in this case it would have. It just angered him upon reflection because he had the answer right from the start. Remember the first mistake? When prices began to move faster than normal, the warning signs were there. It of course would have been easy if he was on the winning side, everybody knows how to win. Prices were moving fast and against the idea in this case and the initial hesitation cost 75 percent more than necessary.

Over the years we just got better at recognizing when something was up. Down $1000 wasn't devastating but it happened in about two minutes. Emotions start to flood your mind, like if I lost $1000 every two minutes, that would be −$30,000 per hour. How many people do you know that lose $30,000 per hour? The business would be short lived to say the least. These events don't happen every two minutes thankfully, but trading the professional value markets is in actuality 100 times what an outsider is used to. There is real money on the line, and there is no school or book that can teach you how you are going to feel and react in an environment that is all about winning and losing money.

Now Mike knew the big things, like when the stock market was crashing in 1987, being a student of economics at the time to be a bullish event for 30-year bonds (guaranteed fixed interest flight to quality) and bearish for the U.S. dollar (lower interest rates were coming on the heels of a recession). When the Treasury Secretary resigned, he didn't think that it would create movement like it did. *It wasn't just about learning theory anymore, it was learning about the players involved.*

The Treasury Secretary is an economic advisor to the President that relays and recommends domestic and international monetary policy strategies to help promote a sound, stable financial system. Pretty important, huh! Realizing that if the Secretary says something positive or negative and the direction your market may go becomes easy if you are prepared. If you don't even know the players, how are you supposed to be successful at this craft? You don't have to know their height, weight, and astrological sign, but just become familiar with influential financial posts out there and know when they speak that you should pay attention. Never again would we go into financial battle without being prepared. When studying the influential players, you soon begin to focus primarily on the key Federal Reserve members and U.S. government cabinet members mentioned in the tables presented in Chapter 4.

## 9/11

Learning the early lesson to respect price movement served us well many times over during our careers, but it especially helped on September 11, and once again before George W. Bush was re-elected for his second term.

It was a quiet morning on Tuesday, September 11, 2001. Mike walked into his spot in the 30-year bond pit and began his day just like any other. Shortly after the 7:20 AM CT bell, the trade tone shifted slightly negative originally but no major news was expected that day. He began playing the short side of the market and go with the sentiment as our focus is on being a momentum trader (a trader that goes with the price flow). There was no real substantial price movement so far, and his day was leaning to the positive side. Price action all of sudden got whippy (the warning). Now experience prevailed. The red flag was beginning to flap in the breeze, so to speak. Soon the attention of everybody in the pit began to focus on the huge screen in the far corner of the financial room at the Chicago Board of Trade (CBOT). Ironically the New Room, as we called it coming from the tight quarters of the Old Financial Room, was touted during construction that you could fit a 767 jet with plenty of room to spare and house us financial adrenalin junkies. Smoke was billowing out of one of the World Trade Center Towers.

Of course on the trading floor somebody always throws out a joke. "Somebody forget to turn off the grill after the late night BBQ in NYC?", not yet knowing the gravity of the moment. No real news of what was going on hit the wires yet, but price action continued to whip. News shortly after started to circulate that it might be a hijacked plane just as another explosion ripped through the other tower. The pit roared in unison, "Whoa!" This was not the normal buy 'em or sell 'em language. This was severe! Stocks and USD were crashing and flight to the safety of fixed-interest products much like what we learned in the 1987 crash, but here lives were being lost and thoughts of war became the new chatter. Negative news translates with a tandem price drop with stocks and the USD. 30-year bonds on the other hand move opposite the news. When it comes down to trading, the language is 100 times tighter than a twitter post. You scorch things in your head like for the USD; bad news, sell 'em, good news, buy 'em. Instincts and experience served Mike well at this moment, but since bonds move opposite the news so it was bad news, buy 'em, good news, sell 'em. In this case Mike reversed his short position to protect himself and instinctually bought the first offer he saw to get long.

Headset clerks working for Cantor Fitzgerald said the phones from the New York offices just went silent. Putting the gravity of the moment aside, if you are short the market and prices begin to rise from news or a geopolitical event, look to the ask or selling price. The bid price and other buyers are now your enemy. When your body gets a shot of flight or fight endorphins, your initial reaction is not thinking about the horrific nature of the event like 9/11. Mike's first response was to protect and reverse the short position he was in and get long. Get ahead of the others in the pit he thought! This isn't the time for limit bids; it's time to go to buy at the market and find an offer (seller) fast! Mike bought into the first offer he found in the 30-year pit that day and reversed his position from short to long as the flight to safety ensued. There was no need to elbow his colleague this time. Our job is to protect number one first, but as the facts of the new reality of our world began to settle, it left a bad taste in your mouth. Profiting from death, especially when it was some of your colleagues, caused Mike to exit his now profitable position and walk out of the pit. As further news reports were released people just started to leave. Soon thereafter the bad taste turned to a new fear as headlines mentioned that more hijacked planes were reported in the air and rumors that the Sears Tower was threatened caused officials to close trading. Forever etched in our brain was the scene on LaSalle and Jackson that September morning with mobs of people on the street looking to vacate downtown Chicago. Driving, catching a bus, cab, or train was next to impossible and so began the silent five-mile walk home.

Acting instinctually during extreme conditions and knowing what to do without hesitation will save your butt. Even if it goes bad, don't panic. Take a deep breath and act. Don't think of the money; just do what you are supposed to do to correct the situation and the moment. *Ask why later!*

## GEORGE W. BUSH'S SECOND TERM IN OFFICE

Another moment seared in Mike's brain was back when Bush II was bidding for re-election. Kerry was kicking his butt in the poles. We were getting negative employment data losing 100,000 to 300,000) every month, all while still at war inside Afghanistan and Iraq. With jobs being lost left and right; it didn't look good for Bush II. The markets one Friday morning were expecting much of the same: More job losses, but the actual data came in that day at 300,000 jobs added. JTN, the trader standing next to Mike said, "Bush II just got re-elected." *Talk about a statement from just seeing a number. The action of prices that day didn't lie to us. It didn't matter if you liked him or not; that's not how traders think. We place no initial judgments or stereotypes on events while in a trade.* Upon reflection of the event we may take issue or debate it with friends and family and then vote, but this isn't the time to hesitate. It's all about reacting as we sum things up into simple one word questions or statements; bearish or bullish? Price will quickly give you the answer!

Bond prices dropped what Mike initially thought was 96 ticks in a matter of seconds (equivalent to $3000 per contract). Since the computer was now in Mikes hands in the pit during this time, we coined ourselves hybrid-traders (a term we used to identify a trader that traded both on the screen

*Play at Peak Times* **73**

and in the pit simultaneously). Mike would feel some of his first effects of price action on steroids. Up to this point he had never seen a drop of this magnitude. Twelve years in the business this point facing wars, new presidents and Federal Reserve chairmen changing the guard, and never a move like this. 9/11 didn't even compare and this was just an employment report. Welcome to the eye-popping computer-induced speed of price action. Trying to watch the pit and watch the screen had its challenges initially. It was new. Remember the *-ings* we mentioned in the introduction to this book. How about not realiz*ing* that your trade count was off before the employment release, leaving Mike with an unwanted long position running in his book (thankfully only one)? As he realized the mistake, he naturally exited as soon as he realized the error for a −76 tick loss ($2375 loss). What time was it? It was 7:31 AM, 11 minutes into the day, one minute after the report was released, and the perfect storm of a plus 300,000 payrolls figure dropped prices to record depths. In the aftermath Mike realized that the low in the computer actually fell five handles or −160 ticks ($5000 per contract). It could have been worse, but Mike's human fingers and eyes never saw it and in this case actually saved him $2625. Mike called me after that, angry but not shaken. He told me that he still had his head screwed on tight and felt he could go in and compete. He came home positive with his best day at the time, netting $4000 by day's end. Prices had bottomed and shot back up in a blink at super speed and it was time to adapt to the new movement of price action.

*The situation could have been worse and it woke us up to be careful with our pens and mouse clicks as it could cost thousands.* We learned to make absolutely sure by double checking and triple checking our positions, pending orders, and open trades while using or before turning on or off the computer. There are no take backs or crying. Suck it up and move on. **Cover your butt first** and **get yourself on the right side** and then discuss it. Don't hesitate!

## READING THE NEWS

When a report hits the news wires and the actual result is far away from the forecast or an event occurs that takes the market by surprise, the faster prices will move to offset the imbalance. Better yet it taught new lessons. When a market starts to get whippy and then move drastically in one direction, respect it. Don't ask questions and the reasons why. Ask those questions later. *It's equally important to note: "Never let a lesson slip away without some reflection at day's end to improve for tomorrow."*

We don't like to get long or short just prior to a release, and gamble on the report's outcomes. We might trade immediately following the economic reports, but it is pure gambling at times. Mike watched a trader who stood near him from 1997 to 1999. He was such an amazing reader of the news, but lost so much money during these reports. As soon as he saw the report he would bid or offer immediately in the direction prices should go. When he finally found somebody who was willing to play with him, prices moved sharply against him. This is equivalent to submitting a buy/sell market or buy/sell stop order into our computer during this time. Buyers and sellers are not that confident and liquidity is thin. Wild price swings are and should be expected so getting the price you think you deserve will most often not be the case. Our colleague was forced out due to losing too much money on the price swing against him, only to find in the aftermath that his instincts were initially right. He just jumped in to soon. The party was over on the initial move and the idea was to wait for prices to come back to the starting point of the move. *It happens so many times that if we missed the initial wave it became part of our strategy to wait for the prices to backtrack to the starting point of the whip, post report.* Now with information about the strength or weakness of the report in hand, we could decide to take on the position confidently.

## FEAR OF MISSING A MOVE

This is not an easy thing to do (wait) as thoughts of missing a move are a huge obstacle and a primary cause for failure. We thought long and hard at home about how to handle getting caught in the whipsaw that is commonly seen on known upcoming calendar reports. One day we just began to write down the price the market was trading at one minute prior to the big news event. *Our hunch was that we could see the result and get the same price that we wrote down one minute after the news came out.* We realized that this happened many times and it told us why gamble. You build up so much anxiety prior to the report that your decision-making process gets blocked. This way you can see the news result and then decide if you still want to jump into the water. The only difference is that the speed and window of opportunity on the computer is open only for a short amount of time, so a decisive response is vital. Remember the policemen and firemen analogy. *We don't start trouble, but when it is time to act, we need to spring to life.* The main difference as a trader is the fact that a fireman and policeman have to go fix the trouble no matter what. As a trader you don't have to join the party if it doesn't feel right or you missed the bulk of the anticipated party. Act now or join the party on the next swing. Don't ever fear missing a move when markets are open 24 hours a day, six days a week. You will not catch them all, but there will be plenty of chances.

## CHAPTER 7

# Preparing for Known Events

There are three important lessons to prepare for known events:

1. Understand each report and the time that it is released on the calendar.
2. Know the key players that talk about and make decisions on those results.
3. Understand your emotions in stressful real-time situations

We believe it is important for you to get to know all of the events and people on the lists provided. If you were to ask us which are the most important known events on the calendar to plan for, we would say the early report events at 5:30 AM PT/7:30 AM CT/8:30 AM ET rank number one and the 7:00 AM PT/9:00 AM CT/10:00 AM ET reports rank number two. All reports take a back seat eight times a year to the most important calendar event, which is the Federal Reserve meeting (FOMC) that informs us on their decision to raise, lower, or keep stable the Federal Funds Interest Rate. Running a close second in terms of market attention is the first Friday of every month, when the Unemployment Jobs data report comes out.

## FED FUNDS

During the FOMC meeting, the Chairman and Board set the Federal Funds Interest Rate. The federal funds rate is simply the lending rate (most times over-night) that private banks charge each other for loans. The target rate is set and influenced by the Federal Open Market Committee (FOMC). The FOMC meets eight times a year, at which they decide a rate level based on current economic conditions. They base this decision on the strength or weakness of the U.S. economy and the global economy. The Fed will turn to the employment data to give them clues to help them make a decision on the proper rate adjustment. When the economy is running strong and jobs are plentiful, as from 1990 to 1999 and from 2003 to 2007, the Fed may hike interest rates to keep inflation under control. When the Economy is running weak and jobs are scarce as in 2000 to 2003 and 2008 to 2011, the Fed may lower interest rates to stimulate spending and growth of the economy. *Sentiment: The U.S. dollar (USD) price tends to get stronger with higher interest rates and tends to get weaker with lower interest rates.*

If the Federal Reserve decides to decrease rates, economic activity should and eventually will increase. An example would be the housing industry would pick up. Mortgage loans would be cheaper, thus creating an increase in existing home sales or new home sales. From 2002 to 2006 we saw a huge boom in housing. As rates increased to slow things down from 2005 to 2007, we witnessed the start of the pullback in housing sales and of course in 2008 they began to fall and even collapse with widespread foreclosures. As economic conditions worsened, the Federal Reserve began dropping rates to try and stimulate spending and ease downward pressure on our economy. See Table 7.1.

**TABLE 7.1** Theoretical Price Response Chart

| Event | Increase | | Decrease | |
|---|---|---|---|---|
| Interest Rates | Currency prices | ⇧ | Currency prices | ⇩ |
| Employment | Currency prices | ⇧ | Currency prices | ⇩ |
| Event | Increase | | Decrease | |
| Interest Rates | Stock Index prices | ⇩ | Stock Index prices | ⇧ |
| Employment | Stock Index prices | ⇧ | Stock Index prices | ⇩ |
| Event | Increase | | Decrease | |
| Interest Rates | Bond prices | ⇩ | Bond prices | ⇧ |
| Employment | Bond prices | ⇩ | Bond prices | ⇧ |
| Event | Increase | | Decrease | |
| Interest Rates | Gold prices | ⇩ | Gold prices | ⇧ |
| Employment | Gold prices | ⇩ | Gold prices | ⇧ |
| Event | Increase | | Decrease | |
| Interest Rates | Oil prices | ⇩ | Oil prices | ⇧ |
| Employment | Oil prices | ⇧ | Oil prices | ⇩ |
| Event | Increase | | Decrease | |
| Interest Rates | Corn prices | ⇩ | Corn prices | ⇧ |
| Employment | Corn prices | ⇧ | Con prices | ⇩ |

*Preparing for Known Events*

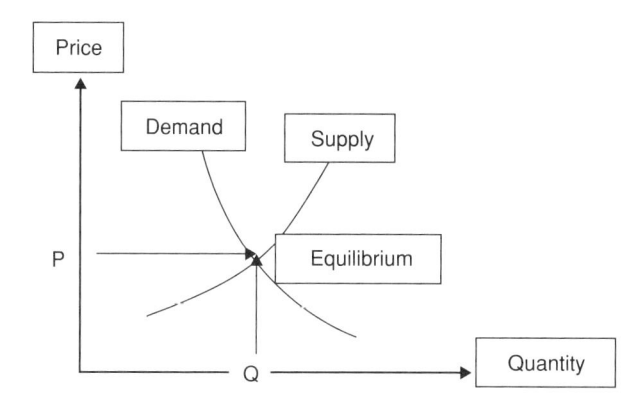

**FIGURE 7.1** Supply/Demand

On the consumer side of the equation, as *supply* increases producers in turn drop their prices in order to attract the consumer to buy, but when *demand* increases, producers increase the price on consumers. The 30-year bond contract becomes a great example of the supply/demand curve. When the U.S. Treasury decided to cease issuing 30-year bonds back in 2001, supply obviously stopped, creating an upward swing in prices.

As interest rates are set and held at all-time lows since 2008 and seem to be locked until mid-2013, we are especially seeing a strong bid in Treasuries (long end still yielding a guaranteed 2 to 3 percent in 2011), and gold (hitting $1900 in 2011). Who wants to invest in a currency with basically a zero rate of return for carrying it? The Federal Reserve is buying back debt as their new weapon (QE stimulus packages) since rates basically can't go any lower. This is done in hopes that it will help the housing crisis and reignite spending by the consumer. The fear with this scenario is that low rates breed inflation, which will continue to be friends of treasuries, gold, oil, and grains. See Figure 7.1.

As the supply and demand curve depicts, when prices go up demand begins to exceed supply and when supply increases price drops to try and spur consumers to buy the product.

## THE PURPOSE OF THE IMF AND THE FED FUNDS TARGET RATE

Many currency traders and governments look to the International Monetary Fund (IMF) to promote financial stability around the globe. Their purpose is to oversee the actions of each of the 187 countries included and to help facilitate international trade to build employment growth and reduce poverty around the globe. It will be interesting over time to see how they will handle the U.S. and European debt crisis and restructure their reserves of USD and Euro (EUR), which make up the vast majority of their holdings. The USD is thought to be the premiere currency, but downgrades in August 2011 by ratings agencies can continue to send shockwaves across the globe as increased cries for a more balanced holding of the world's major currencies emerge. Just as markets have an uncanny way of correcting, so will the IMF, if need be. No matter what currency you begin to analyze you must first get a handle on who controls the actions of the interest rates relating to the pair. In the United States we look to the Federal Reserve.

As the Federal Reserve keeps its target rate held from 0 to 0.25 percent until at least mid-2013, this continues to put a ton of money in the banks hands with an extremely accommodative policy. Of course the wild daily swings that the computers have offered to our markets keeps our focus on ideas from day to day and week to week. Swinging for the fences is for the homerun hitters, and from our knowledge how that works for traders is that they may have a good stretch but they get weeded out very quickly when they strike out. Their fate is very similar to that of the great home-run hitters we had in baseball the last decade. Those that were good at it cheated with steroids, so if their back didn't go out trying to hit the long ball, they were caught red-handed with their hand in the fast-track cookie jar, scarring their name forever.

Whether a weak USD policy is politically motivated or not, our government continues to spend at a rapid pace, all while fighting wars and in-turn devaluing our U.S. dollar. Maybe behind the scenes it's all in hopes of trying to shrink the trade deficit we have with other countries. We buy from others, but with an expensive dollar other countries will not buy from us. So the battle of currency valuations continues with other countries creating price movements and tons of opportunities for trade speculation. It would be nice to be a fly on the wall in the Oval Office to listen in, but all we can do is react and prepare for anything and everything.

The current rates set by the other key banks around the globe are the European Central Bank (ECB), Bank of Japan (BOJ), Bank of Canada (BOC), Reserve Bank of Australia (RBA), Reserve Bank of New Zealand (RBNZ), Bank of England (BOE), and Swiss National Bank (SNB). See Table 7.2. *Along with the FOMC in the United States the BOC and*

**TABLE 7.2** Key Central Bank Rate Chart as of August 2011

| U.S. | ECB | BOJ | BOE | SNB | RBA | RBNZ | BOC |
|------|------|-------|-------|-------|-------|-------|-------|
| 0.25% | 1.50% | 0.10% | 0.50% | 0.00% | 4.75% | 2.50% | 1.00% |

*Preparing for Known Events* **79**

RBNZ meet eight times a year to set policy and interest rates. The SNB meets quarterly and all others meet monthly.

A market to help you with a sense of where interest rates may be heading in the United States is a hidden treasure at Chicago Board of Trade (CBOT) (now under the Chicago Mercantile Exchange [CME] Group roof) called the 30-Day Federal Funds Futures Market (Fed Funds). Professional traders, hedge funds, and industry firms look to this contract as a guide on where interest rates look to move in the months ahead. The confusing part can be in the pricing, but following this simple step will begin to help. Let's start with where the Federal Reserve had the interest rates in August 2011, which was 0.25. What you need to know is the pricing in the Fed Funds is based from 100. A price of 100 in the Fed Funds would equate to a 0.00 interest rate. Since the rate is set at 0.25, take 100 (base rate of 0), then subtract 0.25 (current rate) and you would typically see a Fed Funds price trading at or near 99.75 in the near-month contract.

Traders speculate and move this price to an area where they feel economic conditions are heading. If conditions look to improve, you will see prices begin to drop and in the case of August 2011 rates continue to remain low as the economic picture looks sluggish. In this scenario, the Federal Reserve tries to stimulate the economy by making money cheap to borrow for banks in the hopes they will lend it out to business owners to grow and expand their businesses. In other words, they are trying to get you to spend your money. Fed Funds prices continue to hover closer to 100 than 99.75 under these conditions. When economic conditions improve like we saw in the 1990s and 2003 to 2007, the Federal Reserve tried to pull back the reigns and get you to slow down your spending by raising interest rates.

Now as you look to future contract months in the Fed Funds you can subtract the prices of each month in question from 100 in order to get a feel for when market participants feel there may be a rate hike or a rate drop. See Table 7.3.

**TABLE 7.3** 30-Day Fed Funds as of August 2011

| Month | Fed Funds Price | 100 − Price = Exp Rate |
| --- | --- | --- |
| Aug 2011 | 99.90 | 0.10 |
| Sep 2011 | 99.91 | 0.09 |
| Oct 2011 | 99.91 | 0.09 |
| Sep 2013 | 99.73 | 0.27 |
| Feb 2014 | 99.47 | 0.50 |
| Jun 2014 | 99.23 | 0.77 |

*Source:* www.cmegroup.com

Scanning through the contract months will give you an idea of where rates may be heading. In August 2011 the economic climate obviously in the United States remains sluggish. We had to skip many contract months just to see a sentiment where it was in balance with 0.25 percent, which is not until September 2013. It shouldn't surprise you since the cap that Fed Chairman Bernanke placed on rates (mid-2013) that a prediction for a 25-basis point rate hike is not in the cards until February 2014 based on August 2011 data. If conditions mend and improve as expected, the Federal Reserve Chairman and the Fed Governors will eventually hike interest rates.

It should be noted that a typical movement in interest rates by the Federal Reserve over the years has been in 0.25 increments (or 25 basis points) in normal conditions. In extreme conditions like we faced during the housing collapse and credit crunch in 2008 and 2009, they lowered rates 0.75 to 1.0 at one meeting, which in my eyes and colleagues' eyes alike was the most aggressive drop in rates that we have ever seen. This was of course on the heels of the Bear Stearns and Lehman Brothers collapse.

Everything is always in flux so there are no guarantees but monitoring settlement prices in the 30 Day Fed Funds can help you visualize what main industry professionals are speculating. *We do feel it is important however to remember that industry leaders are speculating to win, not lose.*

Industry leaders typically have more money than the individual investor and hire research teams to evaluate economic conditions. They in turn place positions based upon this research, which can give you added confidence in where they have priced the futures months. *Monitoring price is surprisingly accurate and can save you thousands in research dollars.* We are not suggesting for you not do research, but sometimes when you try and compete with the big dogs you lose focus and start playing too big too soon. We simply are suggesting you use the tools at your disposal efficiently and effectively. *As your analysis is in agreement with industry leaders you gain confidence in the idea. If your analysis falls out of alignment you may begin to take caution.*

## PREPPING FOR EMPLOYMENT REPORTS AND THE FOMC

As you gain confidence in where you believe the economy is heading, now let's try to keep it realistic. Since most people on Earth seem to adhere to instant gratification, especially in the trading industry, preparing for what may happen today can prove to be a more realistic approach. Our parents, teachers, and coaches taught us all as kids and young adults to stay

*Preparing for Known Events* 81

**TABLE 7.4** Preparing for the Employment Report

| Forecast | Previous | Spread = Forecast − Previous |
|---|---|---|
| 89,000 | 46,000 | 43,000 |

focused and present. If you dwell on the past or get too far ahead of yourself you generally will struggle. As we analyze past trends we have also come to grips with the fact that people focus on the day but generally plan their schedules for the week. This will become more apparent in the next Chapter when we talk about our homework rule, which encompasses a daily mood, weekly mood, and a yearly mood.

Let's focus on the current day and help you prepare for how we get ready for the employment data before it is released on the first Friday of every month. Prior to the release you will read and hear many forecasts from news sources like CNBC, CNN, Bloomberg, and the various newswire services like Reuters or Market News International. We draw from these sources and generally find a forecast. In our example we know a few things leading up to the August 5, 2011, date. The forecast was for jobs to increase by 89,000 and the previous report came in at 46,000. The forecast suggests a higher jobs increase for this month, which is positive for the United States and the USD. The months leading up to this time also tell us that payrolls have been sluggish and 89,000 isn't generally going to create that much of a buzz. Remember back when Mike talked about his experience when Bush II got reelected; the payrolls increase was 300,000. That would be robust to say the least. Let's focus on what we know and begin to prepare. See Table 7.4.

We subtract the forecast and the previous to get a spread differential (or forecast high - forecast low) and then add the spread to the high reading and subtract the spread from the low reading to begin to build a sentiment range or mood with certain outcomes. See Table 7.5.

Typically industry analysts will be fairly accurate and not to far off in most cases, just as a weatherman will come fairly close to expectations. If they were wrong all of the time they would of course get weeded out and eventually lose their jobs, so we can begin to trust a forecast to a certain degree. *People generally realize that forecasts will not be right on the money, but something in-line with expectations is normal. For us, we define in-line with the spread differential between the forecast and the previous result.* Taking it a step further if extreme news came from your source, you might of course get a couple more opinions before making any drastic changes.

**TABLE 7.5** Preparing for Results of the Data

| Forecast | U.S. Dollar/Swiss Franc (USDCHF) Expected Action August 5, 2011 |
|---|---|
| 152,000 = 89,000 (forecast) + 43,000 (spread) | Above 152,000 Bullish |
| 89,000 Forecast | Mixed Bull |
| 46,000 Previous | Mixed Bear |
| 3000 = 46,000 (previous) − 43,000 (spread) | Below 3,000 Bearish |

Because traders are speculative in nature you will see some price movement build in the days prior to the release in accordance with the forecast. In this case you might expect the USD to be edging up a bit because a higher payrolls report is expected. More jobs means more spending and more value to the currency. The problem is that we have noticed that in order to get the makings of a strong bullish move you need to at least surpass the 43,000 spread (89,000 + 43,000 = 152,000). The reason for this is that traders have already been pricing in a scenario of 89,000 and what they need is something greater in order to attract new buyers to the party to help their existing long bet. If they don't get something substantially greater than 89,000 prices will remain mixed bull but leaning bullish with readings nearing 152,000. If readings fall below 89,000 to 46,000, bull bets prior to the report will start to suffer a bit despite the fact that the report is overall still positive. Remember, bull speculators prior to the report need something greater than 89,000. In this scenario if the report came out 3,000 or lower this would take the market by surprise and create a mild panic to pre-report bull bets. You can continue to add an additional layer of 43,000 to 152K to give an extra kick to the upside or subtract 43,000 from the 3,000 extreme to get a further downside drop layer.

Let's put this in practical price terms to help you gauge where and how far action may travel according to the result that hits. In Chapter 4 we discussed how we build the support and resistance levels we use to reflect the current conditions, but for simplicity sake let's use assume that the USDCHF normally has a daily price range of 100 pips. This would not be far-fetched as daily price ranges normally seem to oscillate in 1 percent moves (1 percent of 0.7637 is 0.0076 pips rounded to 0.0100 or 100 pips). If the current USDCHF price was 0.7637 before the report, we can begin to predict how far prices might run according to the actual jobs data. See Table 7.6.

*Note:* Traders and students alike often ask us why the market climbed when news suggested it should fall or vice versa. One thing to note is that

*Preparing for Known Events* **83**

**TABLE 7.6** Projecting Market Price Based on Forecasted Results

| Forecast | USD Action | Price Range Expectation 100 Pips USDCHF 8/5/2011 |
|---|---|---|
| 195,000 | Extreme | 0.7737 (100 pip pop of 100 expected |
| 152,000 | Bullish | 0.7687 (50 pip pop of 100 expected) |
| 89,000 Forecast | Mixed Bull | 0.7637 (expected) |
| 46,000 Previous | Mixed Bear | 0.7637 (expected) |
| 3,000 | Bearish | 0.7587 (50 pip drop of 100 expected) |
| −40,000 | Extreme | 0.7537 (100 pip drop of 100 expected) |

we are speculators in this business and are trying to get in front of the next person to gain an edge on our opponents. It's for this very reason that if a report came in at 56,000 text books would suggest that this is bullish and of course it is. But in this case traders built in a price to read a result looking for 89,000 or better and actually need something of 152,000 or higher to get something solid. See Table 7.6.

Once you have your forecasts in hand, now begin to quiz yourself with what if possibilities. For example, here are 3 scenarios to help you prepare for what the Fed might say or do with interest rates (see Table 7.7) with corresponding forecasts and price moves. Rehearsing the possibilities has helped ease our tension before reports.

**Scenario 1:** Now the Federal Reserve has been keeping rates low and locked from 2008 to 2011 and past experience tells us that a typical rate move is in 0.25 increments. The language they use is more telling these days as traders always look ahead to gain an edge (i.e., Quantitative Easing or Operation Twist methods). In this example when the spread differential is 0 then add and subtract what the Fed may normally do to rates in order to help. If the Federal Reserve did nothing and kept language as it read the last time, a choppy mixed price action would likely occur.

**TABLE 7.7** FOMC Interest Rate Preparations (Possible Expectations with Results)

| Forecast | USD Action | Price Range Expectation 100 Pips USDCHF 8/9/2011 |
|---|---|---|
| 0.75 | Extreme | 0.7648 (100 pip pop of 100 expected) |
| 0.50 | Bullish | 0.7598 (50 pip pop of 100 expected) |
| 0.25 Forecast | Mixed Bull | 0.7548 (expected) |
| 0.25 Previous | Mixed Bear | 0.7548 (expected) |
| 0 | Bearish | 0.7587 (50 pip drop of 100 expected) |
| 0 | Leave rates locked until 2013 | 0.7537 (100 pip drop of 100 expected) Created extreme 500 pip drop August 9, 2011 |

**Scenario 2:** If the Federal Reserve raised rates this would obviously have taken everybody by surprise and we would have seen a dramatic rise in the USDCHF. A dramatic upside result would be due to the fact that rates have been low and nobody on the planet would have been expecting a hike in the conditions we had leading up to August 9, 2011. A 100 pip upside minimum result would be in the cards.

**Scenario 3:** If the Federal Reserve lowered rates to 0, which it already in a sense has done, leading up to August 9, 2011, it would be cause for further decline in the USDCHF. The Fed in this case announced that they were going to keep rates locked at historic lows until mid-2013. A 100 pip minimum drop was expected, but the severity of the language caused a drop of 500 pips. Expect the unexpected!

## PREDICTING PRICE RANGE

Practicing scenarios is all well and good, but as traders we feel it is important to have an expectation of how far prices are expected to run based upon results. If an extreme result hits, what does that mean exactly and how can we prepare? We began to develop this feel by using a simple formula that we have mentioned a number of times already, which is the day session range. When you subtract the high from the low you begin to get a feel for how far prices will travel. Taking one day generally doesn't draw on enough information, so we began to look at what most people (traders or the public) realistically plan for, which is a week. *When taking an average daily range over a week you can start to get a realistic feel for how far price will travel.* Of course this is an estimate, but you will be surprised at how far it will take you. You can also begin to back-test on certain reports on how far prices generally travel, but we feel keeping it relevant and focused on what is on the minds of traders in the current week is more relevant than going too far back in your analysis. Remember that you may be drawing data from times when the computer wasn't involved and it was just open outcry. Stay present!

It took some time, but to keep things simple and balanced we found a rhythm that fit our time tolerance and matched it up with the players in the market by focusing on a 15-minute chart for intra-day. *We got an overview and sense of the action on a daily chart for off-hour homework, but found a groove using the 15-minute chart intra-day to help give us more opportunities than a day chart normally offers.* Applying the same concepts and transitioning to a 15-minute chart aligned our instant gratification need to see more opportunities in the time allotment that we could give, which at the same times seemed to fit with the others we played against from day to

*Preparing for Known Events* **85**

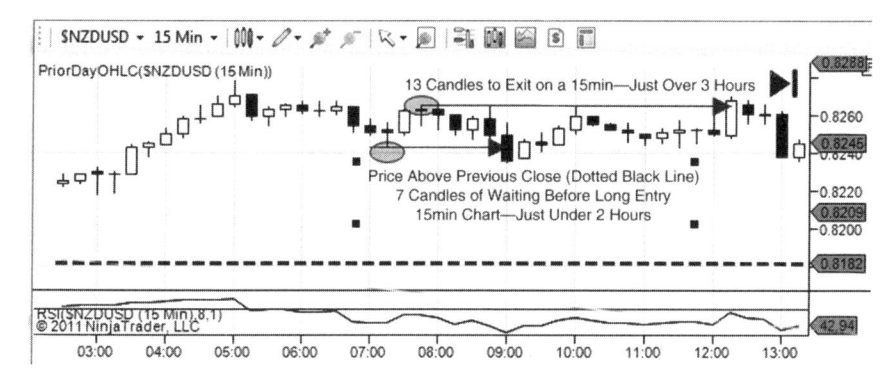

**FIGURE 7.2** Counting 15-Minute Candles between Stand-Out High/Low

day. We intensively studied how long and how far prices tended to travel before we saw a reversal in rotation from stand-out high to stand-out lows and vice versa. See Figure 7.2.

Just as we expressed the importance of a baseline in our examples to build scenarios from where prices were before the report hit, it is equally important to watch time and judge distance. Begin to get a feel for the energy in the market by counting how many candles it took to move from the most recent stand-out high to low to align your time tolerance, whether it is with longer-term swing plays (daily charts) or shorter-term intra-day swing plays (15-minute charts). Understand when a report hits that action can move to the extremes in an instant and when there are no reports, price action will obviously take much longer. Count the candles!

As we keep moving you forward with our strategy, you will see how we piece together what we think about from entry to exit during heated action as reports are released or from the typical daily movement we see when there are no reports scheduled. No matter what condition we face, we know that the action always starts from a baseline and we target the known extremes (highs and lows) to help predict risk, how long it may take, and the distance it may run from start to finish. Since reports are not always on the agenda each and every day, we felt a need to have a structure in place to help guide us all the way through the session and we didn't have to recreate the wheel to find it. The baseline price before a report essentially became the previous close to guide us through the session. Just as we have an annual reset button with a New Year's Resolution (previous yearly close), markets and people have a daily re-set button (previous day session close). We use this benchmark to help us adjust to our 15-minute chart ideas. Some may use the opening price, which in a sense is not that much different in a seamless 24-hour Forex world—when one day ends a new begins. In Chapter 3 we discussed the reasons why we favor the day-end close as a baseline to define direction.

Also begin to take notice of the concepts behind how we factored the spread and then added an extreme layer to the upside and downside in our preparation. The concept behind the baseline is much like midfield in an NFL football game. A team carries heightened strength or weakness at the 25-yard line respective red zone areas (initial addition/subtraction of spread from forecast//previous readings -25 percent of the 100 percent field expectation) and the touchdown areas (extreme result added layer 100 percent high/low), which essentially is splitting the entire field from extreme to extreme into four parts or quarters. The numerical percentages we applied seemed to be in perfect harmony with how many things are viewed in our culture; there are four main temperature readings on a thermometer 0 to 25 (Winter), 50 (spring/fall), and 75 to 100 (summer); there are four quarters in football; there are four quarters in a calendar year; there are four quarters in a dollar; and there are optimists and pessimists feeling half-empty or half-full about the outcome. These concepts will become the foundation that the Rotating Directional System (RDS) strategy stands on to build our key zones using practical numerical percentages. We then balance the weight of these zones against the fundamental or geo-political news to help guide us through this game we call the markets.

# CHAPTER 8

# Risk Tolerance and Developing a Feel for Price Movement

Mike's football coach at Mt. Carmel High School in Chicago used to always say, "If it's to be, it's up to me . . . do it right!" In our opinion everyone has the ability to develop a feel for price action. Although we have been around the markets for quite a while now, trust us, we were not born with these special qualities. They were born out of sheer hard work and experience which, in turn, we used to develop the Rotating Directional System (RDS) strategy, thus enabling us to navigate the markets with success.

In the previous chapters we discussed the fundamentals which give us the confidence to put on a long or a short position. Now we will begin to further develop timing techniques to help discover when it is appropriate to apply those ideas. We will be sharing with you the five rules that consist of the RDS strategy, developed by Mike over the first several years he spent in the business.

Since we are both athletes, we find it easy to relate our trading to athletics and competition. We don't have the same athletic background, but the analogies still provide clarity. It doesn't matter whether you've played a team sport or an individual sport or haven't played one ever, we all at one time or another face an opponent in life, and it's all competition and only one team or person can win. Even though trading seems to be an individual endeavor, we found through our experiences on the trading floors that there are clear and obvious teammates and opponents. *Knowing who our teammates and opponents are at all times in trading is crucial.* We need to know who we can depend on and who we need to stay away from. The health of our teammates gives us an indication of how strong they are and how much power they have to push the market in the direction of choice. A weak teammate will cut and run on us, giving us no hope to help our position. In the trading pit the division was clear. We had noise, facial expressions, and hand signals we could read. They told us who we could rely on, and we became excellent readers of lips and body language. When we moved to the screen we figured out a way to translate these very important cues. This is where a pit trader-turned-screen trader has a huge advantage over someone who has never had pit experience.

## THE TRADING FOOTBALL FIELD

As we begin to dig deep and describe the RDS strategy we will refer to the layout of an American football field to build upon the understanding of the trading field. You will not need to know much about American football to follow along. In fact we use the analogy very loosely.

| End zone | End zone |
|---|---|
| 10 | 10 |
| 20 | 20 |
| 30 | 30 |
| 40 | 40 |
| 50 | |
| 40 | 40 |
| 30 | 30 |
| 20 | 20 |
| 10 | 10 |
| End zone | End zone |

## THE LIGHT BULB WENT OFF IN 1992

Funny as it may be, after four years on the trading floor as a runner and then graduating to a clerk, it hit Mike on a Sunday afternoon while watching an NFL football game. It was the fall of 1992, almost one year before he got his big break to trade and fill orders in the 30-year bond futures

## Risk Tolerance and Developing a Feel for Price Movement 89

pit. Mike was already studying and preparing for the opportunity as if it already happened. He had wanted it badly, and knew that if his bosses would give him a chance he would show them how good he could be. Mike was relating everything in his daily life to trading. We talked so much about trading that our friends started to loathe hanging around us. We became boring. We didn't want to party anymore. We were serious about our goals to become great traders and order fillers, and nothing was going to get in our way.

So, on this fall day while watching his favorite sport, Mike started to listen to the game announcers in the way he was trained to listen to the trader's voices on the trading floor. The announcers voices changed as the teams marched up and down the gridiron. As one team would get closer to scoring the announcers would get louder and more animated. Their voice levels ebbed and flowed based on the position of the ball on the field. The new understanding flashed brightly in Mike's head, much like I'm sure it did in Mark Zuckerberg's head when he began to put Facebook together. The 50-yard line on the gridiron was where players, fans, and announcers began to get excited as a team was driving and threatening to score. *The 50 is the pivotal line to help all of us understand in the heat of the game a place to gauge what team was controlling the action and who might score or eventually win.* The object is to reach the end-zone and the 50-yard line is the halfway point on the 100-yard field. Are we a quarter of the way, half of the way, three-quarters of the way, or are have we reached our goal?

We always want to know who's winning as a player or a spectator, especially if we had to leave the action for a minute. Once we return to the action and check the score, the next question most often is who has the ball and where are they on the field. Speculation about the outcome runs rampant as the action moves back and forth on the field in sports and it is no different when it comes to trading.

*The end-zone objectives on the trading gridiron was the range (High minus Low is 100 percent) and 50 percent was the midpoint (High plus Low divided by 2).* See Figure 8.1. Mike realized emotions in football were similar to those in trading. The only real difference was traders were not physically pounding on each other like the football players. They were instead financially pounding on each other.

As Mike started getting fired up about his analogy, he watched and listened as the action of the game unfolded. He watched the teams get greedy trying trick plays or long passes resulting in erratic outcomes. The team that marched methodically down the field typically dictated the tempo and performed precisely and consistently. Aha! If you already know Mike as a trader today, you know this is the name of his game. He has been and

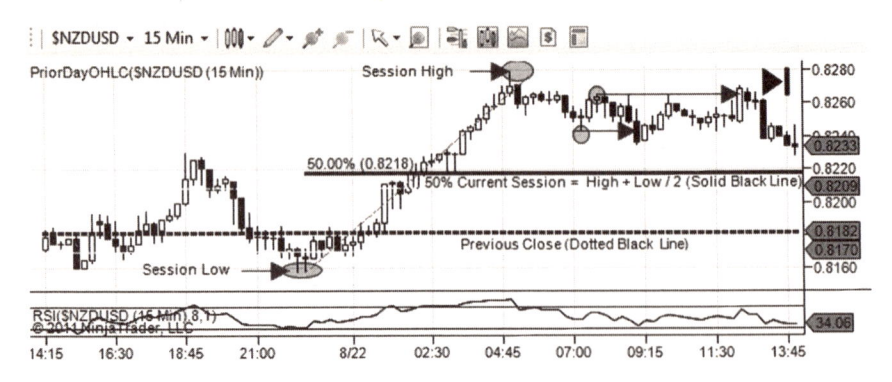

**FIGURE 8.1** High/Low and 50 Percent

continues to be a methodical and consistent trader. Mike has never been a homerun hitter or end-zone-to-end-zone producer, but the base hit or 10-yard style he aimed for added up to a consistent successful approach in his athletic career and it now matched perfectly with his trading career. The methodical team attacked with reasonable, hard-nosed objectives. They did not try to move from one end of the field to the other in one play, but chose to move 10 yards at a time. How was this part related to trading Mike wondered. He went back to the floor the following Monday with his analogy and quickly recognized consistent market shifts after the equivalent of 10- to 20-yard runs (similar concept we tweak to 12.5 to 25 percent of the expected range or simply one- to two-level moves explained as we move forward). See Table 8.1.

The bulls control the top half of the range and the bears control the bottom half. Excitement builds for either team as they move price inside their opponents' red zone as they eye a touchdown.

When you start a task and look at the entire picture, sometimes you tend to get overwhelmed and this wasn't any different when Mike brought

**TABLE 8.1** Trading Field

| High | Touchdown | High |
|---|---|---|
| 12.5% | First and Goal | 12.5% |
| 25.0% | Red zone | 25.0% |
| 37.5% | Field Goal Range | 37.5% |
| 50.0% | MidField | 50.0% |
| 37.5% | Field Goal Range | 37.5% |
| 25.0% | Red zone | 25.0% |
| 12.5% | First and Goal | 12.5% |
| Low | Touchdown | Low |

*Risk Tolerance and Developing a Feel for Price Movement* **91**

his sports analogy to trading. Running the length of the field with opponents trying to drill you into the dirt isn't always going to be smooth and pretty. You don't go out and start a marathon 26.2 miles saying in your head that "Oh my, I have to run 26.2 miles today." You break it into manageable chunks to keep the internal chatter in check to distances like a quarter, half, three quarters, and then the finish. This is much like we handle a calendar year; winter, spring, summer, and fall. Once he recognized the typical movement or rotation in the market, Mike matched that up with his personal account risk tolerance, which we will talk about in depth as we move further into the chapter.

As Mike continued to study the trader's behaviors in relation to the rotation he was noticing, he narrowed down his analysis to daily time frames and applied his thoughts to the 15-minute chart. Looking at these ranges the realistic ebb and flow seemed to rotate 12.5 to 25 percent of the range (equivalent to the concept of the 10 to 20 yard moves) in the time tolerance that most allot to the idea. See Figure 8.2. Fifty percent of the field seemed to take all day and the entire field of movement only seemed to happen on extreme events. In the technical chapter we will talk much more about the time frames we use to build our levels, which ones we use to enter and exit our trades, and when to use them. We will also talk more about the percentages we use and how they relate to those that apply Fibonacci sequences, which in the end is not much different. Laughs generally fill our office when people, traders, and educators say they have unlocked Fibonacci's mystical trading formula. We will dispel this myth. You must understand that the market is extremely dynamic and no magic formula exists when fear, greed, and humans control the action. Levels, whether perfect fractals or Fibonacci retracements, should be thought of as measuring sticks to help gauge what typically can happen. Market tops and bottoms matched

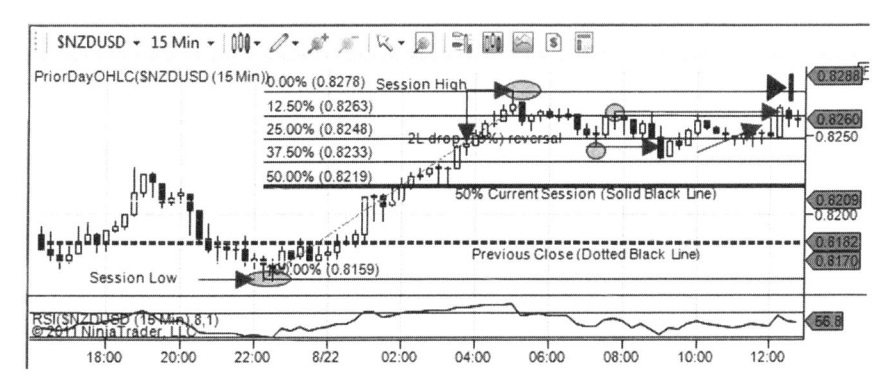

**FIGURE 8.2** 12.5 to 25 Percent Keys (One- to Two-Level Moves)

with the levels provide the better overall lean to help build confidence on the play and how much you might want to risk on it.

Most importantly, when Mike computed and prepared for a 12.5 to 25 percent typical market rotation, his emotions calmed and greed and fear found balance. It became more about grooving with the market like a school of fish moves with the current, and less about the dollars adding up and/or dwindling rapidly.

## YARDS VERSUS LEVELS

The key on our football trading gridiron is how we translate the 10- to 20-yard increments into trading terms. We already declared the midpoint represents the 50-yard line. We then evenly split and assign percentages to the upper and lower half of the field. Each side of the field is broken down into two parts initially and assigned percentages equally spaced 25 percent apart to make up the main end zones (high/low), red zones, and midfield. We call each percentage zone a level. We felt the need to break down the field and lean on the key parts of the field that tell us so much about the emotions of each team up and down the grid. Since it is not always easy to capture half of the field, let alone 25 percent of it on one play, we felt something even more realistic was needed to help us work our way to the objective (high/low). As today's ranges extend and volatility increases, we felt a need to break down the levels one more time in eight equal parts (12.5 percent increments), which was closer to the 10-yard mentality that teams initially target.

## TWO TYPES OF TRADERS

Because there is always somebody willing to buy and always someone willing to sell it creates two types of traders—momentum and contrarian. The question becomes which type is better? We think they are both needed. We want to help you build an approach that allows you to draw from and use the best of each style and show you how we combine both schools of thought.

Momentum traders go with the price action. If prices are falling, we like to be momentum traders and sell first (go short). If prices are rising, we like to be momentum traders and buy first (go long). The problem is to find the best time to buy or sell.

Going against the flow as a contrarian trader is a strategy that some adopt. Trying to pick a high or low is a viable approach at times, but we have found it to be a disastrous strategy in trending markets which Forex pairs most often produce. We will also add here that in the 30 years of combined trading we have never bought the low and sold the high in one trading session. We have held some winning trades that may have surpassed a normal day's range, but buying the 24-hour low and selling the 24-hour high has never happened. It just doesn't happen and if it does happen it is rare and should not be relied on that it will occur on a daily basis. We realize that once you get a taste of connecting with a great trade, you want it over and over, but you soon will need a dose of reality—which the market will assuredly slap you with should you try to match the rare event. It's like hitting a hole in one, although Mike has had a hole in one on an 18-hole course, believe it or not. The point still remains that it has only happened once over 30 years of playing golf, and repeating the rare event isn't something to be relied upon.

Experience has taught us, though, to combine the two strategies by playing momentum with a contrarian twist. We have found a way to put them together to increase our profitability. If prices hit a new session low, rise back toward the newly calculated midpoint and stall (lower lows on 15 minutes), we look to sell at the first retest of the area as a contrarian while at or near this benchmark. After we got short, our objective would be the session low that was established earlier. If prices hit a new session high and fall back toward our newly calculated midpoint, we look to buy as a contrarian at the first retest of the area while at or near this benchmark. After we took on the long position we would target the session high that was established. Both of these scenarios had their direction decided first. When prices are establishing new lows, we think short or if prices are establishing new highs we think long. The idea is to wait but for a pullback rally up (for short) or a dip back down (for long) at or near the midpoint but still on momentum side. We want to wait for a stall in prices or basically see some lower lows to confirm short or higher highs to confirm long. If the resistance area for the short play or the support area for the long play still resides on the proper side of the midpoint (momentum gauge), get after it and target a retest of the session lows for the short or target a retest of the highs for the long. The flip in trend at or near the midpoint will be later defined as the window of opportunity.

## RISK

In our opinion no strategy, no education program, and no trading book would be complete without a discussion on risk. We place the discussion on risk here because we cannot talk about our strategy in depth going forward without this. Our motto is "Trade Strong, Trade Smart, and always make sure you can come back and trade tomorrow!" We have been able to come back every day because our commitment to our risk parameters is adhered to or else we are benched until a more reasonable risk-minded attitude dominates.

Most educators address risk in the following manner: "Make sure you have your risk parameters set. As a rule of thumb, most traders don't like to lose more than 2 to 5 percent in a day." And they leave the student with that. We like to dive in as deep as we can with risk. We developed an interactive risk calculator for ourselves when we first started trading in order to make sure on a daily basis that we did not and would not breach our risk parameters. As educators we share this calculator and talk about risk the way we address it personally. We are aware no two traders are emotionally equipped with the same tools and each person has a different relationship with money. Each person deposits different amounts of money at different times in his or her account. Finally, no two markets trade exactly the same way. Even though the currencies often trend together, some are more volatile than others. When we took all of these factors into account we realized risk tolerance is very personal.

We see this in action when we trade side by side. We use the same strategy; enter trades in the same spots. The difference is where we get out. We definitely don't have the same patience tolerance to hold trades. Our accounts have different balances and we both have different relationships with money.

## THE OLD DAYS

What shocks us most about the evolution of trading is how the brokerage firms used to handle risk. On the trading floor before things were electronic we would card up each trade we made. In other words we would write down on a hard, cardboard trading card each trade we executed. A trade checker would pick up our cards every 15 minutes, check our trades with the other trade checkers of the traders we completed the transactions with, and literally run the cards to the trade punchers. The trade punchers would type up the trades and enter them into the trading system of our respective brokerage firms, which would then send the trades electronically to the clearinghouse of the Chicago Board of Trade (CBOT) or the Chicago Mercantile Exchange (CME) to be matched. Can you see the holes in this

*Risk Tolerance and Developing a Feel for Price Movement* **95**

**FIGURE 8.3** Trading Card

system? Some traders would have massive losing positions but by the time the trades were matched up in the system, the brokerage firm would finally realize they had a trader that was standing in the trading pit trading debit. This happened often and on occasion we would see the risk manager of a firm come into the pit to drag the trader out and stop him or her from trading, but this was still after the fact that tons of money had been lost. Often times a trader could not afford to pay the brokerage firm back, and the firm was liable to come up with the money to honor the trade. See Figure 8.3.

Steph used to be an out-trade clerk before she became a broker. Late at night after the trading day and early the following morning she would get printouts of all the trades executed by the traders in the firm. Steph would have to try to reconcile all the trade punch errors (typos), which would result in unmatchable trades. Since we are all human, there were also many trades that were carded up at the wrong price and the wrong amount and she had to make sure everything was reconciled before the start of the new trading session.

## TODAY

It is much easier for the brokerage firms to manage risk these days. As a trader, if you breach your account balance the computer is set up to automatically close your position out before anything gets out of hand. We personally don't wait until this occurs. We don't use our computer as a back stop. That's too late because if the computer stops you out you most certainly have lost more than the 2 to 5 percent total allocation. We need to manage our own risk and make sure there is still money in the account for tomorrow. The brokerage firms are all competing for your business, too, so they lower the minimum account balance requirements to encourage you to open up an account. We realize these lesser account values are enticing, but when you read on, most traders are shocked to see how undercapitalized they truly are and therefore have almost no chance to succeed.

Overall we will go on record here that in order to trade fulltime for a living you need at least $50,000 of risk capital; meaning if you lost this amount, you still would be able to breathe! You do not need to put this all into your account on day one. In fact we strongly advise you to start trading the micro or mini accounts while you become familiar with who you are as an investor. Let's put it this way: Mike once went to Las Vegas with $3000 of gambling money. Three days, $1000 of risk per day, worst case; nice plan, right? He realized that he could lose and knew he could lose it all but he wanted to spread out his entertainment at the tables with a $1000 loss cap at the end of each night. Wouldn't you know it, he went to the casino floor with all $3000 in his pocket. It didn't pan out that weekend and he was left watching the last two nights. He learned a valuable lesson about risk and himself that weekend. Remove the temptation by keeping a realistic minimum in your account, but enough to free you to trade what you want to trade on any given day. As educators, that is why we love Forex; you can adjust the pip value to a proper setting according to what you carry in your account. We see it as a viable tool for learning without losing an incredible amount of money, based on the fact that you are playing with lower values as you discover who you are when the temptation hits. Trust us, you are going to lose money, especially in the beginning, so why not take it slow and grow?

## PERSONAL RISK TOLERANCE

It was vital we learned from the beginning the value of a price increment otherwise known as a pip or a tick in the markets we traded. We studied the length of time market prices took to travel one level (discussed in detail in the next chapter) and how far prices tended to travel in a 24-hour span.

At the end of the day we calculated the dollar value if we bought the high and sold the low or bought the low and sold the high per one contract. This gave us the worst/best case scenario if we put on a one-contract trade. Preparing ourselves in this way helped us get used to the dollar swings in the market every time we sit down to trade.

We adhere to the 5 percent rule. We never allow ourselves to lose more than 5 percent of our account value per 24 hours. Using the RDS strategy we usually see about one to four trading opportunities per day. We take this 5 percent and spread it out over those four ideas to create a buffer and a strike one (1.25 percent), strike two (2.5 percent), strike three (3.75 percent), and you're definitely out mentality after 5 percent. In other words we are not willing to risk more than 1.25 percent on any particular idea. This is another rule of thumb that has allowed us great staying power in the markets. Since we are aware that everyone's risk tolerance is different, our risk calculator has the option to change these percentages. Remember, the goal is to come back and trade tomorrow.

## INTRODUCING THE RDS RISK CALCULATOR

The risk calculator is an interactive, online device that provides monetary risk breakdowns for the RDS strategy (visit www.rdstrader.com for details). The figures generated by the calculator are very specific in the sense that it breaks down risk from level to level and narrows the big picture as much as possible. As we know markets don't always behave the way we anticipate, so these are only general guidelines broken down as far as possible. We ultimately know what our downside risk is on any particular trade and we never breach it.

Each morning we type in our account value and it generates the amount of money we can risk on each trade (based on the idea that we see four trades per day or 1.25 percent). In the example, we plugged in $50,000 for our account balance. The risk calculator tells us with this amount of money in our account we can lose up to $625 on any particular trade idea (1.25 percent). If we are down $2,500 at any time in the day, we have to turn the computer off. Since there are generally three strikes before you get thrown out, Mike adheres to 3.75 percent, allowing for slippage that may occur ensuring he will not be more than 5 percent down worst case. Let's face it; if you have tried an idea three times and you failed on all of them, it most often signals that it isn't your day anyway and you should

**FIGURE 8.4** Risk Allotment

| Daily Expected Risk / Reward | | | |
|---|---|---|---|
| 50,000.00 | << Account $$ | | Profit/Loss |
| $625.00 | 1.25% | | Single/Strike 1 |
| $1,250.00 | 2.50% | | Double/Strike 2 |
| $1,875.00 | 3.75% | | Triple/Strike 3 |
| $2,500.00 | 5.00% | | Homerun/Out |

shut the computer off. You can also begin to sense when you swing and miss twice that something is up, so start to get a bit more conservative if the market takes you deep in the count. This is where true discipline comes in. We want to be able to come back and trade tomorrow. Your money is your lifeline in this business, so don't destroy your account or career on one bad trade. See Figure 8.4.

On the upside you can think of each percentage on your winning trades as a single (1.25 percent), double (2.50 percent), triple (3.75 percent), and a homerun (5 percent). Once we get a sense of the money we can risk, we look to the main section of the calculator. In the left-hand column titled "Markets" it lists all the markets we provide support and resistance levels for each day, including our 10 favorite and widely traded Forex markets: U.S. dollar/Japanese Yen (USDJPY), Euro/U.S. dollar (EURUSD), Euro/Japanese Yen (EURJPY), British Pound/U.S. dollar (GBPUSD), New Zealand dollar/U.S. dollar (NZDUSD), Australian dollar/U.S. dollar (AUDUSD), U.S. dollar/Swiss Franc (USDCHF), U.S. dollar/Canadian dollar (USDCAD), Euro/Swiss Franc (EURCHF), and Euro/British Pound (EURGBP). The 20 futures markets we cover include: EUR, JPY, GBP, AUD, CAD, CHF, USD Index, E-mini S&P 500, Dow, Russell, NASDAQ, 30-year bonds, 10-year notes, five-year notes, corn, soybeans, wheat, oats, oil, and gold. For example purposes we will focus on the Forex markets, specifically the EURUSD. See Figure 8.5.

If you don't have $50,000, but you have $5000 to start you can adjust the pip values down to as low as $0.10 micro pips to adjust to your risk tolerance. See Figure 8.6.

The column to the right of the Market list is the "Tick/Pip Value" column. This shows the value of a single price movement (tick/pip) in each market listed. Remember we mentioned it is critical we know this about each of our chosen markets. We need to know how much money is at risk every time we put on a trade and the market moves in our favor or against us. Now this is a really interesting column because the futures markets

## Risk Tolerance and Developing a Feel for Price Movement

| Markets | Tick/Pip Value | Level | Level | Trade Size |
|---|---|---|---|---|
| EURUSDFX | $ 10.00 | $ 380.00 | $ 1,520.00 | 1 |
| USDJPYFX | $ 12.40 | $ 161.20 | $ 644.80 | 1 |
| USDCHFFX | $ 11.08 | $ 398.88 | $ 1,595.52 | 1 |
| GBPUSDFX | $ 10.00 | $ 390.00 | $ 1,560.00 | 1 |
| NZDUSDFX | $ 10.00 | $ 320.00 | $ 1,280.00 | 1 |
| EURJPYFX | $ 12.40 | $ 359.60 | $ 1,438.40 | 1 |
| AUDUSDFX | $ 10.00 | $ 380.00 | $ 1,520.00 | 1 |
|  |  | 1 | 4 |  |
| Markets | Tick/Pip Value | Level | Level | Trade Size |

**FIGURE 8.5** Risk Matched with One- to Four-Level Range Expectation (Professional)

have static tick values. What we mean by this is no matter what we do, we cannot change the value of the tick when it comes to actually trading. These values are set by the laws governing each contract. However, this is where Forex is not only a great trading tool, but it is an amazing learning tool to use with real, live trades. When we first started trading Forex we were able to risk small amounts of money compared to the standard way we learned to trade Futures in the beginning.

When we look at the Tick/Pip Value column on the risk calculator we can actually plug in values like $0.10, $1.00, or $10.00 for the value of any of our 10 Forex markets.

The next two columns to the right of the Tick/Pip Value are the "Level" columns. The first one defaults to one level of movement for each market. This gives us an indication, in general, of the amount of money at risk for better or worse over approximately 15 minutes to an hour depending upon price action. The next column shows a four-level movement and dollar value, which is how far we expect price to move for the session. Twenty-four-hour market action isn't guaranteed to move these distances as price could deliver more or less than what we see on the risk calculator.

| Markets | Tick/Pip Value | Level | Level | Trade Size |
|---|---|---|---|---|
| EURUSDFX | $ 0.10 | $ 3.80 | $ 15.20 | 1 |
| USDJPYFX | $ 0.12 | $ 1.56 | $ 6.24 | 1 |
| USDCHFFX | $ 0.11 | $ 3.96 | $ 15.84 | 1 |
| GBPUSDFX | $ 0.10 | $ 3.90 | $ 15.60 | 1 |
| NZDUSDFX | $ 0.10 | $ 3.20 | $ 12.80 | 1 |
| EURJPYFX | $ 0.12 | $ 3.48 | $ 13.92 | 1 |
| AUDUSDFX | $ 0.10 | $ 3.80 | $ 15.20 | 1 |
|  |  | 1 | 4 |  |
| Markets | Tick/Pip Value | Level | Level | Trade Size |

**FIGURE 8.6** Risk Matched with One- to Four-Level Range Expectation (Micro)

Its overall purpose was to give us a sense of what can happen to help alleviate the tension that generally comes about as we enter trades. As ranges widen or tighten from day to day, these amounts will change as the volatility of the particular market changes from day to day.

## USING THE RDS RISK CALCULATOR

We come in with a mentality of something a bit more realistic in terms of objectives and initially target one level of profit or one level of risk. A one-to-one ratio is respectable in the beginning. As you learn how to lose and recover you can hold your losses to a minimum of one level (12.5 percent of expected range) while trying to stretch your gains to a double (two levels— 25 percent of expected range), triple (–three levels—37.5 percent of expected range), or homerun (four levels—50 percent of expected range or normal day session price movement). Overall we see the market rotate one to two levels consistently and feel this is a more realistic objective. On our winning trades we to try and make one to two levels (12.5 percent to 25 percent of the range matched with 1.25 to 2.5 percent account value on upside) and stop ourselves out for a loss on trades that go one level against us (12.5 percent of range matched with 1.25 percent account value on downside).

So let's take into consideration that you have $625 to risk that matches to 1.25 percent of your account. As we match and balance this idea around a normal price rhythm of one level we see that we can adjust the pip value to $1 and trade up to 16 lots (EURUSD or $16 per pip total) which would expose us up to $608 over one level according to our risk calculator adjustment on August 23, 2011. See Figure 8.7.

If you had the setting at the standard professional one lot at $10 per pip, one level would put us under budget at $380 and if we did two lots

| Markets | Tick/Pip Value | Level | Level | Trade Size |
|---|---|---|---|---|
| EURUSDFX | $ 1.00 | $ 646.00 | $ 1,292.00 | 17 |
| USDJPYFX | $ 12.40 | $ 161.20 | $ 322.40 | 1 |
| USDCHFFX | $ 11.08 | $ 398.88 | $ 797.76 | 1 |
| GBPUSDFX | $ 10.00 | $ 390.00 | $ 780.00 | 1 |
| NZDUSDFX | $ 10.00 | $ 320.00 | $ 640.00 | 1 |
| EURJPYFX | $ 12.40 | $ 359.60 | $ 719.20 | 1 |
| AUDUSDFX | $ 10.00 | $ 380.00 | $ 760.00 | 1 |
| Markets | | 1 | 2 | Trade Size |

**FIGURE 8.7** Two-to-One Risk/Reward Ratio Range Expectation Matched with One- to Two-Level Range (Micro)

it would put one level at $760 and over risk budget, which is a no-no. One standard professional lot becomes the total you could risk according to the expected volatility on August 23, 2011. This can be very limiting along the way. Let's say you want to take some profit after you achieve one level. If you just did one standard professional lot at $10 per pip, your idea would be over at the point upon exit. If you had 16 lots at $1, you can take off 10 (equivalent to what you would have had with one standard professional contract) and have six more left to let ride to increase you upside potential. As the saying goes, there is strength in numbers!

## THE WAY MIKE LEARNED FUTURES

When Mike first went on his own to trade his own account in 1997 he needed to put up a $50,000 Treasury Bill for collateral, $50,000 into a trading account, and had to pay $5,000 per month for a seat lease, which gave him the right to stand in the 30-year bond futures pit and trade. He hadn't even opened his mouth and he was already down money. If you know the 30-year bonds at all, you know the value of a tick is $31.25. This meant that if he bought one contract at 120-08 and sold it at 120-09 he would have made $31.25. At the time Mike first started there were 1,000 traders in this pit. Do you think he was able to get the attention of anyone to trade anything with him if he was looking to trade one contract at a time? No way! Mike had to trade 5 or 10 contracts at times in order to just open a position. Right away he was getting out of four or nine depending on what he had to start with, so he could get his position down to a reasonable level. Mike was plenty capitalized to trade more than one at a time but when you are unsure of yourself in the beginning, why risk more than you should. As you learn and gain confidence you can and should step up your game. So, when he had to take 10 contracts and the market went from 120-08 to 120-09 before he could blink he was up/down $312.50. In two ticks he was at his 1.25 percent risk tolerance on his account. Ten lots according to his 1.25 percent ($625) risk tolerance gave him very little room as the bonds at that time were moving about a full handle (32 ticks/$1000 per one lot) per day and roughly around half of that over a one- to two-hour stretch.

One price increment move in 30-year bonds which could take literally one second in time showed him more money than he had ever been used to making or dreamed of making in one second let alone per hour. As exciting as it was, not every trade was/is a winner and this scared him initially. The risk calculator began to ease the anxiety over time. Even though Mike found success, we are aware the failure rate in trading is ridiculously high, and it's not surprising because people don't understand the risk involved. They have not properly prepared to adjust their tolerance with what the market will throw at them during the session. So, when we found trading Forex would allow a trader to change the value of the price increment all the way down to $0.10 at a time, we were overjoyed. Perhaps this could lower the failure rate!

When Mike moved off of the trading floor in 2004 he was concerned with his own failure rate. He had spent the first 15 years of his career trading 30-yearr bond futures very successfully. He had also spent the second half of that 15 years providing support and resistance levels for a number of other markets, although he did not trade them. When Mike left the trading floor to trade on the computer screen the bonds were trading four ticks a day. That was the whole range. He was terrified. He could not make the same living that he was used to making. Mike had to try something different but he was scared. And, that is when he started trading Forex micro and mini lots. He got used to the movement of the currencies, addressed the risk using his parameters, and started applying his RDS strategy. Mike built up his confidence again and realized he could truly trade anything at that point. Mike started trading other markets and enjoyed all of them.

Once we became successful at trading Forex, the next step was to add to our size. We refer back to our calculator to see what kind of monetary risk we are exposed to as we change our contract size. Does it match with our 1.25 percent risk per trade? Are we properly capitalized? Demo accounts have never served us in terms of trading strategy. We found that we do not behave or react the same way on a demo account as we do with a live account. Demo accounts breed a bit more recklessness and we always win on the demo account because there is nothing at stake. This is not real life. Practice how you will trade live. If you have never traded live before, then you are not a trader yet, and trust us, trading live is a whole different ball game. Our bodies go through an emotional ride when live money is at risk.

## NO VACATION FROM DISCIPLINE

Before we close our discussion about risk, we want to tell you a story about Bryan Farming (name has been changed but the story is true and relevant). Back in the early 1990s as a recent college graduate, Bryan came to us to explore our trading education program. He had a few college friends that were doing well in the S&P500 Futures pit and he wanted to try it, too. They recommended he come talk to us. After chatting with us for a few hours Bryan decided he didn't need the education and went ahead to apply for membership to trade on his own accord. Steph recalls several months later sitting on the Membership Committee, a committee selected by the Chicago Mercantile Exchange Board, to vote on prospective members. As a committee member she was privy to bank statements and credit reports of each individual who was petitioning to become a member of the exchange. Steph came across Bryan's paperwork and saw everything she needed to see. She knew his debts, how much money he had in the bank, and who his friends were. He seemed properly capitalized, but Steph knew after talking with him he had no idea how to manage the risk. No plan in place.

Sure enough Bryan became a member and jumped right into the S&P 500 Futures pit. Within several months Bryan had lost more than $60,000 and came crying to us, real tears! We felt bad. Luckily he was smart enough to stop before he was thrown on the street, but it was close. We sat down with Bryan and asked him what he was willing to do. Could he pick himself back up? Was he willing to stay the course we recommended? Eventually we were able to get Bryan on the right track and he became quite a successful trader, but not without dedication and hard work. We did not allow him, nor did he allow himself, to take a vacation from his discipline. Bryan followed our plan like a perfect student. He made his money back, and when he felt he had made more money than he ever imagined, he quit. It was an unbelievable experience for him, but he was so shocked by the pendulum swing of the money he had lost and gained that he had enough. Today he is successful salesperson happily living with a beautiful family of his own.

We often talk about Bryan and his introduction to trading because this still happens often. People just don't realize how undercapitalized they are and where the risk really lies. They don't break it down. Having a solid strategy and trading Forex micro or mini lots can slow down the losing process while you gain experience, all while learning live with real money and giving you the best chance for success as you grow to full-time trading. We are seeing a steady incline of success as this result, and we wish we had this opportunity when we first started.

## FIVE KEYS TO SUCCESS

Before we begin to discuss the core of the RDS strategy, we want to mention five areas we have identified that have helped contribute to our success:

1. Preparation contributes to timing
2. Experience contributes to strategy
3. Risk management contributes to longevity
4. Fear balances greed
5. Win some, learn some

As in any endeavor, the key to success is preparation. When we prepare for each trading day, we give ourselves the confidence to put on the trade, hold the trade, and either take profit when it is time or have the intelligence to take a small loss. We know how to address each of these steps because we have prepared. Think back to your school days. When you had an exam, how did you prepare? Did you retake the quizzes, redo your homework from the section, and look over practice exams? And, when you did all this how did you feel when you walked into the classroom to take that exam? What if you didn't do all that? Did you feel as confident? *We enjoy feeling like we did all we could to prepare for each trading day just like we did in school, although preparation here is even more crucial because this is your money, in your own hands.*

When we prepare, our understanding of the markets is clearer and it gives us the confidence to enter the trade at the right time. When we have prepared we are calmer while we are in the trade and can see the trade objectively as time goes on and price action moves forward. Before we enter our trade, we have a clear idea of where we would like to get out and we can watch for that target with an open mind. If the trade goes against us, we have prepared for that as well. We know how much money we can lose according to our risk parameters and still come back and try again.

Our goal is to share our experiences with you so we can help shorten your learning curve. Of course you are going to have your own experiences and will hopefully learn from all of them, the good, the bad, and the ugly. Most people have to make their own mistakes. How many times did you touch the hot stove when your mother told you not to? We tried once and that was enough. Losing money is painful, and hopefully you will not make the same mistakes over and over. The goal here is to learn from your mistakes and ours!

## Preparation Contributes to Timing

In the very beginning when Mike began to make his own trading decisions, he paid close attention to the traders around him. He listened to what they were talking about and watched when they got active and when they got quiet. He studied facial expressions and watched body language along the way to get clues as to when his colleagues were confident and when they were struggling. When he heard a term used and didn't know what it was, he would look it up. Mike read everything he could get his hands on. When someone would leave a chart up on the CQG terminal outside the pit, he would print it out and study it. Mike tried incorporating many different ideas into his developing strategy.

## Experience Contributes to Strategy

Sometimes his strategy would become what we call today the "Scotty Major syndrome." Scotty is a friend and a long-time student of ours that came to us one day in need of some support. We took a look at his homework and in an instant saw the problem. Scotty had been using so many indicators that his homework looked as if a young child took over with a few crayons. Scotty was extremely smart, but tended to over-analyze the task at hand. It was a big, scribbled mess. Over time Mike had realized how important it was to keep it simple, and we shared this with Scotty. It made a colossal difference in his trading. You know the acronym K.I.S.S. (Keep It Simple, Stupid)? You might wonder, though, if you have to keep it simple, which pieces of the puzzle fit best? A strong strategy does not mean a complicated strategy.

## Risk Management Contributes to Longevity

In regard to risk, we will talk about it in depth later in this chapter, but for right now, *without risk management you will never be a successful trader, never!* Risk management is something we had to develop in the very beginning. We could not rely on our brokerage firms to manage risk for us. We feel we address risk differently and more in depth than most educators. This is why we are still around, trading our own accounts, and why we still have clients with us that have followed our strategy for many years. On a side note, you do not have to be a life-long client with us to trade our strategy. Some stick around because they love the energy and constant reminders we bring to their attention of how to be patient, when to be aggressive, and when things are getting a bit too risky.

## Fear Balances Greed

We have mentioned Warren Buffet's quote, "Be fearful when others are greedy, and be greedy when others are fearful." This quote is one that we strive to follow every day. Living by this motto has provided us with some very lucrative opportunities that we took advantage of in our trading and investing overall. We have bought three different homes together over the last 20 years. The three purchases have all occurred in fearful times and the first two sales happened in greedy times. We used our "preparation which contributed to timing." We purchased our third home during fearful times and we are still in it since the greedy times have not surfaced again, yet. When we trade, the fear factor always creeps up. It is an emotion we can't escape. The same goes for greed. When these two are in balance we make sound trading decisions.

## Win Some, Learn Some

Finally, the fifth area that we have identified in contributing to our success is "win some, learn some." You may have heard this one a little differently "win some, lose some." We prefer to look at our losses as opportunities for growth. Most traders fail to accept the fact that not every trade is a winner. We have plenty of losing trades, and ultimately land on top each week, each month, each year. Celebrate your winners, but quickly move on as it seems every trader knows how to win but the real question is; does every trader know how to lose?

It's our losers that take up the most space in our trading journals and in our heads. Not that we want to dwell on mistakes and become depressed, we want to learn from them, so that when we are faced with a similar situation we will be able to handle and cope with it better the next time. And it assuredly will happen again without question. The market has a funny way of checking in on your progress. Every day the market seems to whisper "just checking!"

Steph recalls a trade early on in her screen trading career that she took. It was in the AUSUSD and for some reason she did not attach a stop to it. That was her first mistake. She was short and the trade went against her 68 pips, which was well beyond her risk parameter. And, if that wasn't bad enough, the FOMC meeting results were announced, the market broke, and it turned into an eight-pip winner, but she did not get out! This was another controllable mistake!

> **Tip:** Whenever you take gut wrenching pain on a trade and it pulls you to the brink and beyond your risk tolerance, you hold it, and price fortunately turns back enough to bring your head above water, take the out! Remember that the entry was poor to begin with and others along the same ride will be glad the market let them take a breath of air.

Of course the trade went against her again, but this time it was in her face 88 pips after stubbornly hanging with the trade going on six hours now.

> **Tip:** Remember to put a value on your time and consider the two-hour concept we spoke of last chapter. If the trade hasn't hit your profit target and you have been under water the entire time since entry, the trade tends to get worse.

Steph had this trade running for 12 hours, which was completely out of her comfort zone for holding onto a position. She usually doesn't hold on to trades for more than a couple of hours and is, most often, out within 30 minutes to an hour. But, here comes the best part ... she added to this losing trade before she went to bed for the evening. Now she entered a stop on the first entry which, of course, was hit while she slept. The first trade final tally was down (160 pips). OUCH! When she woke, up the second trade was (75 pips) against her; no stop, again and she decided to finally do what trades call "puke that one out" (exit the trade with a loss). The recap in her journal went like this, "This was a train wreck of a trading situation. I did not follow my plan. I was thinking about not using stops because I heard someone at another firm say their clients use mental stops. I need to do my own thing. I put in the second trade thinking it would help me out. WRONG!"

> **Tip:** Do not add to a trade in an area where you told yourself you were wrong. The loss most often compounds upon itself and is a ticket to blowing up your account and hard earned money unnecessarily.

She added to the trade in an area that was not within her plan but now stubbornly married to the play, she thought she would only get stopped out on the first entry and see what happened on the second one. Her idea was to end the whole debacle when it hit 5 percent of her account. She did not have a stop in, so of course the second entry exceeded her intended loss percentage but thankfully wasn't more than my 5 percent downside threshold. One bright spot!

Steph continued to write, "The sad thing was that the market did come down one-half hour later. This was the first time I hit my downside limit in my account. It doesn't feel too good." The next journal entry was important though as she took another trade in the AUDUSD, and this time it was a buy. It went like this, "The buy in the AUDUSD later was golden. I bailed when I was up 60 pips. At least I was able to get back in there!"

## WRAPPING IT UP

As we close out this chapter we highlight the points made necessary to move forward with the upcoming introduction to the five core RDS Rules. We recall on a daily basis the five areas that contribute to our overall success:

- Preparation contributes to timing
- Experience contributes to strategy
- Risk management contributes to longevity

- Fear balances greed
- Win some, learn some

Moving forward, comparing our charts to a football field and relating our pit trading experiences to the charts, we can gauge who is winning the current trading session with what the next chapter explores with the first of our five rules known as the homework rule. Of course we always want to keep in mind our risk parameters and the maximum amount we are willing to risk on any particular trade idea (1.25 percent). This allows us to assess daily if we are properly capitalized for the market of our choice. We will be introducing the manner in which we build each level in the following chapters to close the loop even tighter to assessing risk.

# CHAPTER 9

# Why Technical Analysis Works

Stephanie sometimes says "I eat stress for breakfast." We laugh at that, but it's a good attitude to have! After laying out fundamental analysis tips (parity and the annual reset button) we now will focus in more depth on our five key technical analysis rules. We refer to all of our rules as our five internal advisors, as we wear all of the hats when controlling the decisions to buy and sell. We are the risk manager, the economist, the forecaster, the computer technician, the Internet technician, and the buyer and seller using the charts and execution platform. Would you want it any other way? Remember that nobody cares more about your money than you do and these sometimes tedious and difficult hills to climb are the necessary ingredients to success. Hang in there, as these skills are not that tough to acquire. Your brain, an Internet connection, and a desktop computer or laptop are the basic ingredients. Most everybody has a cell phone as well, and you can even use that to monitor action while off running daily errands. We are here to harness and unlock the inherent skills that you already possess but just haven't tapped in to yet.

Everybody looks for timing and that is why technical analysis is not only a necessity in the trading recipe but also it is a prerequisite. *Technical analysis* uses a series of past data points that specifically represent two key elements used in every study: *time* and *price*. The wheel has already been developed, probed, and prodded for centuries. We are not going to stand on our pedestal and change these tools already seared into your brain, but we are going to point out efficient ways to use what is known to help you execute your plan with confidence. Our combination of how we use our discretionary trading methodology will make the difference and help us and you stand out amongst the pack.

## WHY FIVE RULES?

All of our rules have been hand-picked through trial and tribulation by Mike. Believe me when I tell you that I have witnessed Mike break down charts by hand and plot points on graph paper for hours just to give him a sense of what, how, when, where and why. He has broken down moving average convergence-divergence (MACD), Bollinger bands, Gann fans, Fibonacci, percentage fractals, pivots, point and figure, pitchforks, relative strength index (RSI), stochastic, and market profile configurations just to name a few. At times I would find myself tossing and turning at night and not finding Mike in bed yet as I yelled out, "Give it a rest Mike and come to bed"! I also need to mention that Mike isn't the kind of person to just study trading recipes; he needs to apply them in live situations and with live money. You will never learn how it works for you if you don't apply it. This doesn't mean try it once and forget it if it doesn't work that one time. If the idea resonates, we are quite aware that it won't produce a positive result 100 percent of the time. Mike will never be accused of not putting his money where his mouth is when teaching. He is one of the few trader/educators out there that will send out when he is buying, selling, or doing nothing along with the who, what, when, where, and why along the way. We are not teachers who can't do, we are teachers that teach clearly and can do!

We understand that there is so much information to draw an opinion from and it can get maddening. Just Google "trading indicators" and you will get more than 25 million results. That's crazy! Prices go up and down and there are only so many ways you can add up one plus one, but 25 million? Well Mike has thrown out all of the redundant information and draws from five practical common sense technical rules and calculations to build confidence to answer the only *three key questions you need to answer throughout the day or your career: "Buy? Sell? Or do nothing?"*

Students and colleagues often first ask Mike "Why five rules?" In life and in trading one rule on how to handle things just isn't enough in our dynamic ever-changing world and financial marketplace. As things change having only one rule can become obsolete or naive. We absolutely agree with Three Dog Night when they sang *One is the Loneliest Number*. One rule doesn't draw from enough information to give you sound confidence to rely upon in all situations. With two rules you can run into the problem of one signaling go and one signaling stop. What then? Confusion then begins to dominate. Having three rules starts to give you a majority and begins to lead you on the right track. But just think of it this way, if you went to the doctor and one doctor gave you good news and the two others gave you bad news, you might cling to the good news and ignore the other two pessimists. It's in our nature as humans to try and ignore the pain. You will never get good at this game unless you take the painful medicine, learn from it, and then in turn do it better the next time. We avoid four rules as we can fall in tie situations again, so we settled with five rules. Five is a nice fit as it ensures a majority to settle all arguments and draws from enough different schools of thought to give us a solid opinion. And for any of you Fibonacci traders out there it follows the rhythm of adding the results to get the next number in the sequence; $0 + 1 = 1$, $1 + 1 = 2$, $1 + 2 = 3$, $2 + 3 = 5$, and so on. Beyond five rules we find that there are just too many chiefs in the boardroom and nothing gets done. When you face a decision to add more than five rules, it's time to bring Donald Trump to fire some of the excess fat in the chain, as too much can hinder the decision-making process.

It's like we mentioned earlier about one of our friends and students, Scotty Major. Avoid the syndrome of drawing from too many schools of thought as confusion ensues. We couldn't even see the price of the market on his charts because there were so many indicators on the screen. He actually would have tried to fit all 25 million Google indicators on his screen, if he could. Over-questioning and over-analyzing generally points to fear and that is an entirely different issue that we will address later in the Performance Evaluation chapter of the book. As we analyze a trader's approach, we always seem to find redundancies when a student carries more than five rules. We do not want you to hesitate while in the heat of the moment, and success depends upon your ability to act decisively without regret.

## INTRODUCING THE RULES

We have already displayed how price confirms the story of who is winning fundamentally and we will begin to reveal technically how the *homework rule* gives us insight and timing as to which side of the field to play (long or short). As price comes in alignment with the fundamental direction we can now reinforce our idea and time it to build confidence. We would like to formally introduce you to the five rules.

1. Homework
2. Neutral

3. Distance run
4. Window of opportunity
5. Relative strength index

Along with our fundamental knowledge, these five additional advisors will help us predict with foresight and visualize possible patterns, price levels, and opportunities well in advance. Michael Jordan sat in the dark visualizing how he was going to make the basket and Michael Radkay visualizes typical retracement patterns looking like Sprained Ankles—(bear flags to traditionalists) or Flipping You the Bird—(head and shoulders to traditionalists). Mountaintops, city skylines, take-offs, landings and turbulence, hitting a wayward tee-shot or jump-shot, and touchdowns or even ripped sheets of paper remind Mike of the markets. I think we need to get him checked out. (Find these fun favorites and more at: *www.rdstrader.com/patterns*).

Before getting into each rule in detail, we must first remind you of the key components of a chart to ensure proper understanding of how to implement them in what we have successfully applied to treasuries, equities, grains, metals, and energies and now to currencies. Taking your game to any market will be the continuing key to success as money ebbs and flows in and out of sectors.

## CHART BASICS

The majority of technical studies rely upon the price data, which is organized by the open (start), high, low, and close (finish) of a particular period of time. Typical intra-day time frames studied are organized into many trader favorites such as the 5-, 10-, 15-, 30- and 60-minute and longer term daily, weekly, monthly, quarterly, and yearly charts, to name a few. This can get to be quite confusing as charts packages often offer multiple time selections. We cringe when we hear teachers and traders say they watch a five minute confirmed by a 15 minute but not before seeing what the 60 minute is doing against the daily and so on...it's tiring to say, but equally tiring when we watch these traders try and make a simple decision to buy or sell. Not to take away from the work of Elliot Wave theorists, either but the ones who practice it tend to spout out things as confusing as we just mentioned like "Did you catch that fifth wave and hedge with the three-wave correction?" We have sat through some of these sessions. At least from the ones we have listened to, you only hear them say something clear and precise when the trade works, but when it loses, they often revert to sayings like "That was merely a correction to a Super Wave of the

# Why Technical Analysis Works 113

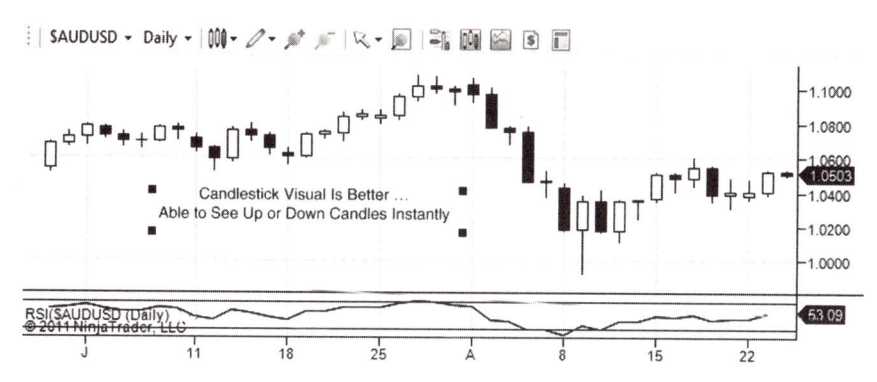

**FIGURE 9.1** Candlesticks Visual

Super Cycle D and a continuation pattern of the short term three wave based from the five-wave cycle." What?

Let's get back to making things simple. Prices go up and down over time, period. The open, high, low, and close are generally built using two common forms called a bar chart or a candlestick chart. They are essentially the same thing but we focus on candlestick charting. Now this book is not about candlestick patterns, but visually we think you will agree as you compare both styles (candlesticks and bar charts). Candles shine through and tell the story about the time period more prominently as the base (area between open and close) versus the bar chart dash to the left (open) and the dash to the right (close) display. Price action above and below the base is called a shadow or wick. The extreme upper shadow top is the high price and the lower shadow extreme bottom is the low price for that time period. This again is very similar to a bar chart. We just track candles because of their visual superiority. Both chart types in the end will lead you to the same place and track the exact same information—see Figures 9.1 and 9.2.

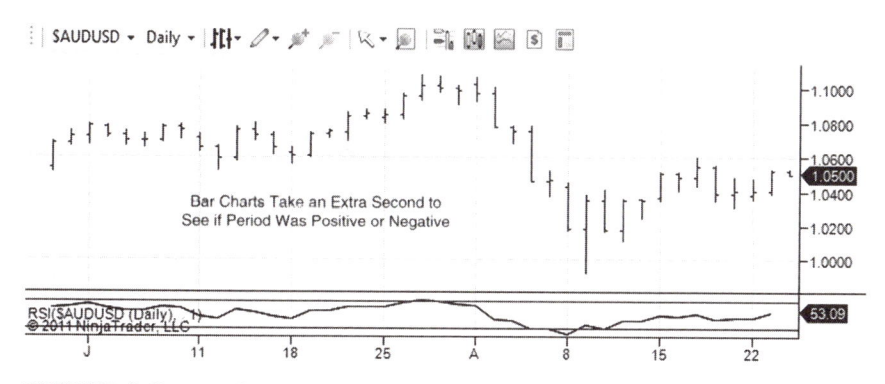

**FIGURE 9.2** Bar Chart Visual

Whether price over the period of time referenced was positive or negative, you can visually see better from wherever you are standing or sitting. Bar charts show the same key elements, but we have found that sometimes it takes an extra glance and that extra glance can cost you. Throughout this book we are going to continue to keep it simple and focus on how and why we use our two favorite time frames: 15 minutes for intra-day perspective and daily for our homework and wider-term perspective. We also will narrow our RDS homework rule using the current day with the RDS weekly for guidance.

## CHART PATTERNS

The basic chart patterns that become apparent are uptrends, downtrends, inside candles, outside candles, double tops, and double bottoms. Get to know them as they occur every day.

An *uptrend* is simply defined as the candle highs and lows are getting higher. This tells you that buyers tend to be winning at the moment. When you first begin to notice an uptrend developing by comparing the current candle to the previous candle, it most often signifies higher prices to come. Eventually all things that go up must come down as Newton tells us, so don't get greedy or too stubborn when you begin to see a downtrend. See Figure 9.3.

A downtrend is simply defined as the candle highs and lows getting lower. When you first begin to notice a downtrend develop by comparing the current candle to the previous candle, it most often signifies lower prices to come (see Figure 9.4).

When doing your analysis you sometimes come up against an *inside candle*. When you compare a candle to the previous one and you see that

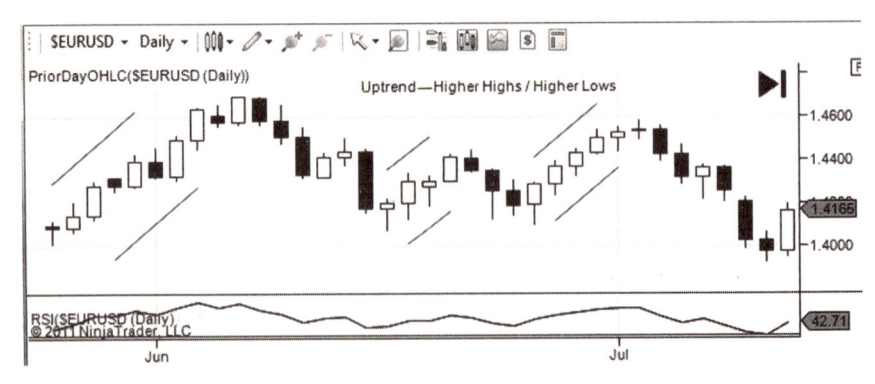

**FIGURE 9.3** Uptrend

# Why Technical Analysis Works

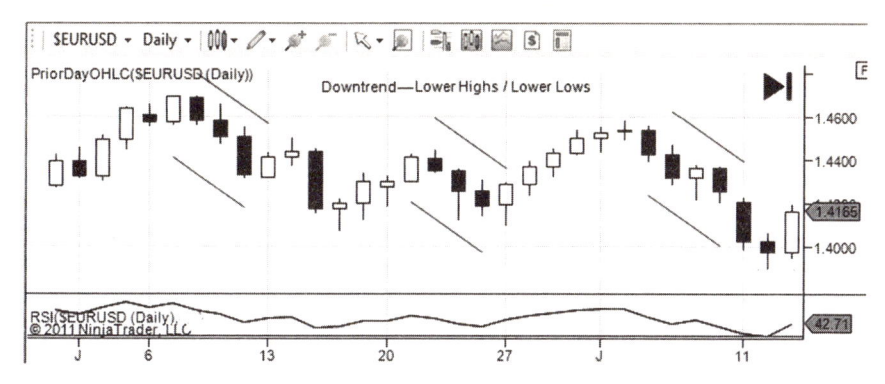

**FIGURE 9.4** Downtrend

the lows are getting higher and the highs are getting lower, you start to scratch your head. This type of candle does not confirm or deny the trend. In a sense it is much like the market is confused or taking a break. We do not put too much weight on this candle type. Basically we discount it, but don't go as far as erasing it from existence. We will go back to the prior candle before the inside candle was formed and continue to consider the original direction of trend to still be intact (see Figure 9.5).

The opposite of an inside candle is an *outside candle*. When you compare a candle to the previous one and you see that the lows are getting lower and the highs are getting higher, you know that you didn't scratch your head being confused but appropriately you felt like you just went through a washing machine. There was something for everybody in this time frame. The importance in the aftermath is where price finished on the candle. If prices closed on the top half of the candle or near the high, it is sometimes referred to as a *bullish hook reversal*. Candlestick pattern followers will be reminded of an *engulfing bullish* signal. The sellers were

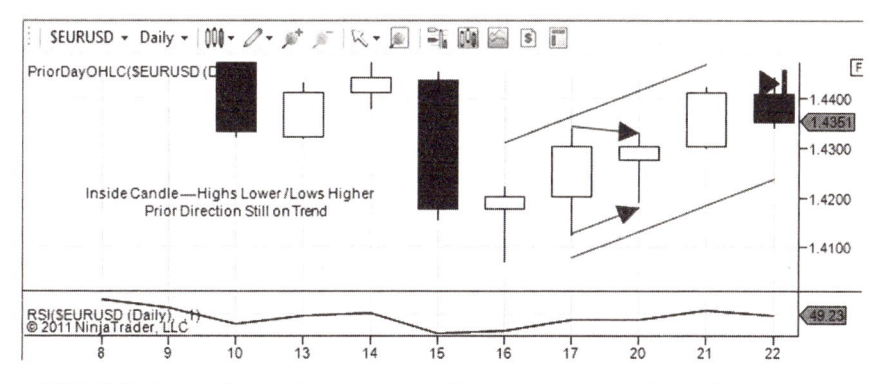

**FIGURE 9.5** Inside Candle (doesn't confirm or deny original trend)

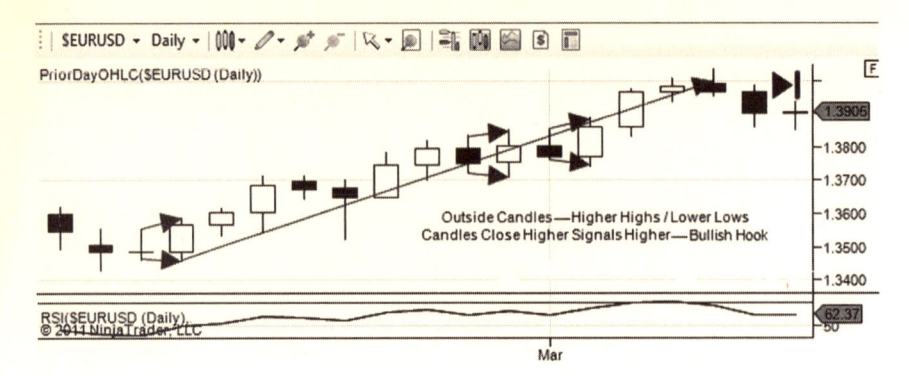

**FIGURE 9.6** Outside Candle (bullish hook)

lured in as price dropped to make lower lows, but as prices snapped upward the hook was set deep in the sellers' bellies as they were dragged to new highs. Prices are expected to continue upward at the next candle. See Figure 9.6.

On the flip side, if prices finish on the lower half of an outside candle or near the low, it is sometimes referred to as a *bearish hook reversal*. Candlestick pattern followers will be reminded of an *engulfing bearish signal*. Much like their bullish counterpart, the buyers are lured into a long position as new highs are made, but as prices begin to drop dramatically the hook is set to drag the buyers to new depths. Prices are expected to continue downward at the next candle. See Figure 9.7.

You may hear of other traders waiting for the candle to finish developing before participating, and these candles are the very reason why. At times we get anxious and want to jump on board, but sometimes waiting for the completion of the time segment confirms the direction and the safer

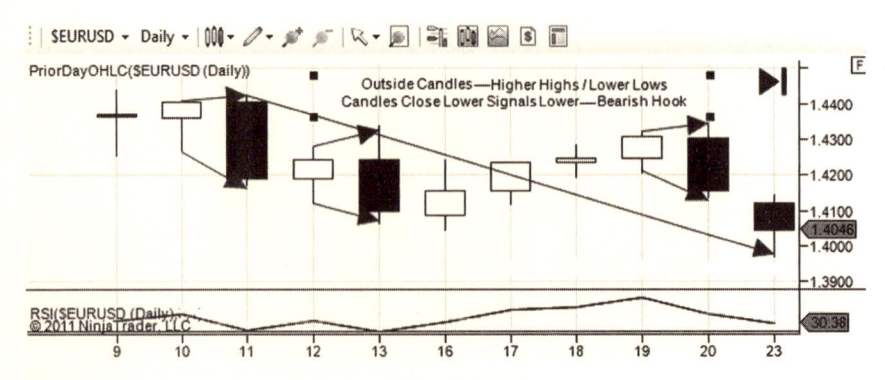

**FIGURE 9.7** Outside Candle (bearish hook)

# Why Technical Analysis Works

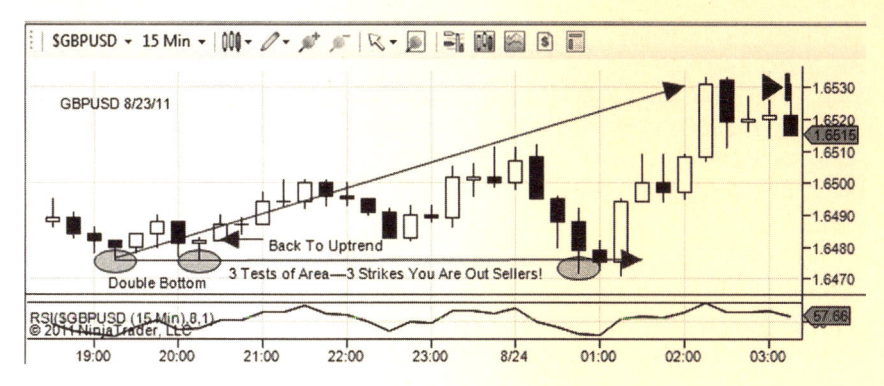

**FIGURE 9.8** Double Bottom (W pattern)

play. It's not always best to be first in line. Being first makes you the pioneer and the riches can be great, but anticipating to soon can leave you hanging out to dry. We will help you with this further when we talk about the window of opportunity rule and apply it to where the set-up is on the field for foresight confidence.

*Double tops* and *double bottoms* become significant because the line in the sand between buyers and sellers is being drawn at or near the same price. As we retest an already established low and price fails to finish or move lower and we see a reversal back to higher highs (uptrend), a confirmed *double bottom* is formed. We call this a *"Win" or "W" Pattern*, which is great for the bullish eyes to see. See Figure 9.8.

The same type of excitement builds for the bearish eyes when you see a *double top*. As prices near an established top and fail to finish or climb higher preceded by lower lows (downtrend), prices have formed an *"M" or "Miss" Pattern*. See Figure 9.9.

**FIGURE 9.9** Double Top (M pattern)

At our web site, www.rdstrader.com/patterns, you can find our favorite patterns along with others that traders watch to help them gain perspective and insight as to what upcoming price action might deliver. However, we feel that you have what you need by following and understanding the basic patterns that we have described. The real question that begins to surface is anticipating how long trends last.

## TIMEFRAME

Most traders come to us and ask what time frame do we use when we pull up a chart? We typically answer the same way: As we have a strong understanding of what other traders look to and where they gravitate. Remember when we mentioned the restaurant story and how long most are willing to wait for their dinner guests? Our frustration level begins to surface after 30 minutes to an hour of waiting. In our instant-gratification world, the window of tolerance in trading seems to hover from a couple of minutes to two hours. This fits aligns similarly outside of trading as YouTube video clips of two to three minutes to two-hour feature films. If they are longer, we all tend to get fidgety and lose interest. The vast majority get annoyed after driving for a couple of hours in traffic and most begin to lose patience after flying more than a couple of hours in a plane. It's the same way in trading. You will begin to notice during our three key sections over the 24-hour clock—Asia, London, and the United States—that price action is at its greatest volatility during these first couple of hours of each respective day-session time zone. These first couple of hours begin to give us a solid picture of what the players are thinking today. Price never lies, remember? Focusing down further with the microscope we get our feel for direction with what we have called "The First Hour Magic." We choose to look at this key first and second hour with a 15-minute chart (a chart that captures the open, high, low, and close over 15-minute segments). We choose a 15-minute chart because for the last 20 years Mike has always tracked the specific questions people always ask him. He says, "Don't take our word for it, and begin to understand the audience around you." The three questions are:

1. What time frame do you currently watch when trading Forex or Futures? Overwhelmingly the majority of the audience always shouts out answers between a one-pip/tick chart (a chart that marks every single price up move and down move) and a 30-minute chart. Yes, we do get answers outside of that range but the majority is firmly entrenched between one-tick and 30-minute intervals. The leverage of these products is so high that it forces traders to monitor the action closely. We just take smack in the middle (15-minute time frames) to get a nice overall

view of how traders break down the action intra-day; not too close and not too far away.
2. How long do you hold on to trades, good or bad? Overwhelmingly the majority of our audience and our colleagues alike fall within holding a position (long or short; good or bad) for a couple of minutes up to one to two hours. Yes, again, we have some fall outside of that range, but it surely is not the majority of the audience.
3. For those of you that hold trades for more than 24 hours, what is the average length of time you are in swing play? Most shout answers between one and five days, which just so happens to confirm our thought on the RDS weekly homework adjustment to align with swing players.

Having this knowledge of other traders helps you and has helped us. We just always ask. This gives us an approximate time horizon for how long we may have to wait for a trade to come to our price and how long we may have to wait for action to reach our objective. This immediately calms the anxiety and allows us to pre-plan as best we can scenarios to build our foresight skills, which are so vital to a trader's arsenal. Price action begins to give you hints about the trade the first 15 minutes and if it hasn't moved accordingly to the desired spot within the time tolerance allotted (one to two hours), we begin to cut the cord on the idea or set a one-cancels-other (OCO) profit limit and stop loss and go stretch our legs for a bit. Remember that you begin to make impatient knee-jerk decisions when anxiety builds.

**Pre-Trade Checklist**

We have much to cover, but this is an appropriate time to begin our mental rehearsal that is much like a pilot begins to do prior to takeoff. We want to be able to return tomorrow, so building good habits needs to start immediately.

**Pre-Trade**

1. Close your eyes and take up to three complete breaths...deep, in through the nose and all the way down to your toes...exhale.
2. Drink some water and feel each drop permeate through your brain, down through your neck, into your arms and chest, down into your stomach, and finally into your legs and toes.
3. Relax your heart rate. Your best decisions and performance appear at a time when you are calm and relaxed.
4. Make sure your equipment is functioning properly (Computer / Internet, Trading Software, etc.).

(*Continued*)

**Pre-Trade Checklist** (*Continued*)

5. Make sure your environment is conducive to concentration and without distraction.
6. Have a news source running. Platforms generally come equipped with a news feed like Market News International or Reuters. You can also turn on the TV and tune into CNN, CNBC, or the Bloomberg channel to keep you informed of current pertinent events.
7. When you are calm, you are patient and have the ability to wait for your clear, well-thought-out entry and exit prices.
8. Don't force and chase the action...it leads to frustration and bad decision making...let the market come to you.
9. Don't think you are missing something...if you are prepared to trade more than one market, another opportunity will be around the corner in the next 15 to 30 minutes.

**During the Trade Evaluation**

1. If the trade immediately goes in a favorable direction in the first 15–30 minutes: The trade is most often worth something...shooting for your objective should be on your mind.
2. If the trade immediately goes against you: The trade usually gets worse...don't be afraid to exit the trade even if you can afford to hang with it longer.
3. If the trade just sits there, it is normally not worth that much: When you get some profit, take it or set a one-cancels-other (OCO) profit limit and stop loss and go stretch your legs for a bit

**Developing a Trader's Memory**

1. Commit to memory and learn something about every trade, whether it was a winner or loser.
2. If the trade immediately goes your way, you may have bought a temporary low or sold a temporary high, points to remember and possibly repeat the next time the market revisits these levels.
3. If the trade immediately goes against you, you may have bought a temporary high or sold a temporary low; don't get discouraged as these are points to remember and possibly reverse or avoid the next time the market revisits these levels.

Later in the book we will discuss trade evaluation and the Intellectual Investor (II) versus the Emotional Investor (EI), but if you begin to wait for your spots, you will have an abundant amount of the necessary mental and financial energy needed to complete the journey of the trade.

## FIRST-HOUR MAGIC

Leverage in trading the currency markets is high enough and the potential it offers can give you much of what you want in the first two-hour segment of time. Most currencies will move about 1 percent per day, so for example, if the Euro/U.S. dollar (EURUSD) was trading 1.4000 that would equate to 140 pips of movement in 24 hours. At the standard professional rate of $10 per pip per contract that would equate to potential risk reward exposure of $1400. If your settings are at $1 pip, that would equate to $140. We feel that realistically capturing 12.5 to 25 percent of that move is very much within our grasp within one to two hours (our tolerance and most traders tolerance anyway). Remember that the big dogs get tired as well and if you are starting to get on board with our tolerance philosophy of the one- to two-hour instant gratification, you will begin to see the light and give yourself an efficient, cost-effective chance at making the money you want.

You just have to play smart and in the perimeter of where the big dogs gave you the signals so you can have your bat ready to swing well in advance when action comes to your price. We predetermine direction with our homework rule and then wait to see where the market has built tops and bottoms to indicate where we should consider a buy or sell. When we trained traders at the University of Trading and as we still do today, we always say: *"Know where you are getting out before you get in!"* You pinpoint the stand-out top and bottom, choose the side you want, establish risk/reward according to the expected price move and time, set it up on your execution screen, and wait for the entry and wait for the exit. It's all pretty easy on paper, right?

*As we adjusted our ideas to fit our time tolerance (one to two hours) we began to notice some outstanding opportunities using the clues of the peak highs and lows built during that **first-hour rhythm.*** Noticing on the trading floor how hyped up everybody was during the first hour segment helped us realize that traders are ready to play during this time and when it comes to money everybody has what's called a *tell*. This is a poker term that is used to describe when somebody reveals their hand without actually showing it to their opponents by movements and shifts in their demeanor and body language. *Now as we can't see everybody's movements when looking into the face of a computer monitor, you can use the standout high and low established during the first hour to help you with the real-time chart tell.* Price doesn't lie and big dogs possess the same emotion of greed in all of us and can't help but tell the world where they really want to make a stand in the market. You may never think you

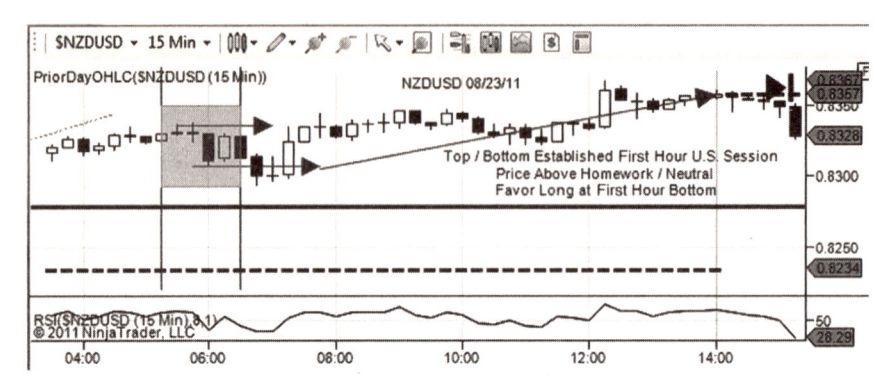

**FIGURE 9.10** First-Hour Magic

will get a chance to buy or sell these areas, but you will be surprised at how often you get a shot (Figure 9.10).

There is essentially no difference in the concept when applying the stand-out tops and bottoms to longer-term swing plays, as the only difference is time and having the ability, patience, and resources to hang on to see the idea play itself out.

# CHAPTER 10

# Defining the Rotating Directional System

Our strategy, RDS, stands for Rotating Directional System. RDS is a five-rule-based discretionary trading methodology that establishes risk management first. Our style offers the trader a trend-side philosophy that predicts time and price objectives using counter-trend reversals as a guide for entries, exits, and overall worth of the trade. After appropriate RDS risk-management parameters have been analyzed for the market of choice, levels of participation are developed from recent market volatility, average momentum, and retracement zones. As prices reach a specific zone objective, new rotation significance is placed on this area. This continues to give the trader an overall updated directional sense of what can be expected for upcoming price action. The zones also post guidelines for price follow through and/or reversals.

Before entering each trade we put the position of the market up against rule one, the homework rule, and four intra-day rules.

## RULE 1: THE HOMEWORK RULE

In order to understand the homework rule we need to make sure you have a solid understanding of the Japanese candlestick chart. We know most of you are adept at this, but as educators, we want to make sure.

The candlestick chart is a tool that gives us an indication of exactly where the market is at any point in time and where the market has been, as well. We prefer to use this type of chart over a bar chart or a point-and-figure chart because the colors give us a great visual of the market. We do not expect you to memorize or even become extremely familiar with the hundreds of well-known studied candlestick patterns out there. We only refer to the most commonly used patterns such as uptrends, downtrends, inside, and outside candles. Remember when we originally built our strategy we did not have the luxury of a computer screen in the pits with us. We had to use our memory, paper, and a pen. Adapting to the screen made it that much easier when we added visual representation.

There are four key components of a candlestick:

- Open—start of the base
- High—greatest price and top of the wick
- Low—lowest price and bottom of the wick
- Close—finish of the base

For the purpose of this book, a white-colored candle base denotes a positive finish (opening is at the bottom of the base and the close is at the top of the base). A black-colored base denotes a negative finish (opening at the top of the base and the close is at the bottom of the base). There is also one more component that is not often discussed, but in our strategy it is extremely important. It is the range. The range is found by taking the highest point of the candle and subtracting it from the lowest point.

Each candle begins to tell a story about price action over time. As you get a feel for how far prices typically travel over time (range), you will begin to understand what type of money is at risk. See Figure 10.1.

You will find that most candles vary in shape, size, and color. Rarely do they look identical. Some are black, some are white, some are big, and others are very tiny. You can tell so much about the market by reading these segments of time individually or collectively. For now we need you

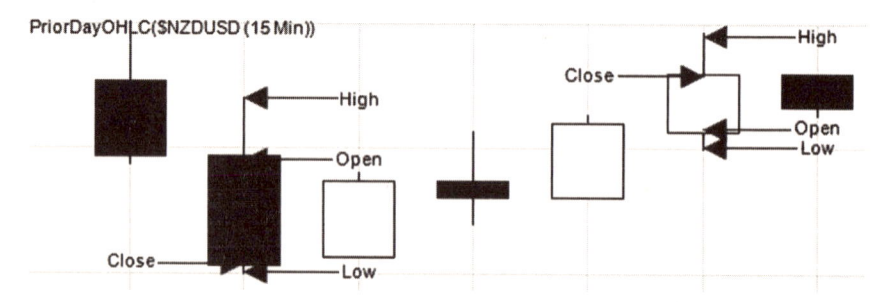

**FIGURE 10.1** Open/High/Low/Close

*Defining the Rotating Directional System* **125**

to be able to glance at a chart and recognize who is winning: buyers or sellers. This will give you the first indication of "feel for price direction."

*We can begin to determine who is winning by using our first tool, the homework rule, denoted by a solid black line. This tool is the first of the five rules we use to give us confidence to enter/exit any particular trade. It is simply the 50 percent market of the current session (high plus low divided by two equals 50 percent).* We place this line on our charts each and every day and we adjust it as many times as needed as price action establishes a new high or low.

Referring back to sports, in most athletic competitions the object of the game is to advance to your opponent's side of the field and score points. The main difference we must be aware of is the fact that professional sporting venues do not lengthen or tighten their playing fields, but the financial markets are more dynamic as trading ranges can be large one day and small the next. The trading field changes size in accordance with the economic volatility and conditions of the time. No matter what the size of the range we always want to have an idea of who is winning, the buyers or the sellers. We look at a chart similar to a football field (see Figure 10.2).

When price action (the candles) is above the homework rule (current day midpoint), we know the buyers are winning. When price action is below, the sellers are winning. Knowing the 50 percent marker helps our trust of direction when considering a long or a short as it confirms and keeps track of the winning team.

We call it the homework rule because we need a starting reference point to judge the action as each new day begins. It's simple, we calculate this mark at the end of each trading session to use for the next trading session initially by taking the high of the previous trading day, adding it to the low of the previous trading day and dividing by two. *Reminder: Forex sessions begin and end at 2 PM PT/PM CT/5 PM ET.* We take this number

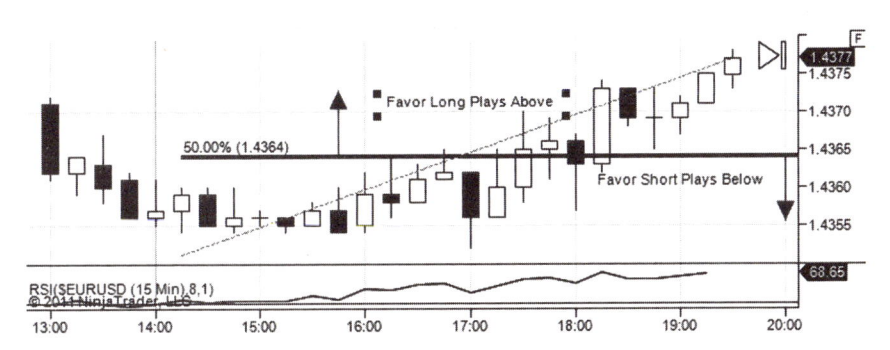

*10 pm UK*

**FIGURE 10.2** Current Day Session Favor Long Above/Short Below Session 50 Percent

and draw a horizontal black line on our chart to denote this area. *After prices absorb the first couple hours of the day session and begin to near the end of the prime Asia session hours we transition and begin to use new highs and lows built from the current session that started from 2 PM PT/4 PM CT/5 PM ET to adjust our homework line.* If new highs/lows are made we recalculate as many times as needed throughout the remainder of the 24 hour session. The computer charting software we use (as most do) has a study that can capture the median (same as 50 percent) and calculate it automatically for you or of course you can use your brain, Fibonacci retracement drawing tool, or even a handy calculator. You can always find charting and execution platform solutions at www.rdstrader.com.

## RDS Weekly Homework

The RDS strategy puts a strong emphasis on the homework rule (current day 50 percent marker) and uses it as an adjustment mechanism throughout the trading session; however, we do take into consideration 50 percent markers for other time frames. The reason the homework rule is so important compared to other 50 percent markers of longer-term time frames is because it is a present tense indicator. We of course are more interested in staying present as we don't want to look too far behind or too far ahead. The issue that comes to light is that at times during the heat of the moment just focusing on today can be a bit narrow-minded. We don't want to forget the bigger picture and reverse our thoughts on a whim during all the back and forth action that typically occurs throughout a day session. We needed a bigger-picture 50 percent filter to help keep our footing. The bigger picture that met our tolerance and matched with what seemed to be on the forefront of the news and traders' minds was the weekly outlook.

*We tweak the weekly chart data slightly and use the last five trading days to capture what we call the RDS weekly.* Typical weekly charts capture Monday through Friday action but the problem with a weekly chart is that if it happens to be Tuesday it is only capturing Monday and Tuesday, thus defeating the purpose of keeping a wider viewpoint on these days. We settled on what generally stands out in a trader's memory anyway, which typically consists of the last five trading days.

Here is a quick little test; see how quickly you can recall what you ate for dinner last night. How about the night before last, and the night before that, and so on. Unless you eat the same thing for dinner every night you tend to get a little slower on each response. We feel that after you have gone through the last five days your short-term memory begins to transition into long-term memories. When in long-term memory you tend to recall stand-out meals and categorize them into meals you love or meals you hate. Translating this into trading language you tend to focus on today

## Defining the Rotating Directional System

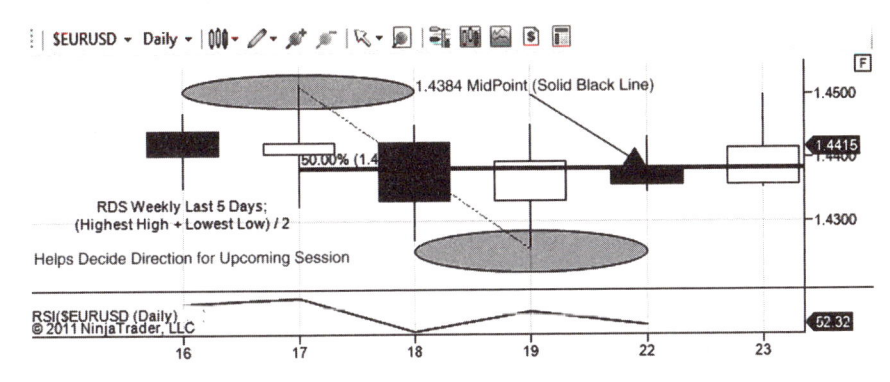

**FIGURE 10.3** Homework Rule with RDS Weekly

present tense, recall short term up to five days, and then transition into longer-term ideas or yearly thoughts. Seems like yesterday that you just graduated from high school or college, right? It's nothing more than a little compressed data in a neat little zip file in your brain. We are not doctors of the brain, but we have asked and tested enough colleagues and students on this concept to know that we are on the right track with this logic.

For our purposes we tend to focus our intra-day trading ideas with a homework rule that consists of two parts; *the current session 50 percent and the RDS weekly 50 percent to help* gauge and trust direction of either a long or short. See Figure 10.3.

We now apply the RDS weekly on our 15-minute intra-day chart and track it along with the current session homework rule. See Figure 10.4.

There was an earlier long Mike took on this day when action was above the current day midpoint and RDS weekly. As prices tested the support

**FIGURE 10.4** Homework Rule Current Session with RDS Weekly on 15-Minute Chart

point it failed and stopped Mike out. Action found support at the RDS weekly midpoint and upon confirmation Mike went long again and ended up making money this session. If he limited his thoughts to only the current session midpoint he may have gotten short due to action falling below. This reversal would have created chaos on the ensuing rally. The bigger weekly picture was still pointing long above 1.4384. Mike entered his long from the RDS weekly area and covered it at the current session midpoint area (the place where action failed as support becomes resistance). He sat quietly the rest of the day after the wild ride as action remained mixed in between the current session and the RDS weekly midpoint. You will also learn how Mike applied another layer of our strategy with the neutral rule in the next section to help give him a majority to continue favoring a direction.

## RDS Yearly Homework

As an additional reference point we mentioned a longer-term thought as well. Traders who watch day charts and play longer term swings can add the yearly 50 percent marker to their arsenal to help build confidence for long or short plays. You can take all three of these midpoints into consideration and look for price action to be above all three to boost confidence to go long or if price action is below all three you can feel a bit more confident about a short. Having three layers assures a majority to help guide direction. Since the yearly is a bit farther out than our time tolerance favors, we add something more current, which will be defined as our neutral rule (next section) with the RDS weekly and daily homework rule to guide direction. See Figure 10.5.

We continually get signals to maintain a more current focus, since the pace of our world is gearing to more and more instant gratification. For our purposes we continue to find success by siding with the ever-growing

**FIGURE 10.5** Yearly 50 Percent Marker Homework Rule

*Defining the Rotating Directional System*  129

fast-paced mindset-of-the-masses mentality, so leaning with the relevant midpoints like our current session and RDS weekly homework to confirm the direction is favorable.

If a trade is setting up that doesn't have the longer-term yearly midpoint in agreement but has our current session, RDS weekly, and neutral rule in place, we will still enter a trade with confidence. We don't totally dismiss long-term information, but you must understand that long distance information tends to be forgotten in today's climate. Humans have a natural need to move on and dismiss the events of the past and concentrate on the current task at hand. Could you imagine if all we could do is cry every day about a past sad event that happened years ago? Thankfully our bodies have natural chemicals that kick in to help us settle down. Since the markets are controlled by people, price action will rise, fall, and settle down daily with an ebb and flow that matches the financial mood of the time. Staying present as much as possible has kept us in the game for the past 20 years.

Not every trader has a one-to five-day outlook like we do. Some trades span out to bigger swings in the market. There is definitely opportunity to think bigger. Just make sure that when you look for bigger moves that you are aware of the risks and the time these ideas take to play out. Time horizon adjusted to your style is quite easy. The concept of the midpoint and football field doesn't change, but the length of time you span your idea across does.

As we have mentioned the New Year's Resolution thought earlier, we feel that if you move to a longer-term mindset, most lean on the one-year clip cycle. Warren Buffet seems to match up with this as he has mentioned a five-year time horizon much like we mention our five-day horizon to gain perspective. If you adopt a longer term model, just be prepared to build up your tolerance for the time and energy it will take and try not to get caught up in the frenzied daily back and forth rhetoric that you will have to overcome. However it is important to not completely shut yourself off from the news because something may happen to fundamentally change your thoughts along the way

In closing thoughts about the first RDS rule, the homework rule, it is one we adhere to and use with great respect to guide us with our directional sense up and down the financial gridiron.

## RULE 2: THE NEUTRAL RULE

In the last example and in some of the previous examples we have been hinting of the neutral rule. Whenever we are making a decision that could cost us money we always want to dot Is and cross Ts. Just relying on the

50 percent daily/RDS weekly can sometimes leave us mixed and on the sidelines but adding a tie-breaker rule to the mix gave us a majority. We feel this rule controls the 24-hour sentiment each and every day and the combination of these three directional guide posts has made us quite a bit of money over the years.

It still rings in Mike's ears as ZIM screamed to Mike in the 30-year bond pit at 2 PM Central, "Where did the bonds go out?" ZIM wanted to know where prices closed (settled) for the session. Mike shouted the price back to ZIM as he in turn relayed the information to the person on the phone. When Mike first entered the trading floor January 3, 1989, he was introduced to ZIM. He managed one of the biggest 30-year bond decks in the business. They were referred to as Plaza, which later became known as Solomon Brothers, and then Solomon Smith Barney. ZIM's desk shot billions worth of bonds into Mike's hands and into the 30-year bonds pits, when Mike worked for the largest independent Brokerage firm called NANCO.

Every single day since Mike started working for NANCO until he left the group in June of 1997 to become a self-funded trader, ZIM like clockwork at 2p Central asked Mike, "Where did the bonds go out?" Now we can stop right here and we hope that the manager of billions and billions of dollars asking for seven years straight where did the bonds go out would start to tell you that this price was a pretty important price to know. Not only the closing price in bonds but any market for that matter, because through the years Steph heard the same shouts from the desks at the S&P 500 pits, NASDAQ, and we collectively have heard it as we happened to be walking by the other desks in the grain room and currency quadrants. *The closing price at day's end becomes our second rule or what we call neutral.* See Figure 10.6.

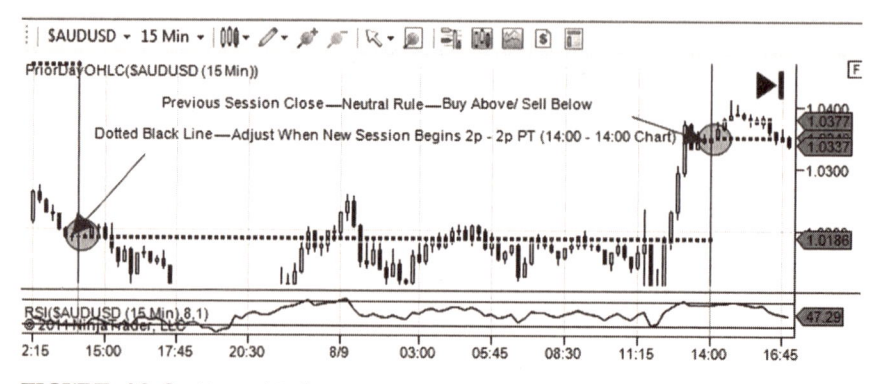

**FIGURE 10.6** Neutral Rule

In Forex this can be found at the transition from yesterday to today which occurs at 2 PM PT/4 PM CT/5 PM ET.  *10 pm UK*

## The Closing Price Is the Neutral Rule

If that wasn't enough to start building importance, it was one of the four key prices from the open, high, low, and *close* we mentioned earlier. Remember that we are not reinventing the wheel or in our case the open, high, low, or close, we are just here to help organize the information that you can use to make sound buy/sell decisions. The closing price has much significance for starters as this price is where every open position (long or short) is marked at the end of the session. A trader's statement will reflect a bottom line value and their trading account will reflect the balance based from the closing price. After the session was complete the upcoming evening session or next day when the trader saw his statement with the open position it would be reflecting a result relative to where price was currently but referenced from the previous closing price. Naturally this price was known and enters the brain of every trader. If you start watching CNN, CNBC, or Bloomberg you will always see the reporters talking about how much a specific market is up or down on the session. The net change or percentage change they are announcing to their audiences comes from the previous closing price.

This price is a sentiment meter. *If current prices are above neutral a positive or bullish sentiment is building.* Long positions (buys) would tend to be making money more often than not. *If current prices are below neutral, a negative or bearish sentiment is building.* Short positions tend to be making money. Through Mike's studies of forecasting through college, he began to notice that when price action held above the previous closing price after the first hour of the session, it tended to finish higher and if price action started below and held through the first hour, prices tended to move lower.

Mike mentions this to students all of the time "when reading trading books, begin to notice what trading authors always reference." We can't say it enough times, "the wheel has already been built"; you will be hard pressed and wasting valuable time and energy trying to discover a new way to track price. It has been done. Almost every technical study out there needs the neutral price, no matter what time scale is being referenced. If you got into the nitty-gritty of how to calculate all of the studies out there, you will find that it entails using the last price of each candle referenced in the study. As you think about it practically and compare neutral to everyday business, don't you hear bosses always ask about the bottom line? They of course want to know how things are going at the start of the day

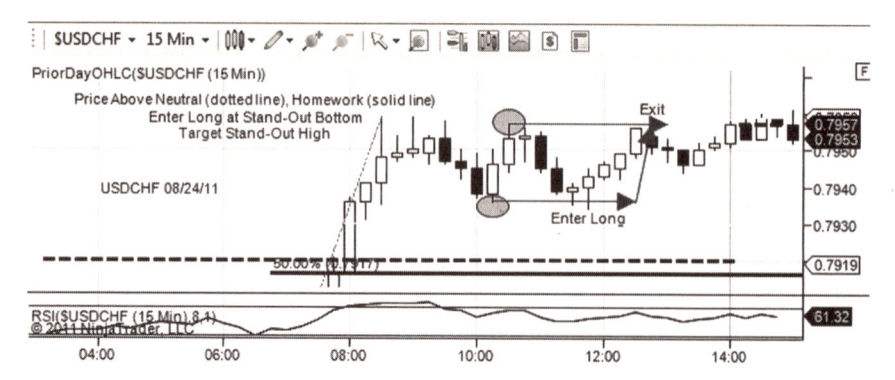

**FIGURE 10.7** Bullish Play: 15-Minute Charts Using the Previous Close

(open) but every boss's concern falls to the all-important question: Are we still in business at the end of the day?

Nothing is foolproof, so you will want to time the idea and not just blindly get long when prices are above neutral or get short when prices are below. We could be sitting near a stand-out top or bottom and going with momentum may get you long at a top or short at a bottom. That stings! We want to enter long into the market at or near a bottom, if the neutral price is below that entry spot. On the flip side we want to sell near a stand-out top as long as the prior close price is still at or above this area. See Figures 10.7 and 10.8.

When we add the homework rule concept to the picture it adds to our confidence in the idea. From the prior chapter we have highlighted our three favorite 50 percent marks: the current day, RDS weekly (last five days), and year. We feel using the RDS weekly captures the relevant audience for the majority real-time perspective. When we laser our focus to the current action, comparing the RDS weekly to the current day

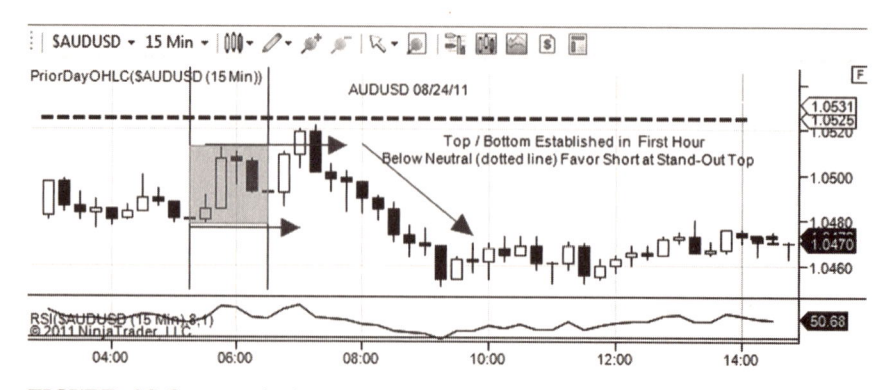

**FIGURE 10.8** Bearish Play: 15-Minute Charts Using the Previous Close

## Defining the Rotating Directional System

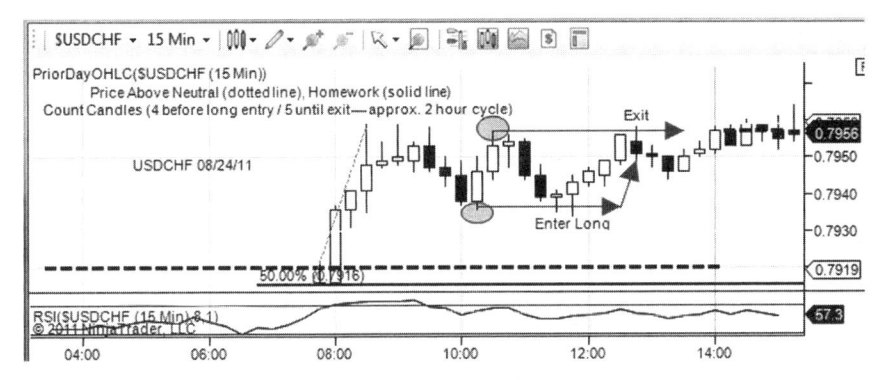

**FIGURE 10.9** Count Candles and Prepare or Time

homework 50 percent and the neutral rule, it provides us with the confidence in direction as we retest a stand-out top/bottom for the first time.

Be sure to prepare for the length of time it may take for the trade to get to your entry spot by counting how many 15-minute segments it took the stand-out area to develop, as this can provide a good measure of how long you may have to wait to enter. Once you get the price you want add that same length of time to give you a feel for how long it may take to reach your objective. See Figure 10.9.

## Waiting

It is vital that you begin to prepare yourself for the waiting game as it is the hazard that most struggling traders can never overcome. It reminds Mike of his good friend Arthur, a seven-figure account holder. This guy swings some money around to say the least. Arthur ran into a slump and couldn't pinpoint the reasons why. The trader picked the direction in accordance to what we have been talking about, but many times he was entering into a position in the middle of the road between a stand-out top/bottom. When Mike asked him why he entered in the middle, he said that he wanted to get a feel for the market and enter. To some degree I completely understand this thought process, you do need to get in there to know what's happening. The problem is that it got him started in the middle and most often got him over-leveraged into an idea way too soon, because when the trade got to the spot he truly wanted he didn't have enough bullets to play the area due to earlier entries. Mike then asked a series questions that changed the trader's life.

Mike: "What time did you physically sit down to trade today?"
Arthur: "At the open."

Mike: What time did you enter your first trade?"
Arthur: *"Two minutes later."*
Mike: "What time did you enter your first trade the last five days?"
Arthur: *"Oh pretty much at the same time every day."*
Mike: "Over the last five days how many winning days did you have?"
Arthur: *"One winning, three loss, and one break even"*
Mike: "Arthur do you realize that the spot we wanted to enter the market on your winning day hit right on the open when you first sat down and the other four days the spot we wanted didn't hit until one and two hours later and it was setup mixed, at best ? Arthur, you have a patience problem and a hint of a gambling problem. You need the action right when you sit down!
Arthur: *"I see that."*
Mike: "If you waited for the spot that we would have wanted on all five days, you would have had three winning days and two break-even days."
Arthur: *"I see that."*
Mike: "Arthur, do you only trade the dollar index?"
Arthur: *"Yes."*
Mike: "Add the game plan and prepare for some of the other currency markets we cover and when the dollar index isn't set up when you sit down, instead of forcing the action right away on days that you have to wait begin to look to the others first. Use the pent up energy looking for the best setup."

Mike just gave Arthur a positive distraction by giving him something to do while he waited. This helped him use his energy to look for the best setup and broke his slump immediately.

## Short Term Memory: Five-Day Concept

Having some knowledge about our neutral rule now helps us explain how a trader thinks and how the students and colleagues we have watched and taught think. You will be surprised at how much you can begin to assume with a good deal of accuracy about how another trader thinks. We have been asking, listening, and teaching and we constantly take mental and written notes. Mike has told me time and time again that he feels his sociology and psychology courses in college taught him more about the markets than his economic books have taught him. Sociology and psychology taught him about group and individual behavior; great tools to possess when trying to anticipate the next price move.

When applying the neutral, homework, and RDS weekly rules to the markets, we hope that the light bulb is starting to go off just as it did for

Mike. He hand picked fact-based concepts that helped define direction that matched with the financial world's short-term memory span of a week. You may not take our word instantly, but as you study charts and price action you will find a week becomes very significant in strategy. You may even notice the weekly concept when thinking about your daily life. If you begin to look at your planner or schedule on your calendar, you might tend to notice that the things you have planned for today are pretty firm and as you go out in time you will begin to have less and less confidence in the schedule due to the constant changes life brings. For the most part your schedule for the week seems to hold in place. As we have mentioned many times already, it's much like our weatherman analogy as they tend to only offer what is relevant to their audience, which is a weekly forecast.

If you ever did any private sessions with Mike you would most definitely be asked the question point blank, what did you have for dinner last night? How about the night before? The night before? And so on. It's not that he cares about what you eat, he cares about what you can remember and how fast you can recall it with accuracy! Mike is merely trying to get you to realize what you remember and as you get into the heat of the moment (a trade); your mind will instantly shoot to flight-or-fight instincts. Our brain is a defense mechanism as well as a helpful problem solver. If we remembered every single good and bad moment, it might hinder us from making a timely decision. That's why we have a so-called highlight reel or short- and long-term memory to help us filter and process what is needed at the moment.

## Yearly Neutral with Yearly Homework Rule

We realize that every trader doesn't want or need to trade every day and there is an audience out there that is only looking for a handful of ideas per year. The beauty of the two rules is that you can take the same philosophy from the intra-day 15-minute charts and build it around an idea that captures a longer-term perspective that fits your mindset. So many struggling traders lack the ability to think outside the box and adjust the proven concept to their time frame tolerance. You can apply the neutral rule and the homework rule, but shift it to a wider perspective as we mentioned in Chapter 4. As we move outside of the week, we feel a trader's mind moves to long-term memory or to a time that we are all familiar with, which are yearly highlights. Whether it is media driven or from our birthdays each year, we all seem to have that yearly reset button. With the annual switch within all of us we transfer our intra-day philosophy to pinpoint big picture swing plays as well.

We tag the closing price on the last day of trading for the year and monitor price action from that point forward. With the yearly neutral set in

**FIGURE 10.10** Bullish Play: Daily Chart Combining Yearly Homework Rule and Yearly Neutral Rule

place until the next December 31, we just simply adjust the yearly homework 50 percent as a new yearly high or low is established. If price action is above the yearly neutral and the yearly homework mark, we favor bullish (buying) positions and if price action is trading below our two key directional sense rules we favor bearish (selling) positions. See Figures 10.10 and 10.11.

Be sure to prepare for the length of time it may take for the trade to get to your entry spot by counting how many days it took the stand-out area to develop, as this can provide a good measure of how long you may have to wait to enter. Once you get the price you want add that same length of time to give you a feel for how long it may take to reach your objective. Now this isn't foolproof, but this exercise alleviates tension and anxiety while waiting. If prices haven't reached your objective in the time allotment you have

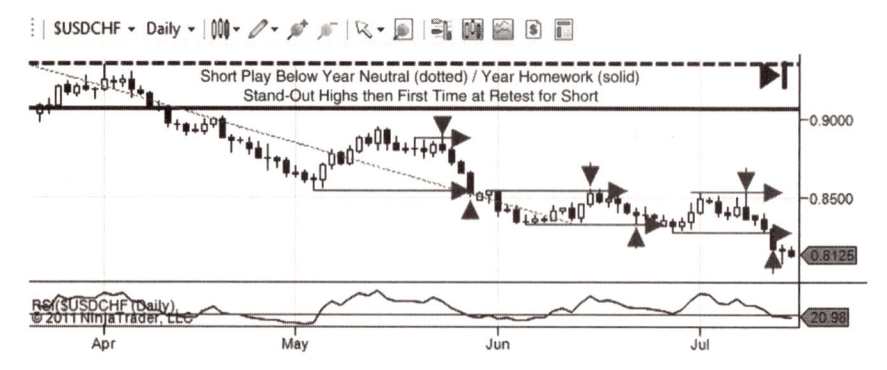

**FIGURE 10.11** Bullish Play: Daily Chart Combining Yearly Homework Rule and Yearly Neutral Rule

set, then the choice is to do one of two things. Attach a stop and limit to the positions (one cancels other [OCO]) and go stretch your legs, or have the courage to exit as prices should be where you targeted and most often times there is a reason for them not being there. Watching where new stand-out tops and bottoms form while in a position can help you adjust to new global occurrences along the journey. Life and opinions change minute to minute and in a computerized trading world it now changes in seconds.

## The Measured Move

Since trading is about speculation as well, we felt a need to add this aspect to our trading strategy as well. As our trading style matured we found a need to help develop foresight skills a bit further and forecast daily price targets that matched our style with our competitor's as well. Forecasting targets and preparing ahead of time for realistic 24-hour price moves was an equally important match against the homework and neutral rules. We noticed at times as the session stand-out top/bottom was met, that we sometimes left money on the table after realizing prices had a little more gas in the tank. Markets seemingly displayed a consistent energy and at times a top or bottom may have developed in a tighter range intra-day. As you enter and shoot for the stand-out top/bottom we found that by also predicting how far prices may typically travel from day to day helped us extend the trade for bigger gains. We could take some profit as the initial target (stand-out bottom/top) was met and then ride the remaining position to the forecasted range target. When you exit a trade that surely had the ability to offer more profit, as a competitor it leaves a bad taste in our mouth. It's like being in the clear and on your way to running in the end-zone but your opponent took a last-ditch grab and caught a piece of your shoelace, catching you inches short of the overall goal (actually happened to Mike when returning a punt in college). Here is how we anticipate and forecast what we believe the range potential will be for the upcoming session.

## Forecasting and Building the Field

Every trader struggles with what time frame to use when he or she begins to chart market movement. Questions usually asked are: Do I look at daily, weekly, monthly, quarterly, or yearly charts, and so on. From earlier we have expressed that we can see all that we need to know from daily charts to do our homework and monitor 15-minute charts during the intra-day session. As our focus shifts to homework, using only one day of time doesn't always capture enough data to get a true read. If we go back too far, that

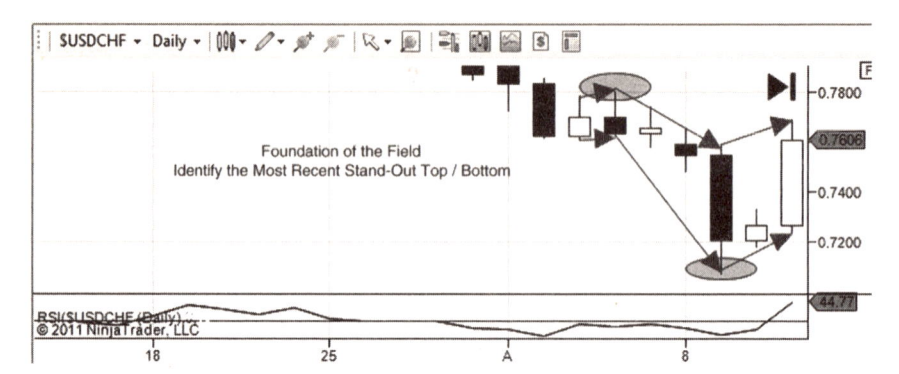

**FIGURE 10.12** Identifying the Most Recent Stand-Out Top/Bottom to Build the Field

information gets us thinking too much in the past. So what is that perfect amount of time?

What we discovered through years of trading is to use basic uptrend and downtrend analysis from daily charts to build our initial footing. In the beginning let's not predict and let's focus on when shifts actually do occur. The *recent stand-out high/low* simply takes into account when the market shifts from an uptrend to a downtrend or vice versa. When prices rise from a low and consistently make higher highs, obviously the idea is to stay long (buy) with the trend. When prices fall from a high and consistently make lower lows, we want to sell and ride the short and stay with the trend. See Figure 10.12.

As you monitor action from day to day through time and analysis you will begin to see that tops and bottoms on daily charts usually trend on average for approximately five days, but remember that technical analysis is not an exact science. Thinking of it as an exact science will take you down along with the countless others that regard it in this manner. We use it to gauge or measure when buyers or sellers are strong and when they get tired and go to sleep.

## Five-Day Cycle

We feel the five-day cycle (number of trading days in a week) is a great indicator of time for the majority of traders. There is no secret formula or a magic number, but for some reason things seem to gravitate around a five-day cycle. Trend shifts can and do last longer or shorter than five days, so again take caution to not take it as an exact science but as a great reference point to consider. Countless hours of study led us to think about the reasons why. Conclusions of five days came from everyday life and then it later infiltrated into our trading recipe. See Figure 10.13.

*Defining the Rotating Directional System* **139**

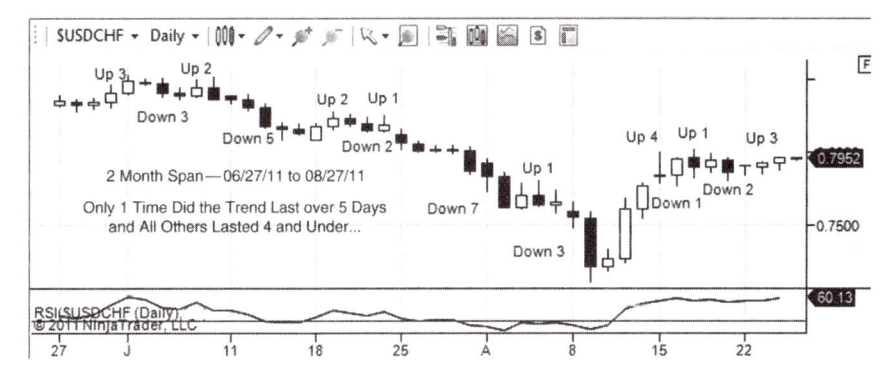

**FIGURE 10.13** Average Trends Seem to Rotate Approximately Five Days

*The key to a sound strategy is to find a number that price action hits but doesn't hit every day.* If the event was achieved every day, you wouldn't be able to weed out what was relevant and what wasn't, but as you back-test through data a number will become apparent. This number for us is five. Later in the chapter we will reference back to show you an alternative way to use our concept to help anticipate how far we expect prices to travel mathematically by using a five-day average range. First, we will show you how it is built from actual confirmed highs/lows.

## Eight Key Zones of Measurement

As we see daily highs and lows getting higher when compared to the previous session, we wait to see where prices stall (hit a top) and start to transition down with lower highs and lower lows. Circle the stand-out top of the move and as the downtrend stalls (hits a bottom) and prices start to shift higher with greater highs and greater lows again circle the stand-out low of the downtrend.

First thing we do is **break the range from top to bottom in two parts** to get our midfield (same as homework 50 percent concept). Since our calendar year is divided in quarters and there are four quarters in a dollar, four quarters in football and basketball, we get a sense of key zones on the trading field so we break down the range yet again, but this time in four equal parts: the low, 25 percent, 50 percent, 75 percent, and the high. These are the meat of the range and will later help us define our two-level rotations (25 percent of the field). We begin to map this key area on a chart to represent where we might want to enter. As a team moves into the opponent's red zone (25 percent from the low or high), the emotion and excitement of the offense builds and on the flip side the defense gets worried. If the majority of the action is spent on a particular side of the field the defense tends to be in trouble in trading and any competition that involves a winner or a loser for that matter. A continuation of the route on the losing opponent is expected.

Price movement from low to 25 percent to 50 percent to 75 percent to the high doesn't always happen in moments. It takes time to move to these key zones and just like anything we have a time tolerance that we discussed. In order to match price potential and balance it with time we have identified yet one more important and last breakdown of the range, which is eight equal parts (12.5 percent of range). The entire map from top to bottom or vice versa would look like: 0 (low/high), 12.5 percent (1st and goal—1/8), 25 percent (red zone—1/4), 37.5 percent (field goal range—3/8) and 50 percent (midfield—1/2), 62.5 percent (field goal range—5/8) 75 percent (red zone—3/4), 87.5 percent (1st and goal—7/8), and 100 percent (low/high).

Remember that in order to build a solid strategy you need to identify what seems to happen every day and what can happen but doesn't happen all of the time to get a solid feel for what can be expected for the upcoming session. In all our years, we always see the market move back and forth a handful of times around one level (12.5 percent of range), similar to a single in baseball. There are at times two to three two-level rotations back and forth (25 percent) in the day, similar to a double in baseball. We might see one triple similar to three one-level rotations (37.5 percent of the range) and potentially one homerun or a four-level rotation. Realistically this tells us to maintain a 12.5 percent to 25 percent expectations outlook on our trade entry and exits for the two-hour typical life of a trade. See Figure 10.14.

For those of you not feeling the football analogy, let's use a thermometer to drive the same point home on the significance of eight equal parts. Since the temperature during the calendar year for the globe (at least where

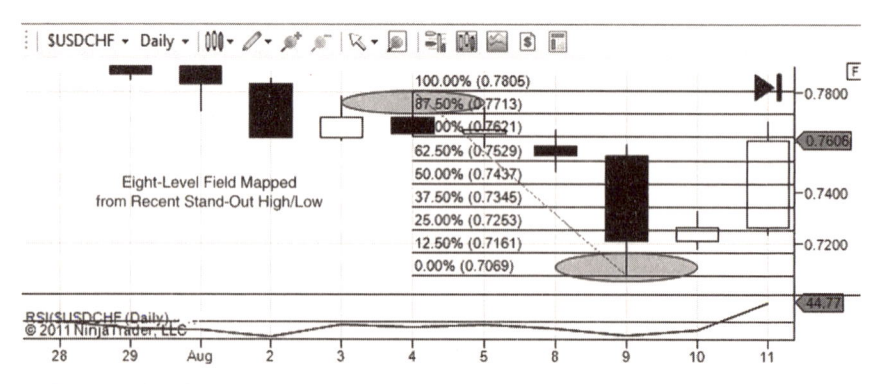

**FIGURE 10.14** Field Divided in Eight Parts

*Defining the Rotating Directional System* **141**

the majority of us live) ranges from 0 to 100, people gravitate to the climate that most fits their personality. No matter where your climate tends to fall on the temperature map 0 degrees is cold and 100 degrees is hot. The sweet spot for warm weather lovers is 75 degrees and the sweet spot for cold weather lovers is in the 25-degree range. Fifty degrees is a nice meeting in the middle that creates an equilibrium that all can tolerate.

Since temperature and life is never constant we do get a feel seasonally for when things are the best. In the winter months the best spot for the snow boarders and skiers range from 12.5 degrees to 37.5 degrees. 12.5 degrees and lower isn't the best because it is getting cold and extra layers to keep warm may hinder your ability to move down the slopes as you like. 37.5 degrees or warmer melts the snow and is too slushy for good skiing, leaving the sweet spot average in the 25 percent area.

On the flip side, warm weather lovers in the summer time might like to go for a run or a swim. The range of temperatures that we see in the summertime generally hover from 62.5 degrees to 100 degrees. One hundred degrees might not affect swimmers from getting in the pool but it sure would if the water was 100 degrees. The same idea would go for runners in 100-degree heat. They would not be able to last too long facing those extreme temperatures. If the temperature in the pool falls below 62.5 degrees it's getting a bit too chilly for people to get in their shorts and jump in at those temperatures. Runners may like it but initially will need a warmer layer at the start. It would take some time to get warmed up and when they do they would have to shed layers along the route. This leaves us with an average sweet spot for warm weather lovers at 75 degrees.

Remember that teams that have the ability to initially push deep into their opponent's territory tend to be able to repeat that task. The losing team that allows this to happen is in a bit of shock and it's likely that it can be done to them again. As seasons change you always get that one day of a blast of heat or a blast of cold to let you know that the season is changing and will be hanging around for the next three months or so. Trading is no different.

## Fibonacci for RDS

At the 37.5 percent (3/8) and 62.5 percent (5/8) points, much like field goal range in football, you will find that these areas are significant for many traders as well. Just as the snowboarder and skiers and the runners and swimmers know the cut-off of their season when temperatures began to rise above the 37.5 degree area (spring/summer to follow) or fall below the 62.5 degree area (fall/winter to follow) respectively, these zones become a foreshadowing signal of what is likely to follow for a trader as well. Some even use the Fibonacci percentages 38.2 percent or 61.8 percent respectively. As price action gets to these zones on the map, participants begin to anticipate direction as confidence builds to move to the nearest extreme (high/low).

Fibonacci was a mathematician who came up with the golden ratio; traders just took it and thoughtfully applied it to a trading range as well as various time sequences. Fibonacci felt his ratio came into play for just about everything. The idea is that you take the numbers in the sequence counting by 1 and add their results to the next number higher. An example would be: $0 + 1 = 1$, $1 + 2 = 3$, $2 + 3 = 5$, $3 + 5 = 8$, $5 + 8 = 13$, $8 + 13 = 21$, $13 + 21 = 34$, and so on. Now you would divide the successive results by each other and you will consistently get the ratio equaling 0.618 or 61.8 percent. After the result arrived at when dividing 5 by 8 or 0.625 the ratio begins to appear: $8 \div 13 = 0.615$, $13 \div 21 = 0.619$, $21 \div 34 = 0.618$, and so on. If you took the whole number of 1 and subtracted 0.618 you come up with the other percentage of 0.382 or 38.2 percent. Fibonacci saw the ratio come into play for the precise measurement needed to build homes and various structures, and he even thought that you could compare the mathematical concept and relate it to the proportions of humans; 0 percent representing the toes and 100 percent representing the head. The torso made up the bulk of your mass (hips 38.2 percent to shoulders 61.8 percent) with the distance from your feet to your head ranging from 0 to 100 percent.

Traders began to apply this ratio as it shows up in trading ranges. We are not disagreeing, but we just want to show you to further explain the concept that the mere difference between 37.5 and 38.2 percent or 62.5 and 61.8 percent is not very much in the end. Remember that no matter what percentages you use in the end that these are speculative areas on a trading range map. The main importance of using either is the emotions traders start to feel at these locations. Don't get too caught up and risk your entire life savings thinking that everybody is viewing the same thing at the same time and will push the market where you want it to go when you want it to get there. If it was that easy everybody would have already done it.

The reason why Mike favors using 37.5 percent or 62.5 percent is because in the trading pit we didn't always have computers. Since the adjustments between 37.5 versus 38.2 or 62.6 versus 61.8 were not that significant, he asked himself what was easier to calculate in his head. The answer was simple; just knowing how to divide by two and the eventual $1 \div 8$ division stuck with him ever since. He just simply took the range and divided it by two to get 50 percent and took the 50 percent and divided the result by two to get 25 percent and taking 25 percent and divided it by two to get 12.5 percent. Without a calculator or a computer in the beginning, he became very quick and efficient with dividing the key zones by two to come up with the level he needed.

## Four Level Moves Forecasted Barring No Economic or Geo-Political Events

The natural ebb and flow of price movement doesn't move from expected top to bottom in an instant and in one direction unless an economic or geopolitical event hits. When this happens, we can sometimes see a run in prices up to amore than eight-level move, which is equivalent of a price move from the daily stand-out top/bottom used to make up the original field.

Movement of this magnitude clearly doesn't happen every day, so expecting it daily will be a stretch and undoubtedly leave you discouraged if you expect it. It's much like when looking into baseball stats you will see that the majority of hits are singles (one level—12.5 percent equivalent) and as you move to doubles (two levels—25 percent) you see plenty but not as much. As you get to triples and homeruns the numbers or chances of hitting them goes significantly down. You can make the same assumptions in poker and the chances of getting a pair (two of a kind), trips (three of a kind), or quads (four of a kind). This helps us define what we prefer to wait for before entry, which is a two-level price move, which basically is starting a poker hand with at least a pair.

As we achieve each significant zone in trading the comfort levels and the emotions will adjust along the scale. This of course isn't an exact science as we have mentioned, but you can begin to develop a sense of what is realistic and what is unrealistic. One thing we can tell you with near 100 percent accuracy is that price movement always achieves a 12.5 percent. We call this a one-level move.

Well into the high 90 percent area price achieves a 2 Level Move (25 percent of expected range). As we search for price movement to establish a three Level Move (37.5 percent of range) we start to see a decline in the 80 percent area but it's definitely not enough to shake us off the idea that it can't happen. four Level moves (50 percent of range) occur in the 70 percent area. Beyond four Level Moves the percentage begins to hit failing marks falling below 60 percent. Establish a boundary of what is likely and at times touch but not every single time. Failing grades of 60 percent or worse doesn't mean it will not happen but expecting a move of more than four Levels isn't something that should be counting on.

## Adjusting the Field to the Neutral Rule

Before we move into appropriate entries according to our strategy we need to make an adjustment to our field. Since we noticed that almost all strategies encompass the closing price in their study (our neutral rule) we want to skew our 50 percent marker established from our stand-out top or

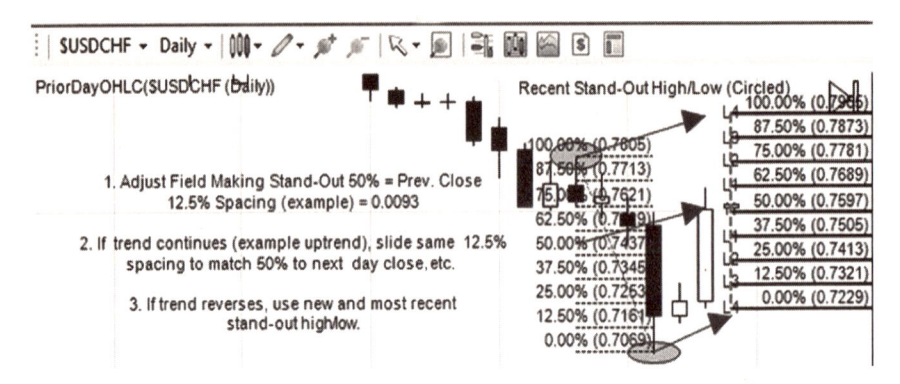

**FIGURE 10.15** Adjusting the Field to Neutral

bottom and adjust the entire field up or down to match the most current previous close price. We feel this puts us in alignment with current market sentiment with a well-known price point to help our directional GPS for bullish or bearish confidence. How far prices may travel over 24 hours, barring extreme geo-political events, doesn't change as we initially prepare our map to fit four levels up from neutral to four levels down from neutral (eight total). See Figure 10.15.

At the end of the session if the trend coming into the day remains intact, you can keep the current level spacing the same. The only change will be to move the entire field to match the closing price. If the trend at the end of the session reverses, you can then readjust our levels to reflect the eight equal parts based from the new stand-out high or low.

### Average Range

An issue that became apparent with our stand-out high/low field was when prices closed outside of the extreme due to an erratic movement from an event that took place during the session. Things changed your viewpoint today and sometimes you tend to get a new feel and don't have the confidence to rely on the spacing you made earlier, especially if things remain on trend. It's hard to maintain a 32-pip rotation spacing of levels for example, when you have a blow-out day revealing a more than eight level price run. Price generally will not exceed the blow-out run the next session but volatility is in the air and the spacing you had running will most certainly create five-, six-, or even seven-level moves the following day. Here is how we solved and tweaked our concept.

We didn't completely throw out the stand-out high/low field but we just modified it to have an adjusting mechanism that fit within the normal

*Defining the Rotating Directional System*

five-day memory that we noticed was apparent as well. Mike began taking the high minus the low (range) for each day up to five days. He added them up and divided by five. This gave him a sense of how far prices may travel that day, which in a sense was in accordance with the normal reversal in trend cycle seen and what traders tended to remember anyway. We would add the five-day average range result from Neutral to get an upside extreme and then divide it by four to get our four key levels on the top half of our map. In turn we would subtract the five-day average range result from neutral to get a downside extreme and divide it into four parts to establish the four key downside levels on our map. Some traders may say it's much like an Average True Range (ATR), but at times traders skew the results by only using the base of the candle and excluding the wicks or shadows. *We always say to the exponential smoothers or those that filter out tops and bottoms to "save it for the board room and keep it away from the trading arena. If we can't smooth the losses from our account, we will not smooth the wicks and shadows out of our level calculations."*

We prefer to use the exact information because it paints the most accurate picture. Let's send a nice dose of reality to any of you who are thinking about smoothing your results. Our politicians are the best data smoothers we know. Do you think they would be in office today if they included the food and energy cost in the Consumer Price Index (CPI) and the Producer Price Index data. The U.S. Department of Labor filters out this data because they claim it's too volatile a component to get a true read of inflation. This is a politician's way to brush under the rug the fact that since we have lived in Los Angeles from 2008 to 2011, the cost of gas has fluctuated from about $2.50 to $5.00 per gallon. Our calculator says that is at one point a 100 percent increase in prices. So if prices were to climb 3 percent each year and we started from $2.50 per gallon that would mean the price of gas should have been $2.57 in 2009, $2.65 in 2010, and $2.73 per gallon in 2011. Maybe the next time we should fill our car up and only pay the rate that it should be. See how well that goes over with the gas station attendant. Data smoothers beware when you enter the trading arena! You have been forewarned! See Figure 10.16.

Building the levels from past stand-out highs/lows or mathematically is never going to provide foolproof 100 percent successful results, but matching the time you use with the time traders generally stick around in a position will help you become a pretty solid forecaster. We have had many rave about the accuracy of our levels across multiple markets. They are accurate enough due to the fact that humans are habitual in nature and strategies are becoming more and more computer and formula driven based on open, high, low, and close data. After that it just becomes adding some sugar or salt to the recipe to give you a solid measuring stick.

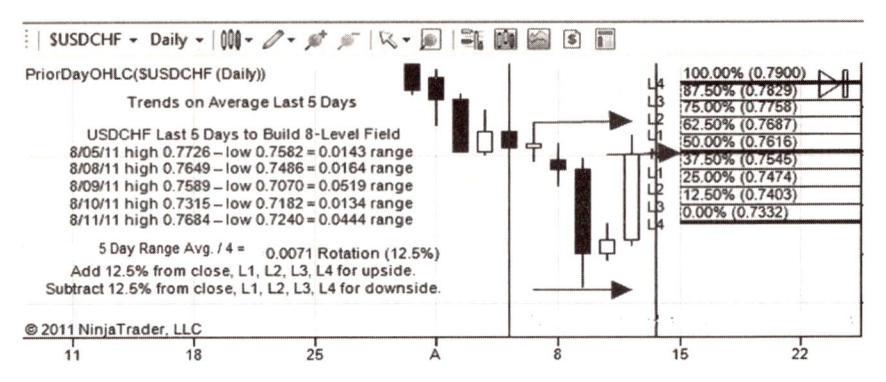

**FIGURE 10.16** Field Built from Five-Day Average Range Adjusted to Neutral

### Perfect Bull/Bear Day Adjustment

We realized that we could have what we call a "perfect bull day" or prices moving from the previous session close and run up to the five-day average range or vice versa have a "perfect bear day" or a price move from the close down to the five-day range result. Again this was not going to happen in one shot. Prices naturally ebbed and flowed in the same two-level rotations we like. Building a field from this angle confirmed that it held the overall concept in place and the levels did not stray too far either way. It also allowed us to be more up to date with current volatility when the trend continued. With the levels set in place and the focus set on the key 25 percent level rotations we called our next rule the distance run.

### RULE 3: DISTANCE RUN; TWO-LEVEL ROTATIONS WITH A FOUR-LEVEL RANGE OBJECTIVE

We of course want to stay on the path and target entries, exits and length of time in a trade on realistic educated assumptions. Some of Mike's boyhood idols in baseball were Pete Rose, Rod Carew, George Brett, Wade Boggs, and Tony Gwynn. They were some of the premier base hit and doubles hitters who had the longest careers in baseball. Now you can choose to identify with the glamorous home run hitters, but you will find that they are few and far between, ending up with bad backs and short careers or fighting a steroid scandal. Base hits and doubles are achievable for the majority of us out there, and I often hear Mike say that he had many at bats in his baseball career and hit only three homeruns. He played all out and kept anywhere from a .300 to .500 batting average, started and played in every

*Defining the Rotating Directional System* **147**

**FIGURE 10.17** Two-Level Move with Homework and Neutral above for Sell Entry

game in his career, and never missed one game due to injury. He just merely concentrated on playing to his strength and got good at getting on base so the cleanup hitters could drive him home.

As the person who makes all of the trading decisions and controls when to get in and when to get out, wouldn't it then serve you well to lean on and wait for the highest percentage spots to enter the price rhythm of the market. We just began to wait for a two-level rise in price from a low before considering short. Our confidence in pulling the trigger climbed when our other advisors were on board; the homework rule (weekly/current day) plus the neutral rule (previous close) still above our head as well as the upcoming window of opportunity and RSI rules. As a target we would shoot for prices to fall and retest recent bottoms to a four-level total range target matched with the realistic anticipated price run measuring stick of one to two levels (12.5 percent to 25 percent drop respectively) for an exit. See Figures 10.17 and 10.18.

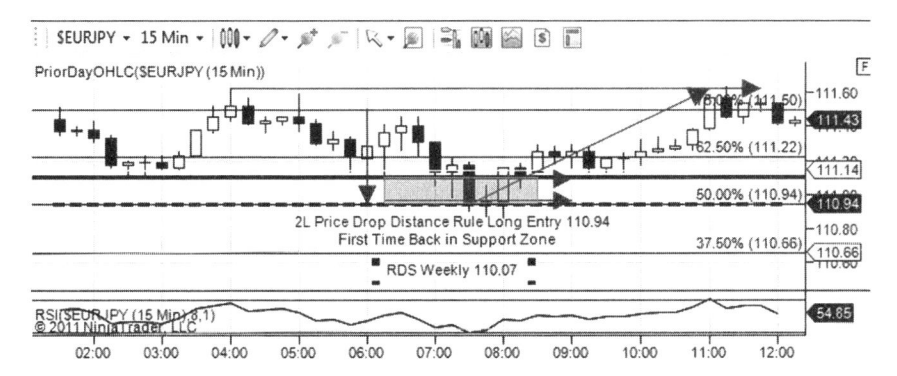

**FIGURE 10.18** Two-Level Move with Homework and Neutral below for Buy Entry

On the flip side we would wait for a two-level fall in price from the session high before considering long. Of course we want to check in with our other advisors, the homework rule (weekly and current day) plus the neutral rule (previous close) and upcoming window of opportunity and RSI rules, before entering. As a target we would shoot for prices to climb to previous tops coinciding with a four-level range target matched to one- to two-level realistic objectives (12.5 to 25 percent respectively).

At times you will get a mixed read, when just using the neutral or daily homework rule. The RDS weekly adds the third layer to helps decide if the idea is still worth trying. The example shows the neutral rule and RDS weekly in agreement with a long play on the Euro/Japanese Yen (EURJPY) on August 25, 2011, but the daily homework was signaling caution. When faced with these decisions, having a majority still makes the idea worth trying. You can always scale back the amount of your entry to match the slightly cautious signal.

## RULE 4: WINDOW OF OPPORTUNITY, TIME TO EXECUTE

In a sense we have already been describing the window of opportunity. After building the field of play and establishing our levels to help us measure price moves, we use our downtrend/uptrend skills from our daily charts and transfer that concept to our preferred 15-minute intra-day chart to help our timing and confidence prior to entry.

Get away from trying to pick bottoms or pick tops; let the big dogs give you a tell and show you a bottom/top. When action shifts from a downtrend to uptrend or vice versa, we call this transition "the flip". We of course will get ready and try to anticipate when this may happen because when prices move into that two-level four-level max distance run we feel price action is going to hit a wall. Now this isn't always certain, but through experience and what we have described so far with field building you will begin to see it and gain confidence with it. As prices have fallen two levels we begin to know what we do not want to do, which is sell, because we feel a bottom is imminent, especially if approaching a stand-out low. We missed the short party so to speak. The feeling here of the sellers is much like arriving to a night club a couple hours late to visit friends. When you arrive sober you are most definitely out of sync. It is not always wise to join the party here. Traders who have joined in on the fall much earlier are up money and beginning to think about taking their money and going home.

On the flip side the concept is much the same; after a price rise of two levels, we do not want to buy at this point, because we feel that a top is

*Defining the Rotating Directional System* **149**

near. As a trader, the three most common questions we ask ourselves all of the time are buy, sell, or do nothing? Once we have eliminated one side (buy in this case after a two-level rise), we concentrate on the preferred side or do nothing. Doing nothing is just as important to a trader as participating. *It's not about how much you make, it's about how much you don't lose.* To take from some poker concepts that transfer over to trading, the object at the end of the day is to have just as many chips or more in your pocket, so there is no need to play mediocre hands. We feel that in the trading world that you should eliminate them entirely, because the market is full of many professionals with smart money lurking out there to take what we call dumb money.

## Buy Window of Opportunity

Let's consider the buy-side window of opportunity first. Buy entry timing is typically safer when we first start to see higher highs and higher lows on a 15-minute chart. Now of course you can apply the same concept to other time frames, but since we prefer a 15-minute chart intra-day we will display it referencing this unit of time.

As we pinpoint exactly where and when a higher high occurs on the 15-minute chart we get a confirmation to place either a buy market order or wait for action to revisit the bottom and using a buy limit order to get long. The window is broken down into three choices after seeing higher highs. See Figure 10.19.

We will make slight tweaks and adjustments to the window if we have not yet seen a two-level drop before placing a long position in the buy window of opportunity (see Figure 10.20).

After you identify the buy window we identify buy entry areas as star one, tar two, or star three.

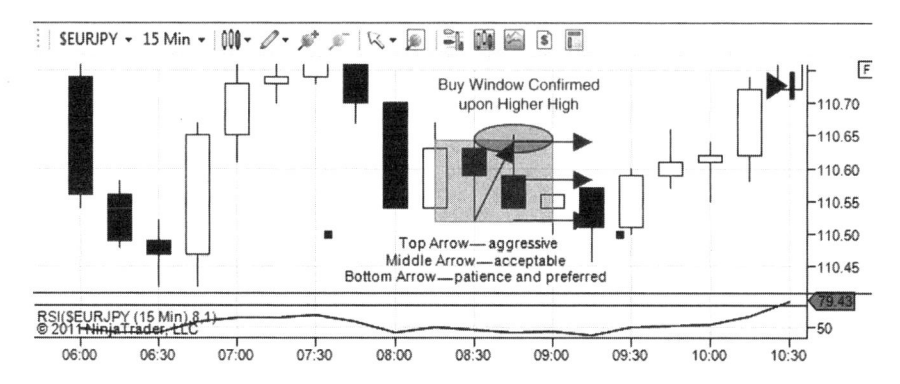

**FIGURE 10.19** Buy Window Three Choices

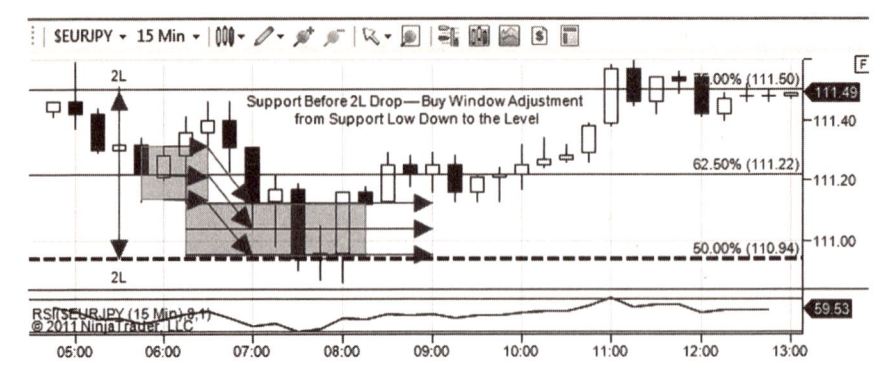

**FIGURE 10.20** Buy Window Three Choices Adjusted to the Level, if We Haven't Seen a Two-Level Fall

Star One: Just as we see higher highs, an aggressive play would be to enter a buy market order immediately. We call this entry star one.

Star Two: Through experience we often see price action make a higher high and then pull back into what we call the window. It's much like taking a battering ram to a locked door. The first hit might produce some cracks (higher highs) in the door but there is a recoil effect as you get knocked back to the area where you started from which is now the stand-out low. We feel that you can most often get a better price from the recoil to the midpoint of the window based from the stand-out low to the price where you first witnessed higher highs. The type of order needed at star two is a buy limit order. We will discuss topics about scaling-in (incremental buys at varying prices within the window) versus all-in (entering at one price only) in the next chapter.

You should note that you do not always get the recoil that you wanted and can be left on the sidelines. This is why we fall into the discretionary trader realm as we feel that a human mind and touch can differentiate between close enough and exact. A black-box computer algorithm cannot make these adjustments. It is a cross to bear for both sides of the coin, but in the end no matter what you choose you need to build a tolerance for the one that got away and realize that plenty will. Try not to get frustrated if you missed a move, as there are approximately 220-plus trading games a year so there will be plenty of opportunity. *We focus and worry about what we get and we learned to not dwell on what we don't get.*

Star three: After we see higher highs we look back to where prices started the upside trend, which in this case would be the stand-out low. Hindsight can be plenty helpful in trading, but most shrug their shoulders and say that it doesn't make me any money. We disagree. In this case you see where the line in the sand is drawn (the stand-out low in this case).

*Defining the Rotating Directional System* **151**

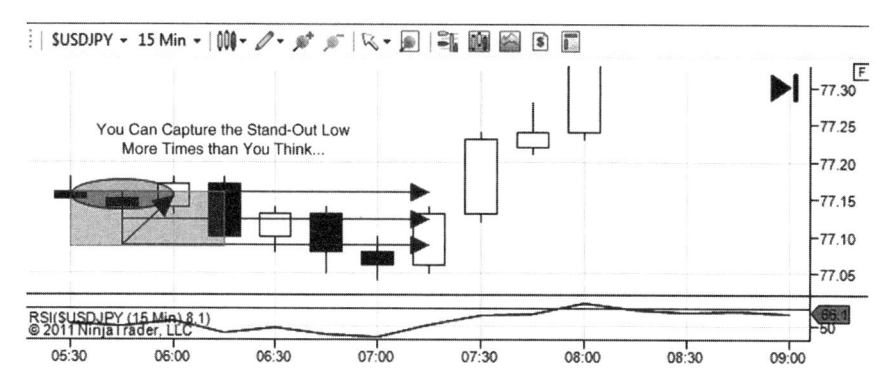

**FIGURE 10.21** Can You Get the Stand-Out Low?

There is no guessing about the bottom. We realize that you didn't get the trade yet, but you do have confirmation about your thought, which is to start getting long immediately (star one), waiting for the middle of the window (star two), or waiting for the bottom (star three). When referring back in time and studying the possibilities, Mike blocks out everything to the right of the chart after seeing the higher high. He wants to show himself and his students the best way possible to not view what has happened in the aftermath. You need to back-test in a way that gives you the most realistic thoughts you would have had prior to entry, after entry, and how things went until exit. See Figure 10.21.

Listening in on many of Mikes classes I often hear him say after he sees a higher high; 'Wouldn't it have been nice if we would have known that was going to be the bottom. How great would that be?" As Mike reveals the next four to eight 15-minute segments (one to two hours respectively) he often says: "You got your wish."

## Sell Window of Opportunity

On the flip side, when considering a sell we look to see where lower lows begin on a 15-minute chart. As we pinpoint exactly where and when the lower low occurs we get a confirmation to get short (sell). Just as we did for the buy window we break it down into three choices after seeing lower lows.

Star one: Just as we see lower lows, an aggressive play would be to enter a sell market order immediately. We call this entry star one.

Star two: After the typical recoil that you most often get, you can set a sell limit at the midpoint of the window. We want to remind you that we will discuss scaling-in (incremental sells at varying prices within the window) versus all-in (entering at one price only) in the next chapter.

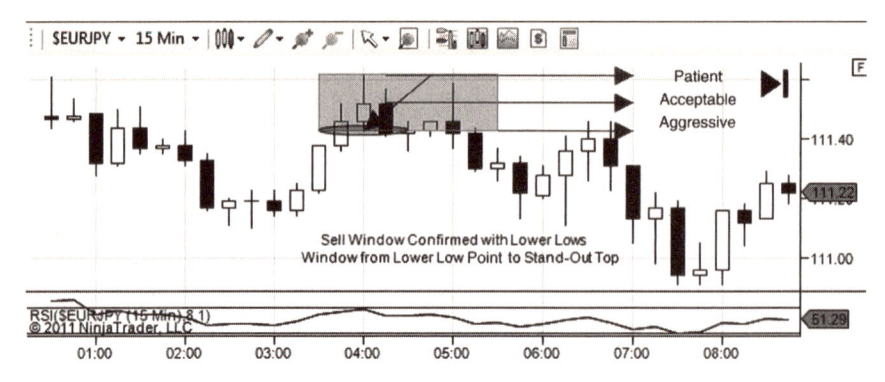

**FIGURE 10.22** Sell Window Three Choices

Star three: After we see lower lows we look back to where prices started the downside trend, which in this case would be the stand-out high. Use the hindsight studying tip that Mike suggested earlier by blocking out everything to the right of the chart after you first start seeing lower lows. Incrementally begin to reveal the next four to eight 15-minute segments to see if there was a chance to actually sell that top or star three. The order type used would be a sell limit order set to the known high price at the top of the window. See Figure 10.22.

We will make slight tweaks and adjustments to the window if we have not yet seen a two-level rise before placing a short position in the sell window of opportunity (Figure 10.23).

This example shows that the flip in trend occurred after it surpassed the two-level rise. There is no adjustment needed to the window, when faced with this scenario. After a flip occurs and your notice that we have the distance run rule fully met and then some, this is when we feel it is

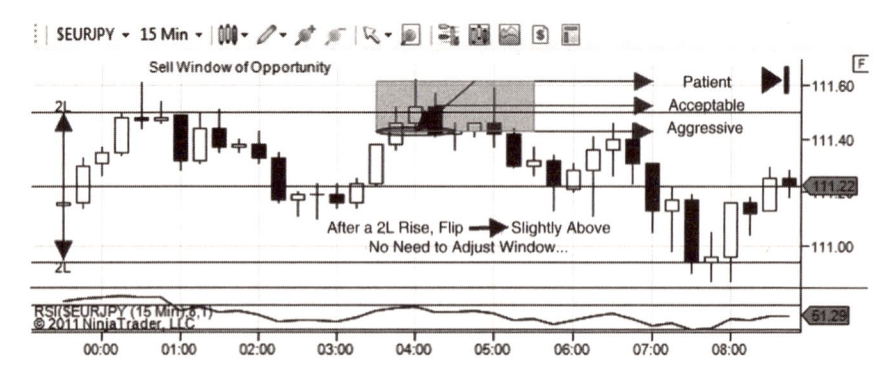

**FIGURE 10.23** Sell Window Three Choices Adjusted if We Have Seen a Two-Level Rise

*Defining the Rotating Directional System*  **153**

better to take advantage of any of the three entry areas within the window. Price action is forecasted to be at it apex already and you can gain confidence that is overbought by confirming your others rules to this point. To make sure we add one final layer to our rules with what we call a traditional technical indicator: the Relative Strength Index (RSI).

## RULE 5: RELATIVE STRENGTH INDEX: THE SECOND OPINION

Earlier we have mentioned our reasons why we believe that price action tends to rotate around a distance run of 25 percent on average but just like a doctor giving you some news, at times you want another opinion. We do feel that it is important to develop foresight skills and as you gain experience with the two-level distance run rule you will soon gain confirmation by using oscillators to help you gauge over-bought and over-sold concepts. Looking at the energy that already exists in the market by using your eight-level measuring stick will give you foresight as to where and when; the oscillator that you are using can give you another opinion.

With so many oscillators to choose from like Relative Strength Index, Moving Average Convergence Divergence (MACD), Stochastic, Bollinger Bands and so on, we recommend making it simple and choosing one. Through the years Mike has studied them all and tried them all in tandem with his other rules, but he seems to fall back on the one he first saw somebody using at the computer kiosk for members on the trading floor at the Chicago Board of Trade (CBOT). We didn't have computers in the pit at the time but we did have a few terminals to look at that had real-time charts and technical studies software on it. Since traders never talked strategy to each other in the pit, the computer terminal was a popular stop before the market opened or when coming back from a break to catch you up on price development.

Early in Mike's career before work one morning he went to go take a look at the charts, but he found that he had to wait. A well-known seven- to eight-figure earner was ahead of him. When it was Mike's turn to use the computer his first instinct was to clear out what the trader ahead of him had left so he could place his Levels on the chart and get a clean printout like he always does. Something stopped him from just erasing what the guy had left on the screen that day. This was a seven- to eight-figure earner. Sometimes you don't have to be a fly on the wall but you can take what one man leaves behind and see if it might be a hidden treasure for you. Mike saw something new to him at the bottom of the screen. It was RSI. Mike scratched his head and uttered, "What the heck is RSI?"

Eager to always learn and if a seven-to-eight-figure earner was taking a peek at it, why shouldn't we take a look. Mike came home that night and began studying oscillators, specifically the Relative Strength Index. We use J. Welles Wilder's Relative Strength Index (RSI) to help confirm or deny an entry in tandem with our other rules. Before going further, *it is important for us to mention that just as our levels are speculative in nature that fit our personality so is RSI.* There is no magic formula and J. Welles Wilder puts his pants on the same way all of us do, so don't hold anything on a pedestal higher than your own personal instincts. Use what mentors have taught us in the past and mold it to fit your personality. This oscillator is used to gauge strength or weakness in the market. In other words, it helps us anticipate over-bought or over-sold conditions.

## Special Note on Over-Bought or Over-Sold

Mike clearly despises the words over-bought and over-sold. There is no such thing as over-bought or over-sold when you have experienced Gulf Wars, changing presidents, different Fed Chairman, tech booms and bubbles, 9/11, housing collapses, credit crunches, flash crashes, and debt limit dramas. In an emotion filled environment you need to remember to focus on what is real and what is speculative. The real factual rules mentioned so far are the fundamental parity price concept along with the homework rule (day, week, and/or year 50 percent), the neutral rule (previous day close on 15-minute and/or previous year close on daily charts) and the window of opportunity rule (stand-out top/bottom). They are clearly defined and reside on the factual side of numerical evidence. The distance run and RSI rules are speculative in nature, which doesn't mean that they are not useful but they are vital to help you build instincts. You have heard of gut-feeling before; the distance run and RSI help you build that vital sixth sense.

Having factual rules and instinct rules working together in tandem creates a balanced approach to risk taking. Too much speculative information creates wild swings and unsustainable adrenalin rushes and too much factual information often leads to stagnant growth bogging down decision making. You may have already noticed that our rules have a mixture of both, but weighted a bit more on the factual side. Formulating a plan weighing a bit more on fact but with some speculative risk-taking elements to it has kept us thriving for the last 20 years.

## RSI Formula

RSI is a measurement of $n$ period previous closing prices that tell you how strong or weak the market has been over $n$ periods. It is just like a gas tank reading in a car. When the empty light flashes, it's time to refuel. In trading

*Defining the Rotating Directional System* **155**

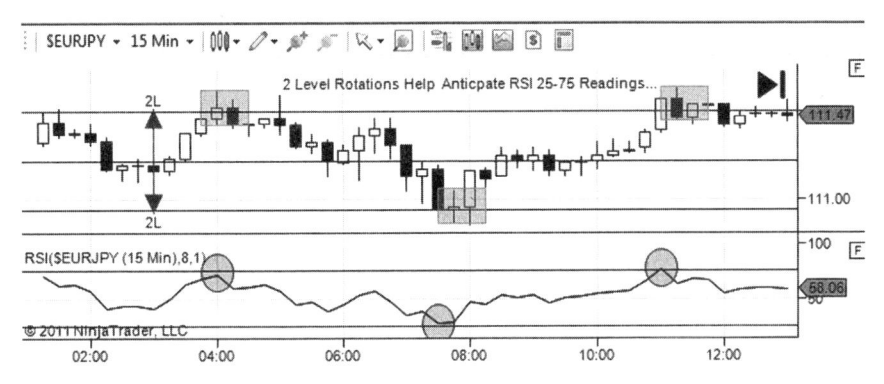

**FIGURE 10.24** 15-Minute Chart RSI Settings—Eight Periods (2 hours)

it is no different, as prices will eventually become exhausted and need to refuel as well. As we have mentioned earlier we prefer intra-day to use a 15-minute chart and feel a two-hour time horizon is on the majority of every trader's mind, so we set $n$ periods to eight as there are eight 15-minute segments in two hours. See Figure 10.24.

If we are looking out at longer time horizons we focus on a daily chart, but adjust the settings to 10. This setting is relevant to us because we realize that there are typically 20 trading days in a month so in turn we cut the month in two parts to get a nice point of interest to represent strength or weakness. Adding another layer to the thought of setting RSI at 10 periods on a daily chart comes from the mere fact that it's rare that we see 10 up closes in a row. It has happened and at times exceeds that number but it is rare. *Remember that any good strategy places a setting that is hard to achieve but not impossible.*

If you want to play with the settings we feel it is important to put it in terms of how people tend to think. For instance, if you want to look at a five-minute chart (one third of a 15-minute chart), you might think to increase the setting by three times the amount (setting of 24 two hours). When analyzing this thought you want more action and you are working with the people who have instant-gratification problems as well. Don't adjust a setting to keep it at the pace of a 15-minute, two-hour style, bump it up to a setting of 12 or one hour on a five-minute chart. You are thinking faster, so make the settings hit faster with a 12 setting on a five-minute chart (see Figure 10.25).

You could always look deeper into Wilder's studies, but the essence of how we read his indicator is that he would take the number of periods in the study (15-minute chart setting of eight periods in our case) and compare the closing prices in each segment. If there was an up-close or prices finished higher than the previous 15-minute candle, he would put

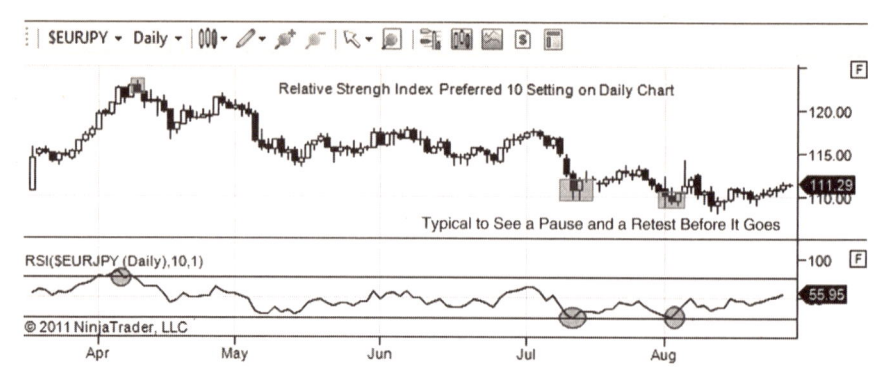

**FIGURE 10.25** Daily Chart RSI Settings 10 Periods (Half Month)

it on one side of the fence. If there was a down-close or prices finishing lower than the previous 15-minute candle, he would put it on the other side of the fence. He would add up the up-close data and divide by eight (numerator) and add up the down-close data and divide by eight (denominator) to get a RS number. He would then put it in his formula that would create a value between 0 and 100. If the value fell to a reading of 20 to 30 or what we middle to 25, prices were thought to be approaching over-sold and likely to turn higher. If the reading reflected a value of 70 to 80 or middle to 75, prices were thought to be approaching over-bought and likely to turn lower.

$$\text{RS} = \frac{\text{Up } n \text{ Close Avg.}}{\text{Down } n \text{ Close Avg.}}$$

$$\text{RSI} = 100 - 100 \div (1 + \text{RS})$$

We of course do not like to pick the top or bottom of the move and feel it is better to get confirmation by waiting for a reversal in trend (the flip). As readings are 25 or lower, we like to see a shift from a downtrend to an uptrend first before entering long (buy window) or if already short, it is signaling to take your profit. If we are getting a reading of 75 or higher, we like to see a shift from an uptrend to a downtrend (sell window) before entering short or if already long, it is time to exit and take profit.

A recap of the rules will begin to prepare us for the next chapter as we put all of the pieces together. We will not only search for high percentage entries for profit but also we will map out our confidence by looking closely at where the setup is taking place to define the mood of teammates and opponents on the field. This will help us stay away from what we consider risky low percentage plays and help us minimize our losses.

*Defining the Rotating Directional System* **157**

### Review of Trade Thought Process

Students find it helpful to review our technical thought process while evaluating whether to be long, short, or out. We favor a majority along the way (three out of five minimum) to help us on both entry and exit thoughts. We may have started the trade with five rules, but along the way we might now only have two on board signaling a time to exit, or we might start with five rules and go down to only three along the way (keeping a majority) signaling for us to possibly ride the winner a bit further. Riding trades will of course take practice to develop the experience of when and where while in a trade.

Equally and in a sense most important is what we get ourselves involved with upon entry. We want to stress the importance of using the rules collectively to form an opinion. One rule alone does not depict a successful strategy in our opinion. As we view the market technically, our first thought when focusing on the 15-minute chart is to decide a direction to favor. Buy or sell by looking where price is currently compared to the following:

1. Homework (current day, RDS weekly midpoints); long above, short below...
2. Neutral (previous session close or settlement price); long above, short below...

    The next step is to look for one of the following:

3. Two-level price run (distance run); two-level fall to consider long (rule one and two equal to or lower than the entry price) or a two-level rally to consider short (rule one and two equal to or higher than the entry price)

    And wait for a flip in trend:

4. Window of opportunity; a flip from a downtrend to an uptrend before considering long (assuming rule one, two, three) or a flip from an uptrend to a downtrend before considering short (assuming rule one, two, three)

    Confirm strength or weakness of the two-level move to sense if you thought is in alignment with current volatility

5. RSI; readings of 25 or lower are thought to be oversold and signaling a possible long (assuming rule one, two, three, four) while a reading of 75 or higher is thought to be overbought and signaling a possible short (assuming rule one, two, three, four)

# CHAPTER 11

# Putting It All Together

The holistic objective of the Rotating Directional System (RDS) strategy is to live large and you will overcome all obstacles to reach your destination. What does that mean? When we moved to Los Angeles and ended up in Hollywood, we knew we were achieving the dreams that we set out to accomplish when we entered this business. As our frequent exercise routine consisted of running outdoors we would venture toward the iconic Hollywood sign not too far from where we live. As we stopped and paused for a breather when we reached the top, we came up with a significant word to identify and reflect on how we got here. Living large has a meaning to us as achieving what we set out to accomplish in this business and our lives. We hope you find something to help remind you of where you want to go and how hard you will fight to get it!

We will be assuming from here on out that you have a strong idea of what our five rules are and how we use them in our strategy. This chapter will focus on the when, where, and how confident we are about price direction of a currency pair or any market for that matter as we relate it to fundamental and geo-political economic conditions of the time. We also assume that you have begun to establish some strong visions of risk/reward and how you are going to handle each contract you buy or sell. Risk will be addressed further in this section but we want to remind you of preparing for at least one to four levels of expected price movement per contract per 24 hours and possibly up to eight or more levels of price movement during extremely volatile moments.

> ### Review of the Rules
>
> **Rule 1 Homework Rule: Current Day/RDS Week Mid-Point**
> - The abbreviation for this rule is HR
> - Prefer long when current price is above both midpoints
> - Prefer short when current price is below both midpoints
>
> **Rule 2 Neutral: Previous Day Session Close (2 PM Pacific)**
> - The abbreviation for this rule is NR
> - Prefer long plays when current price is above
> - Prefer short plays when current price is below
>
> **Rule 3: Distance Run**
> - The abbreviation for this rule is DR
> - Two-level preferred (25 percent) move up for short
> - Two-level preferred (25 percent) move down for long
>
> **Rule 4: Window of Opportunity**
> - The abbreviation for this rule is WO
> - Flip from uptrend to a downtrend before getting short
> - Flip from uptrend to a downtrend before getting short
>
> **Rule 5: Relative Strength Index**
> - The abbreviation for this rule is RSI
> - Reading 25 oversold (cover shorts/possible long)
> - Reading 75 overbought (cover longs/possible short)

*(handwritten annotation: down - up long)*

## MOMENTUM SIDE TIMING

As you study and look to the rules for guidance upon entry and exit, we want you to take note that we prefer to play on what we define to be the momentum side of the field or the side overall that we feel traders tend to be making more money. The homework rule (HR) and the neutral rule (NR) markers make this distinction very clear to us as it is based on fact. Which side price is on (top or bottom) in accordance with our position (long or short) always sends a clear message of right and wrong. Waiting for the distance rule (DR) and the window of opportunity (WO) to develop will also keep you from guessing or trying to pick a top or bottom. If a top

*Putting It All Together*

or bottom is formed and the extreme point resides on the proper side of the NR and HR, we feel a momentum side play is in order. On top of that a favorable Relative Strength Index (RSI) reading would confirm the green light on the play.

If the entry point falls in between NR and HR, signaling a disagreement in our directional indicators, we tend to lay-off the play and look to see if another market is providing a reading that has the NR and HR in agreement. We will discuss later when we feel the best time to play counter trend (contrarian) is in order, but first we want to discuss our preferred momentum side philosophy and when we feel it is ripe for a high percentage opportunity.

It is not always easy to find confidence of when and in what direction to play, but Mike has helped me and countless others when he compares a standard candlestick chart to a market profile chart to gain added insight to your arsenal. Market profile was a concept that Pete Steidlmayer put together years ago. He uses time and price to represent value in the market just as a candlestick chart does, but what's interesting about what Steidlmayer did was that he took a mathematical price distribution (bell-shaped curve) and applied the concept to the markets.

## MARKET PROFILE—RANGE BOUND OR TRENDING

A market profile is formatted to help you identify with ease what prices continually repeat trading over and over again through time. For example, if price trades in a range of 1.4320 to 1.4340 in the first 15 minutes and in the next 15 minutes price trades in a range from 1.4330 to 1.4350, the common prices traded during the two time segments were 1.4330 to 1.4340. The repeat prices are defining a value area, because through time, long and short positions are accumulating in this area and beginning to stand out. As the value area defines itself further throughout the session, it often times forms shapes to help define confidence or lack thereof in price direction. Trading sessions typically paint 3 distinct price distributions that we call; normal, trend (strong) or range bound (flat).

Since we all seem to possess instant-gratification tendencies, we want to scan through our favorite currency markets and focus on those that have trending potential (ability to move) and look away from those that are trading with range-bound potential (flat and sideways). If the action looks range bound, we will tend to move on to another market. If the action looks like it has trending potential, we will continue to monitor this pair. Market profile assigns a letter to each price that was traded during

**FIGURE 11.1** Market Profile

the time frame you are monitoring. As prices repeat in the next time segment, the letter is displayed again to the right. If it happens to be a new price not traded during the session as of yet, the letter will move all the way to the left. Before showing the examples we hope you are not getting the feeling that you now have to go out and buy a market profile package, if your current software doesn't already have it. We want to illustrate the concept and then help you transfer the knowledge and see the same picture which can in fact be easily seen on your current candlestick chart. We adhere to doing our best to keep things simple but at the same time want you to be knowledgeable. See Figures 11.1 and 11.2.

Market profile helped Mike a ton, but as most indicators it offers hindsight information and it left holes to help build vital anticipatory skills.

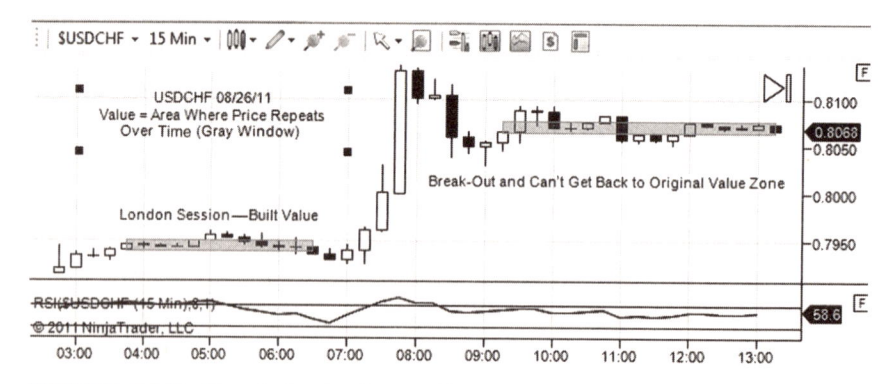

**FIGURE 11.2** Pinpointing Market Profile Pattern on a Candlestick Chart

*Putting It All Together* **163**

Remember that we feel it is important to have a mixture of fact-based indicators; HR, NR, and the WO with speculation indicators like our DR and RSI. We also feel that you can predict what price distribution is likely to deliver by understanding the emotions and mood of buyers and sellers at each particular zone on our eight-level field. As price stalls or tests various levels, we most often can speculate with a great deal of accuracy the picture that price will paint for the remainder of the session. After you have seen the overnight development and the important first-hour action, you now can begin to forecast what might be possible: normal, trend, or range bound. We just begin assigning a mood or feeling to each level on our eight-level price grid. As price moves up or down the field the mood of the buyers and the sellers changes from manageable to nasty when wrong and from normal to dancing in the end zone when right (see Figure 11.3).

We discovered a method to reveal when price is range bound, normal, or trending as we learned the moods of the players trading in the market at these key areas on the field. The only way we truly learned this was by being right in the middle of the action ourselves and witnessing firsthand the expressions of terror and pure joy on the faces of traders in the trading pit at each key level. Sometimes seeing what others look like at their best and worst moments helps internally remind us how to act and not act when faced with similar situations. Because you cannot see the facial expressions of traders on the computer, we will translate how you can rightfully assume who is at their best and worst based on the location of price on the field and what it has done over time to help.

Since emotion is rampant and unavoidable amongst traders, it is equally important that you learn and discover as well who you are in the heat of the moment. *What we have learned is that internal pleasure and pain is equal across all traders.* Some may trade bigger values, but the

| Profile | Trend | Trend | Normal | Non-Trend | NR | Non-Trend | Normal | Trend | Trend | Profile |
|---|---|---|---|---|---|---|---|---|---|---|
| MARKET | (L4) | (L3) | (L2) | (L1) | Neutral | L1 | L2 | L3 | L4 | Rotation |
| EUR/USD | 1.3845 | 1.3891 | 1.3937 | 1.3983 | 1.4029 | 1.4075 | 1.4121 | 1.4167 | 1.4213 | 0.0046 |
| USD/JPY | 79.61 | 79.77 | 79.93 | 80.09 | 80.25 | 80.41 | 80.57 | 80.73 | 80.89 | 0.16 |
| USD/CHF | 0.8249 | 0.8276 | 0.8303 | 0.8330 | 0.8357 | 0.8384 | 0.8411 | 0.8438 | 0.8465 | 0.0027 |
| GBP/USD | 1.5773 | 1.5806 | 1.5839 | 1.5872 | 1.5905 | 1.5938 | 1.5971 | 1.6004 | 1.6037 | 0.0033 |
| NZD/USD | 0.8201 | 0.8223 | 0.8245 | 0.8267 | 0.8289 | 0.8311 | 0.8333 | 0.8355 | 0.8377 | 0.0022 |
| EUR/JPY | 110.86 | 111.29 | 111.72 | 112.15 | 112.58 | 113.01 | 113.44 | 113.87 | 114.30 | 0.43 |
| AUD/USD | 1.0563 | 1.0586 | 1.0609 | 1.0632 | 1.0655 | 1.0678 | 1.0701 | 1.0724 | 1.0747 | 0.0023 |
| USD/CAD | 0.9602 | 0.9623 | 0.9644 | 0.9665 | 0.9686 | 0.9707 | 0.9728 | 0.9749 | 0.9770 | 0.0021 |
| EUR/GBP | 0.8723 | 0.8747 | 0.8771 | 0.8795 | 0.8819 | 0.8843 | 0.8867 | 0.8891 | 0.8915 | 0.0024 |
| EUR/CHF | 1.1501 | 1.1557 | 1.1613 | 1.1669 | 1.1725 | 1.1781 | 1.1837 | 1.1893 | 1.1949 | 0.0056 |
| MARKET | (L4) | (L3) | (L2) | (L1) | Neutral | L1 | L2 | L3 | L4 | Rotation |
| Profile | Trend | Trend | Normal | Non-Trend | NR | Non-Trend | Normal | Trend | Trend | Profile |

**FIGURE 11.3** Field from Neutral; Non-Trend, Normal, or Trend Distribution Likely to Occur

feelings that a smaller trader feels when placed under the same price pressure points relative to their respective trade value in reality becomes no different emotionally. A loss is a loss and a win is a win. A one-lot or 100-lot trader is used to their values, and the sting of loss and the pleasure of profit are relative.

After a market is firmly established and open interest builds and remains solid, you can in a sense cancel out watching volume all of the time. Buyers and sellers will assuredly show up every day and offer enough to take on your action. Not that we don't feel watching volume is important, but the fact is that 100 percent of the time you have access and a method to track the two things you truly need in an established market: price and time (charts). With a chart you can rightfully assume volume. Did you ever notice that volume for the most part in each contract hovers at or near certain levels as the final daily tally is known? Traders are human and are creatures of habit and the amounts they trade are fairly similar from day to day. As we came to this realization, we could easily then just begin to watch facial expressions of the big and small as the market hit key price points on the eight level to gain a sense of their mood.

## TEAMMATES AND OPPONENTS

At this point it is important for us to remind you that when you get long (buy), your teammates are the big dog buyers and your opponents are the big dog sellers. Don't get confused here because after we buy, we only need to do one thing, which is to off-set and flatten our position with a sell at some point. We naturally sell to a buyer (our teammate) when long. On the flip side when you sell your teammates are the Big dog sellers and your opponents are the buyers. This is why we want to play on the momentum side and prefer set-ups that occur on the proper side of the NR and the HR. We want to count on our teammates being in a good mood and willing to fight the fight. Those that want to fight it out are those who are most often making money and more stable in mind, body, and spirit.

As traders it is important for us to also remind you not to forget the fact that you are always in control of when you play, when you exit, and when you wait. We of course can't control the outcome of where the big dogs drive price after we enter but one thing is for certain: We can always try and start our day at the most premium location on the eight-level field we have created.

As the coach of your own team wouldn't it be nice if you had the chance to enter the market at an area where the people you were depending on to help you make money were in a good mood? If they are in a bad mood or confused, why not stay away? Simply speaking, if prices are driving up and

*Putting It All Together* **165**

above NR and HR, buyers are making money, making good decisions, and in a good mood. On the flip side when prices are driving down and below NR and HR, sellers are making money, making good decisions, and in a good mood. It's equally important to realize when the party is over as well, so don't join the momentum party too as prices reach your predicted range potential. Wait for a new cycle to rebuild.

Buyers tend to be in a great mood when price action is two levels above neutral, and sellers tend to be in a great mood when prices are two levels below neutral. Now we are not saying to blindly jump in and buy in hopes of the break-out when price action is two levels above neutral or sell when price action is two levels below neutral.

As we add our rules and see opportunities for entry at level two from neutral or better, we feel the chances of success grow. Even when these trades do not hold up, they tend not to run away destructively in the wrong direction through time. In order to drive the concept home, let's think of an NFL coach. What if we told you that you can be an NFL head coach and every time your team gets the ball and starts on offense, they can begin at your opponent's red zone (25 yards from a touchdown)? A 100-yard field and you only have to go 25 yards to score when your opponent has to go 75 yards. How about if you were in the NBA and you always got to start on offense at your free-throw line and your opponent had to start and run the ball down the entire length of the court before they could score? Now mistakes can happen as nothing is foolproof, but fresh legs and starting at your opponent's 25 would be a great thing! Just look at the stats of any sport where action remains for the most part on one side of the field. The team that controls the best starting spot tends to maintain possession and dictate the tempo because the opposing team is always on their heels feeling as if they are always fighting an uphill battle, while you feel like you are running downhill. That is the type of entry spot we are talking about when we begin to enter the Forex markets or any market for that matter. We scan through our list of favorites to see if there are any setups to enter with rules met at our opponent's 25-yard line. Location of the set-up becomes the tell.

## A THREE-STEP PROCESS: ENTRY, PROFIT, AND STOP LOSS

Whenever we enter the market (long or short), it is important to think of the three-step process: entry, profit objective, and stop loss. Over our 20-year career spanning through the pit trading school at the University of Trading and our current computer trading school at RDS Trader we have always reminded ourselves and our students: *"Know where you are getting out before you get in."* It will be the catchphrase that builds confidence to answer the questions that will arise before entry: how many contracts and how much risk is acceptable. Of course acceptable risk varies from individual to individual, but we will explain risk/reward in terms of levels.

We went into detail about our personal risk-management preferences earlier in the book by setting parameters of 1.25 percent of our account per idea and never breaching 5 percent loss. As a reminder on losing trades strike one is 1.25 percent, strike two is 2.5 percent, and strike three is 3.75 percent. Most often we stop trading after hitting this mark. At this point the writing is generally on the wall as things haven't been going well. Trying three different times and all resulting in loss is a signal to take a personal time out. We build a cushion to 5 percent to allow for any slippage on our third attempt to ensure we don't surpass the dead zone. We feel it is important to never go beyond your threshold and to establish cut-off points that will stop you before hitting the daily financial pain threshold.

## Profit Objective

As we look to enter the market long or short we first wait for a resistance window top before selling and a support bottom before buying. The first time prices move back into the WO, we enter. As we enter we consider of course our stop-loss target, but when looking to the profit side we identify an objective. When turning to ideal buy or sell setup we want to also pay attention to our profit objective. The initial objective would be the most recent stand-out top (for buys) or bottom (for sells) on a 15-minute chart. The next objective is to look for a move to the four-level range target.

When waiting for a two-level distance pullback before entry, it most often times produces a one-level to two-level profit target anyway. This is due in part to seeing, on average, four-level range predictions. *We balance the objective to meet the session extreme to the four-level range target to create the most realistic outcome.* Most often times this naturally occurs within our one- to two-hour time tolerance as well (see Figure 11.4).

*Sometimes you can begin to anticipate a bottom before you see higher highs by noticing what is called a long tail upon completion of the candle.* A tail is the distance from the low to the base, and if it is lengthy it most often tells you that a bottom is imminent. It's the same on the flip side if you see a long upper tail (or shadow) off of a high. This signals a potential top. The U.S. dollar/Swiss Franc (USDCHF) actual long play Mike took on August 26, 2011, (buy example) told him a bottom was likely at 0.8044 before he saw a higher high. He entered long as price fell back down to the bottom of the tail, and then added to the idea as he saw higher highs and took profit at 0.8090 after a two-level run up and price pause. Lower lows at 0.8090 confirmed the top and he exited all remaining longs at this point. See Figure 11.5.

*Putting It All Together* **167**

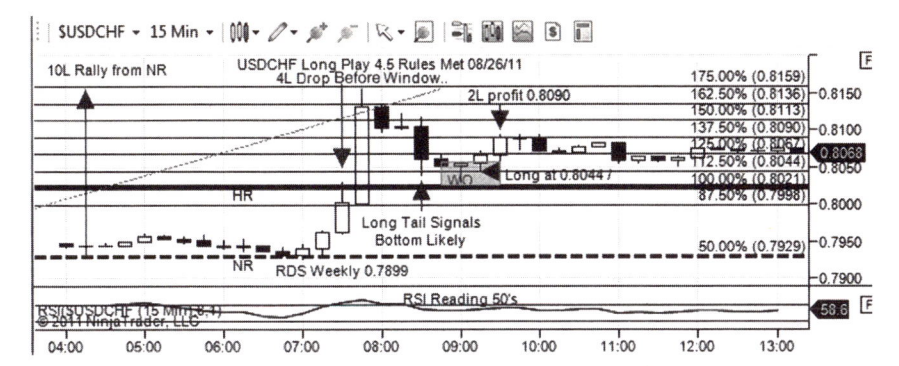

**FIGURE 11.4** Ideal Buy Setups Level Two or Better

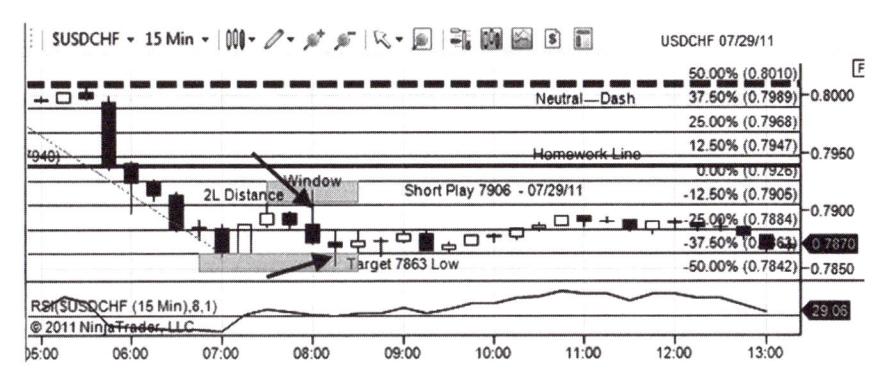

**FIGURE 11.5** Ideal Sell Setups Level Two or Better

While we strive to put ourselves in strong high percentage setups, all trading strategies experience failure at some point, so it is equally important to consider an acceptable loss that balances normal ebb and flow of price action (one level to two levels) along with a 1.25 percent dollar allotment that was originally given to the trade.

## Stop Loss

In theory we want to naturally risk less and make more. This is a goal that in the end you should always strive to achieve. What we feel a realistic model to initially adopt is to **maintain at minimum an equal risk/reward ratio.** The reason to first adopt a one-to-one risk/reward ratio is that so many traders come to us with ratios that consist of enormous losses matched with only minimal gains. Often traders truthfully reveal to us ratios like three pips of loss for every one pip gained and sometimes greater than four-to-one loss-to-win ratios. The reason is mainly due to the fact that it is a natural instinct in our culture to easily accept a win, but it's hard to swallow a loss. We are a society that preaches "Win, Win, Win," not one that teaches loss or how to lose. If this sounds like you, just realize that you are not alone. It is the number one issue traders face. Clients of course come to us in hopes of flipping that ratio back to the positive.

Mike changed his life around as a trader when he stopped focusing on the length of losses. It's not that he forgot about them entirely, but he began to focus and compare them to the length of his winners. When trading Treasury bonds Mike noticed that he was able to make up to four ticks (pips) on a trade. It wasn't that he couldn't make more or the potential wasn't there to make more, he just noticed that he naturally had enough after he hit four ticks. As soon as you start thinking about the money in the trade, your subconscious mind works against you, especially in the beginning. Four ticks in bonds are worth $125 per contract, which is only a small portion of a normal bond range that steadily achieved a 32-tick day-to-day range at that time (not a coincidence that it was 12.5 percent of the expected range). Not many people come from another vocation with the potential of making $125 per contact per 30 minutes to an hour. A tolerance of dollars made and dollars lost at these levels, which are quite small to the trading world needs to be built up.

Mike also noticed that he had some 6-, 8-, and 10-tick losses. He began to get on top of this behavior by looking at previous statements of trades and began to add up the excess loss beyond the four-tick normal gain. When he cut his 6-, 8-, and 10-tick losses into a reasonable and very doable four-tick loss, the bottom line result of what would have been in his account at the end of his first year almost floored him, and me for that matter.

Most look at trying to control their losses and never think about their gains. *Start focusing on what your body allows you to make and set this limit on your losses.* As you get better at hanging with winners and capping your losses, your account magically grows. As Mike capped the loss at four, he then freed up time in his day and naturally began to focus on trying to hang with winners longer. Getting out of losses and getting back on track working with winners actually made us more efficient and increased our profitability. It took some hard initial work to calm the inner chatter that tried to talk him into hanging with a loss longer, but cutting the cord paid off.

This method naturally began to align itself to profit/loss targets matching a realistic rhythm risking only one level (12.5 percent of range matched with 1.25 percent of your account) with a one-level to two-level profit objective (12.5 percent range matched with 1.25 percent account upside to 25 percent of range matched with 2.5 percent account upside). As we

*Putting It All Together* **169**

moved into the currency markets, normal price movement in terms of pips from day to day was greater shifting from Treasury Bonds to Currencies, but not in terms of daily percentage of total value. We noticed a similar 1.25 percent to 2.5 percent total value of the contract daily price flows. As we adjusted to the average range and normal price rhythm of currencies, keeping the range percentages and account percentages in alignment with a one-level risk to a one-level to two-level profit objective.

*Needless to say, cutting the losses to meet your winners and establishing a one-to-one risk-loss ratio is the first step in creating a cure for the financial disease you have built.* As you get your losses under control, you then free up more time to think about what story price is revealing along the journey from top to bottom each day. It also begins to reveal the mood of teammates in the market and the mood of opponents. See Figure 11.6.

During these initial long plays (NR, HR-RDS weekly, WO) things were going very well. While pushing for a breakout through the session highs and possible to the four-level range target, things reversed and stopped the trade out after a one-level loss. As price came back up to the original support area, it now acted as resistance. As lower lows appeared, the ideas transitioned to short-play ideas as action was setting up on the day session HR, and the NR was higher after the WO developed. The target was initially the session low, which hit a few hours later. While Mike got caught up hanging with the long side too long on this trade as he was thinking action would travel to the four-level target, he didn't lose focus on the stop on remaining longs. He could have taken the profit and exited everything, but only took some and was riding. The point of maintaining discipline on the stop is that he remained clear thinking enough to realize that action was now set up for a short side play. Original support now acted as resistance to allow him a three-rule short. He covered it for a profit and

**FIGURE 11.6** Stop Loss Keeps You Seeing the Action

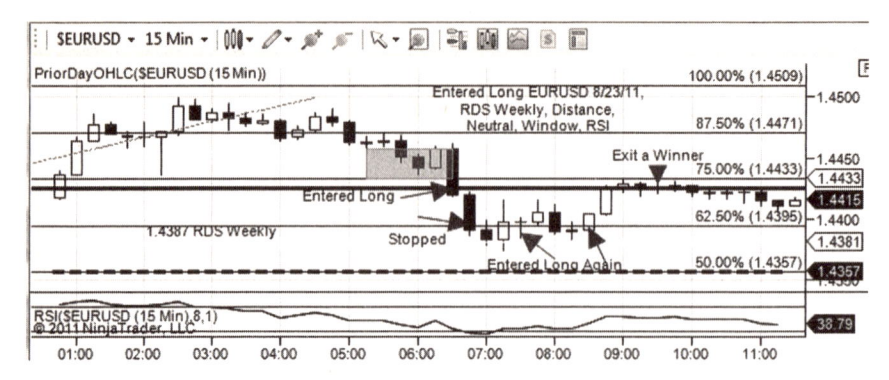

**FIGURE 11.7** Perseverance

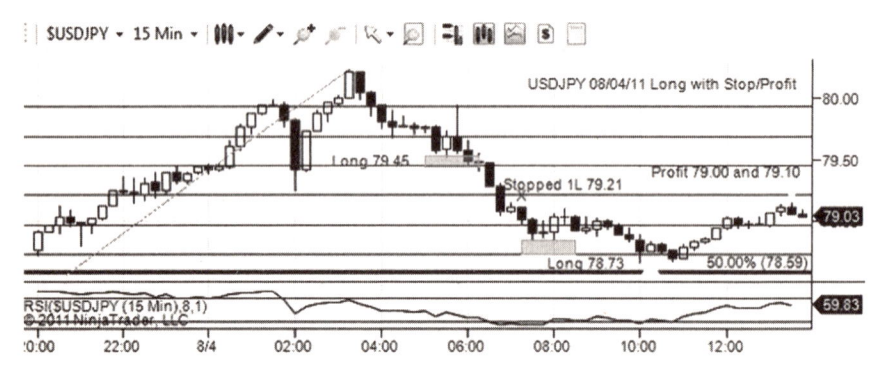

**FIGURE 11.8** Perseverance

finished with a nice overall profit on the session. Don't get uptight after a loss as the market rotates enough to give you the opportunities that you never think you will get after absorbing one. Keep your head about you! See Figure 11.7.

Perseverance is part of the game, as you can see from the action of the last example that Mike faced on August 23, 2011, playing the Euro/U.S. Dollar (EURUSD). See Figure 11.8.

Here you see again how you can overcome loss if you can keep your wits about you as Mike played the U.S. dollar/Japanese Yen (USDJPY) on August 4, 2011. If it was easy, everybody would be doing it.

## LEVELS REVEAL THE ANGRY TELL

Along with our sport analogies, parts of trading are much like poker as well. All professionals look for what poker terms a tell (signs that reveal your opponents hand). Since you can't see the traders' faces in our game today,

*Putting It All Together*  **171**

you can look at other financial risk reward games to help. Whether at the poker table or on the football field, players look into their opponents' eyes and scan for body tensions to give clues of where the play might be heading before it happens. A flinch or stutter at the poker table or a white-knuckled lean on a lineman's hand can be truly telling. Trading in the open-auction markets revealed this to us all of the time. Mike would always tell me that he didn't watch traders that he knew were making money because everybody knows how to win, but you learn so much about somebody when they lose. It's a character lesson.

Over the years we have seen many characters and traders fall to their knees when trading the markets. Mike didn't get enjoyment watching others lose, because he knew that by stepping into this game, he would at times himself lose. He just wanted to know and get a feel for when other traders started to get to their breaking point, and reveal the most useful information: the angry tell. When you are in an environment with a thousand people that you can observe and watch every day, you get to know some of their behaviors pretty well. When money is on the line it's hard for anybody to disguise their tells. You had to get good at it because everybody was watching for signs of weakness. You want their money and they want yours, and any signs of weakness or revealing behavior gave your opponent an edge.

Everybody needs to get angry at some point to truly learn. We are not saying to go out and try to start trouble for yourself, but burning a little fire under your butt is sometimes the right medicine. Mike tells me a story about his behavior during his second week of trading on his own as a local. Mike added to a position that he already deemed losing and outside of his window. Nonetheless Mike let it run and even added to it again, and it cost him! He remembers being so mad at himself that day that he walked out of the pit to get some fresh air and cool off. Another local, ESR, leaned outside of the pit clearly noticing what happened and watched Mike mumbling to himself under his breath and said, "Do you want me to tell JTN that you want your old job back?", laughing hysterically. Nobody feels good when they are getting laughed at, but coming from ESR it was actually in my eyes a little sign of respect for the craft of trading in general. ESR was seasoned and he knew exactly what Mike was going through. ESR was a very candid character and he was beloved by all in the pit, but this day and what he said to Mike scorched such a memory in Mike's brain that it actually provided him the fuel he needed to show ESR and the rest that RDS was here to stay!

You couldn't always tell when overlooking the crowd when somebody was winning, but it was clearly obvious when they were losing. Some of those traits would be; eyes bloodshot, red-face, sweating profusely, picking fights, swearing, and downright nasty behavior. Nobody was 100 percent immune, as the market always finds a way to expose every weakness. Since we have been in the game for some time now, we have seen the six-figure earners as well as the seven- and eight-figure earners all hit their edges at one point or another.

As you get to know some of the traders, you soon pick up on some of their trading habits and personalities. Some simply love to sell and get short. You couldn't talk them into a bullish thought if your life depended on it. On the other hand you also get a sense of those that mainly love to buy or get long. Good luck trying to convince them to join the bear side!

Mike simply began to focus on the behavior of the long lovers when price action was falling and the short lovers when price was rallying. On one particular day when price action was at neutral and moving down to level one, Mike noticed that the body language of a die-hard bull wasn't revealing a thing. All while losing money the trader was still talking about the ball game he went to last night. *However, when prices dropped to level two that day, something began to shift in the die-hard bull's behavior. This trader stopped talking about the ball game and began asking market related questions; the Tell was revealed.* It's much like when we took this concept to the charts, as it is similar to a price flipping in trend from up to down or from down to up. This trader's behavior told Mike much about money tolerance and what traders call *heat*. Sweat on the brow was building on this guy. The size of the trade wasn't the factor, as most mainly stick to their comfort amounts; 1 to 10 lot traders, 25 to 50 lot traders, and 100 lots and up. If they ever exceeded the amounts, most would square their positions to a favorable setting. The pit was designed as a hierarchy as well, so it was easy to monitor and witness if this tell translated across large and small traders. Smaller traders were down in the middle and bigger traders were up top. As Mike observed big and small traders alike who favored a specific direction, their behaviors when losing were all similar and apparent as price moved near level two from neutral. Some even began elbowing Mike when price moved to level two and beyond from neutral and asking him, "What's going on?"

Emotions flared as prices ran to level three or level four against the diehards as the heat got nasty and unbearable for them; understandably so as you get a feel for how much money was evaporating from their accounts. This was where the angry tell reared its head. Mike came home and told me they called a guy "The Heat" because his face got bright red and he resembled the Heat Miser on *The Year without a Santa Claus*. "The Heat's" hair stood up with full red-face equipped with a 1000-yard stare that could burn a hole right through you. It wasn't too hard to know what was going on and what not to do, which simply was don't to follow "the Heat" today. "Just look at him," we would say.

Since you don't have traders to watch on the computer to build this sense, you need to discover where this is on the charts. Our eight-level maps begin to reveal this ahead of time. The location of price revealed the

# amazon.co.uk

Thank you for shopping at Amazon.co.uk!

**Invoice for**
Your order of 2 April, 2012
Order ID 202-2046755-4007526
Invoice number D1ms5przR
Invoice date 16 April, 2012

**Billing Address**
David Brimlow
The Grove, Montexx
Langton Green
Tunbridge Wells, Kent TN3 0AD
United Kingdom

David Brimlow
Langton Green
Tunbridge Wells, Kent TN3 0AD
United Kingdom

| Qty. | Item | Our Price (excl VAT) | VAT Rate | Total Price |
|---|---|---|---|---|
| 1 | **The RDS Forex System: A Breakthrough Method to Profiting from Market Turning Points (Wiley Trading)** Hardcover, 1118095681 (**-P-1-B257C613-**) | £32.50 | 0% | £32.50 |

Shipping charges £0.00

Subtotal (excl VAT) 0%  £32.50
Total VAT  £0.00
Total  £32.50

Conversion rate - £1.00 : EUR 1.21

### This shipment completes your order.

So you can always check the status of your orders or change your account details from the Your Account link at the top of each page on our site.

### Thinking of returning an item? PLEASE USE OUR ON-LINE RETURNS SUPPORT CENTRE.

Our Returns Support Centre (www.amazon.co.uk/returns-support) will guide you through our Returns Policy and provide you with a printable personalised return label. Please have your order number ready. (You can find it next to your order summary above). Our Returns Policy does not affect your statutory rights.

Amazon EU S.à r.l, 5 Rue Plaetis, L-2338, Luxembourg
VAT number : GB727255821

**Please note - this is not a returns address - for returns - please see above for details of our online returns centre**

956/DXmm5prZR/-1 of 1-//1M/econ-uk/7235919/0418-17:45/0416-16:15 Pack Type : C2

*Putting It All Together* **173**

strength of the tell, and it coincided with range bound, normal, or trend days. Remember that we have been saying all along that price doesn't lie. Nobody was immune from showing their weakness when losing in an open environment. *Mike just began to realize that level two on the charts from neutral was when the spirit of the losers was starting to buckle.* This gave further confirmation about the importance of the 25 percent move or two price levels of our eight-level field.

Angry players most often make bad decisions and most times it's hard for them to get out of that funk or rhythm. As a trader who has complete control as to when to enter, wouldn't it be nice if you could always play an angry opponent or know when they were starting to get agitated. Well, you can by knowing where price is located on the field at the time of entry: neutral, level one, level two, level three, level four, or better. *We just religiously mapped our field for what we would normally see each day; four up from Neutral and four down from neutral and became more confident in a setup when rules were met at level two or better.*

There are many different combinations that the current session range can hit our map and meet a majority of our rules. It is mainly important to recognize where the setup actually occurs on the established eight-level field to guide your confidence to enter. A five-rule setup may not feel that good when the setup lands on neutral because the strength and mood of both sides is at the coin flip area. We normally see a four-level range during a 24-hour session, but we must note that these are predictions and are not to be taken as written in stone. Quite often we get a larger-than-expected range due to a world or economic event. During these days and those that follow, the ranges are simply adjusted for as they occur. Since we adjust to the recent stand-out high or low on a daily chart and compare that with a five-day average range, the levels will adjust to the increased volatility. This ensures that we have established appropriate and relevant spacing of our levels to help our daily range projections. See Figure 11.9.

| Buy Mood | Nasty | Angry | Edgy | Manageable | NR | Normal | Interested | Crush | Exalt | Buy Mood |
|---|---|---|---|---|---|---|---|---|---|---|
| MARKET | (L4) | (L3) | (L2) | (L1) | Neutral | L1 | L2 | L3 | L4 | Rotation |
| EUR/USD | 1.3845 | 1.3891 | 1.3937 | 1.3983 | **1.4029** | 1.4075 | 1.4121 | 1.4167 | 1.4213 | 0.0046 |
| USD/JPY | 79.61 | 79.77 | 79.93 | 80.09 | **80.25** | 80.41 | 80.57 | 80.73 | 80.89 | 0.16 |
| USD/CHF | 0.8249 | 0.8276 | 0.8303 | 0.8330 | **0.8357** | 0.8384 | 0.8411 | 0.8438 | 0.8465 | 0.0027 |
| GBP/USD | 1.5773 | 1.5806 | 1.5839 | 1.5872 | **1.5905** | 1.5938 | 1.5971 | 1.6004 | 1.6037 | 0.0033 |
| NZD/USD | 0.8201 | 0.8223 | 0.8245 | 0.8267 | **0.8289** | 0.8311 | 0.8333 | 0.8355 | 0.8377 | 0.0022 |
| EUR/JPY | 110.86 | 111.29 | 111.72 | 112.15 | **112.58** | 113.01 | 113.44 | 113.87 | 114.30 | 0.43 |
| AUD/USD | 1.0563 | 1.0586 | 1.0609 | 1.0632 | **1.0655** | 1.0678 | 1.0701 | 1.0724 | 1.0747 | 0.0023 |
| USD/CAD | 0.9602 | 0.9623 | 0.9644 | 0.9665 | **0.9686** | 0.9707 | 0.9728 | 0.9749 | 0.9770 | 0.0021 |
| EUR/GBP | 0.8723 | 0.8747 | 0.8771 | 0.8795 | **0.8819** | 0.8843 | 0.8867 | 0.8891 | 0.8915 | 0.0024 |
| EUR/CHF | 1.1501 | 1.1557 | 1.1613 | 1.1669 | **1.1725** | 1.1781 | 1.1837 | 1.1893 | 1.1949 | 0.0056 |
| MARKET | (L4) | (L3) | (L2) | (L1) | Neutral | L1 | L2 | L3 | L4 | Rotation |
| Sell Mood | Exalt | Crush | Interested | Normal | NR | Manageable | Edgy | Angry | Nasty | Sell Mood |

**FIGURE 11.9** Moods

**174**                                              THE RDS FOREX SYSTEM

Since we always have three choices, buy, sell, or do nothing, we feel it is best to have an idea of the range of feelings that your teammates or opponent may be experiencing upon entry. The first letter of each mood from neutral to level four reveals an acronym to help you remember who you are playing with and against at all times and what mood they may be experiencing.

## BUY/SELL LOCATION AND TEAMMATE MOOD

Since the mood concept is the same whether we enter with a buy or a sell, we have wrapped the long/short set-up locations together. The numerator if you will reflects the buy-side and the denominator reflects the sell-side mood in our explanations. See Figures 11.10, 11.11, 11.12, and 11.13 for illustrations.

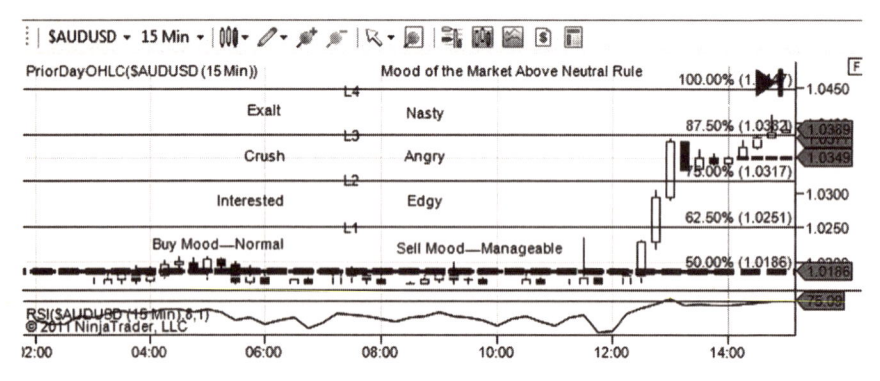

**FIGURE 11.10**   Field Pinpointing Buyer's Mood

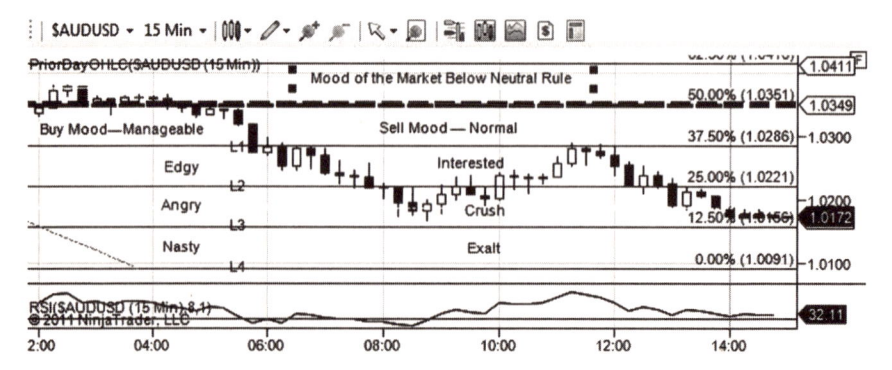

**FIGURE 11.11**   Field Pinpointing Seller's Mood

Putting It All Together    **175**

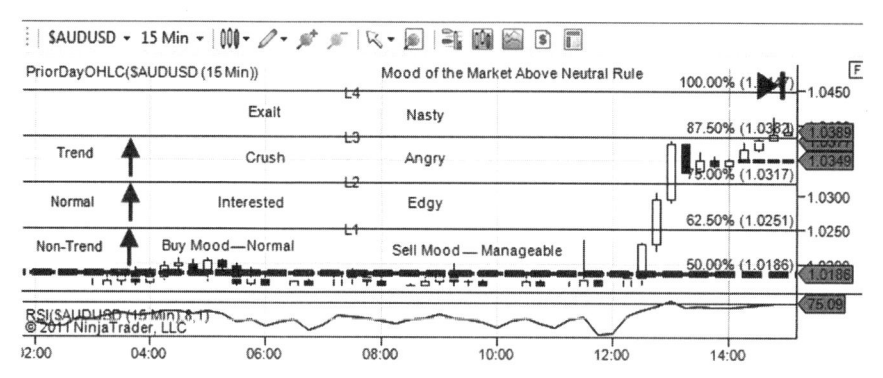

**FIGURE 11.12**   Combining Mood with Profile Above Neutral

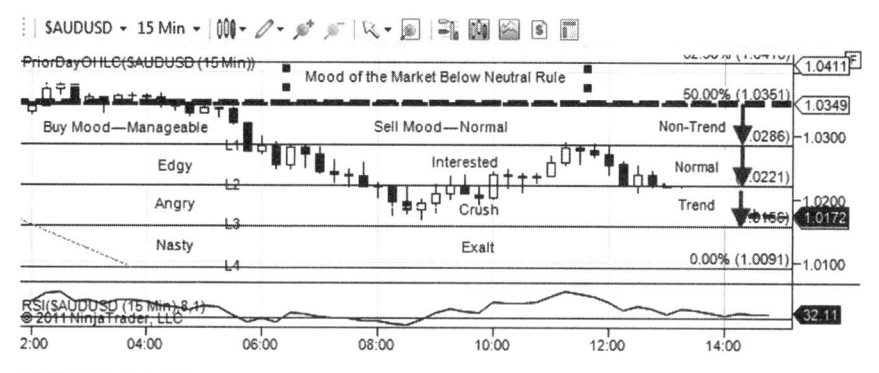

**FIGURE 11.13**   Combining Mood with Profile Below Neutral

## Neutral Side Setup

When a bottom/top *window* is established after a *two-level distance price drop/rise, RSI near 25/75,* and the entry price lands on *neutral,* the willpower of the teammates you are counting on to make you money is not as strong to defend that low. *Getting involved with a buy/sell entry here is not the wisest choice, and tends to wind up being a 50-50 proposition at best, even with the rules met.* We are not in the game for coin-toss results. Since the market is bigger and has more money than we do, we do not want to take sides against an equally matched opponent, as both sides have not made or lost much and maintain the ability to drive prices in either direction. Typically when you see a setup on neutral anyway it tends to be on the wrong side of the 24-hour session *homework* marker and as price nears neutral the team driving it there has momentum on its side. It is better to sit on the sidelines or look to see if another pair is setup better. Sometimes dong nothing is making you money as well.

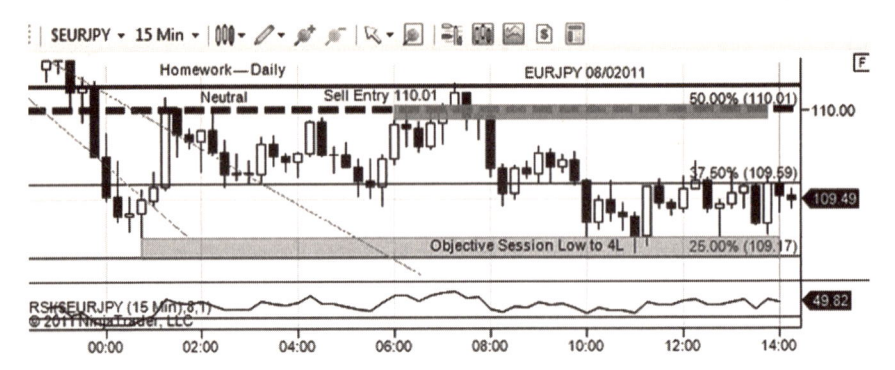

**FIGURE 11.14** Neutral Sell-Side Setup EURJPY 08/02/11

On the other hand, if you decide to get involved with a neutral setup, we feel the chances of success are greater when our directional sense indicators favor the idea (neutral and homework rule—daily and RDS weekly). The mood for the winning side from neutral to level one is normal and the mood for the losing side is manageable (see Figure 11.14).

The chart depicts the sell entry that took place for the EURJPY at 110.01 on August 2, 2011. The shaded gray area is built from the earlier resistance top to the next level higher (neutral in this case) to give us an entry signal. After resistance is formed and as we consider this entry spot, we know the price is near a two-level move higher from the session low, landing on neutral but the session homework rule is higher giving us the confidence to participate short. RSI wasn't reading exactly what we like but we did have a solid majority of our rules met. As a discretionary trader you will have to make decisions when things are close enough to the speculative rules (distance and RSI) before participating. In this case we did and our objective (lower shaded gray area) is built from the session low to the next level lower or four-level range target. When all rules are not exactly met, you always have the choice to scale back the entry size to ease some of the anxiety should you decide to participate.

### Level One Setup from Neutral

When rules are met and the entry price lands on level one above/below *neutral*, the mood is optimistic to defend that bottom/top that was established. Our confidence getting involved with an entry here is feeling a bit better, but be careful as you may see the entry spot landing on the wrong side of the 24-hour session *homework* rule. If the *homework* rule lands in favor of the entry, we feel the trade is worth executing as your teammates continue to have control of the action. There is not a substantial winner at

*Putting It All Together*  **177**

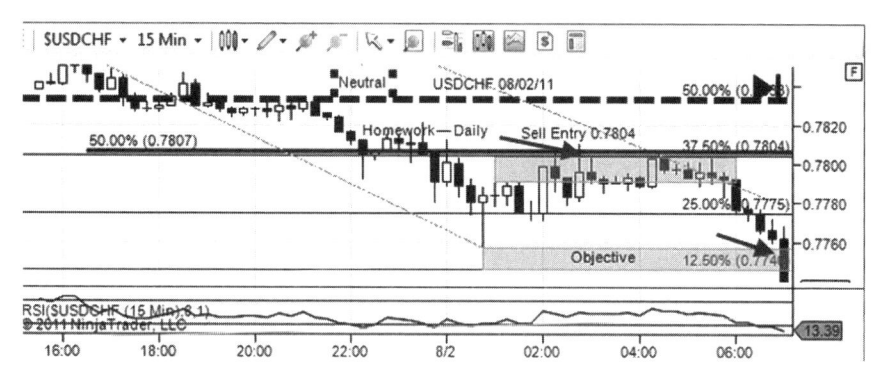

**FIGURE 11.15**  Level One Sell-Side Setup USDCHF August 2, 2011

this point, so we tend to scan through other pairs to see if there is a better fit that day. The mood of your teammates is positive, but straddling normal to interested and the mood of your opponents is beginning to shift from manageable to edgy (see Figure 11.15).

The chart depicts the sell entry that took place for the U.S. dollar/Swiss Franc (USDCHF) at 0.7804 on August 2, 2011. The shaded gray area is built from the earlier resistance top to the next level higher (level one below neutral in this case) to give us an entry signal. After resistance was formed we noticed that the pullback from the low was near two-level (25 percent of eight-level field) landing on level one. The session homework rule is higher, giving us the confidence to participate short. Our objective (lower shaded gray area) is built from the session low to the next level lower or four-level range objective.

## Level Two Setup from Neutral

As prices top/bottom after a firm four-level price run and pullback at least two-levels to form a bottom/top window with RSI near 25/75 and price lands on level two from neutral, we feel the mood of our teammates remains strong and their lead on that day is well established, making it hard for your opponents to overcome. Our confidence getting involved with an entry here is solid, as the setup most often occurs on the proper side of the 24-hour session homework rule. The mood of your teammates is clearly interested, with thoughts of crushing, as your opponent's mood is edgy with hints of anger.

This setup doesn't happen every day, but it does happen often enough. If you have the patience to wait for it, the play pays dividends more times than not. As we get deeper into the chapter we will discuss time in more depth and when it is time to weather profits and losses. See Figure 11.16.

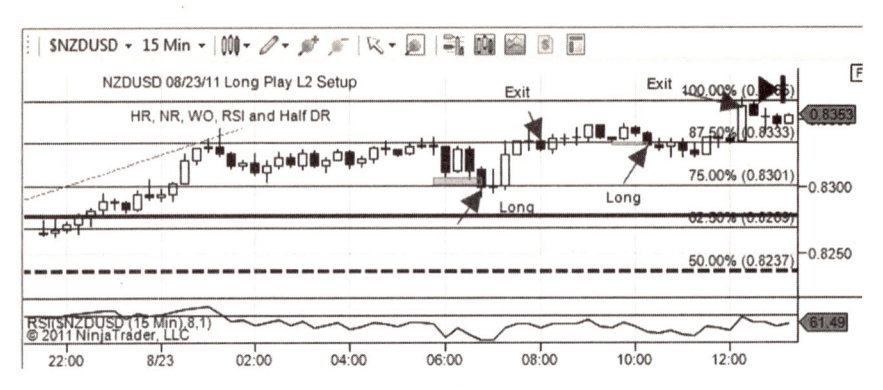

**FIGURE 11.16** Level Two Setup

## Level Three, Four, or Greater Setup from Neutral

As prices travel outside level four on extreme days you might see setups after 25 percent retracements that give you entry signals that land on level three, level four or greater from neutral. The mood of your teammates from level three to level four is moving from crush to exalt and the mood of your opponents is moving from angry to nasty. The same concept remains, so if you have the energy, time, and focus, keep playing. *Just keep in mind that prices have the ability to run extreme distances on these days and the overall mood across the spectrum is in the giddy zone for the winners and in the numb and state of shock zone for the losers. Never let your guard down and think you invincible!* See Figures 11.17 and 11.18.

We know many traders who have ripped their mouse cords out of their computers and at times have broken their monitors or keyboards when on the wrong side of extreme days. If you decide to enter on the momentum side when playing the angry opponent, the objectives when short continue

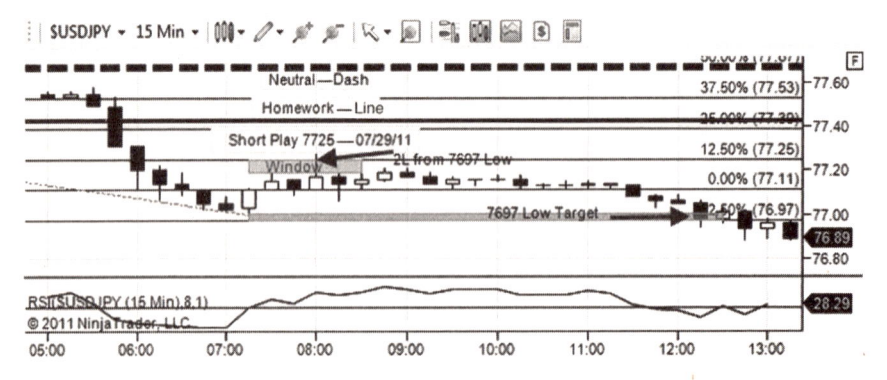

**FIGURE 11.17** Level Three Setup

*Putting It All Together* **179**

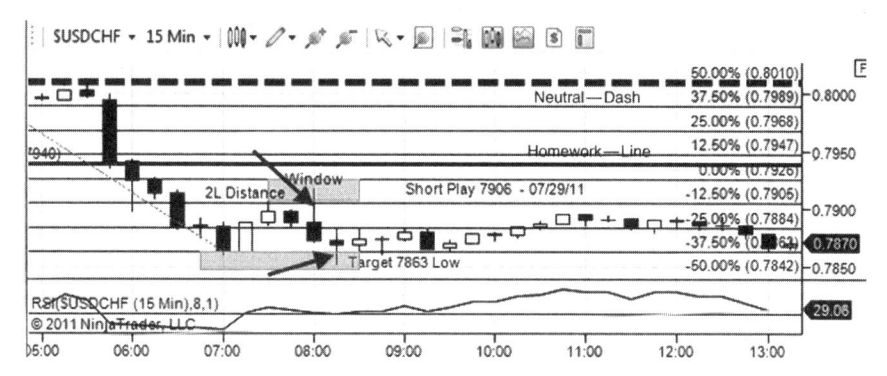

**FIGURE 11.18** More than Level Four Setup

to be the session low to the next extended level lower or when long the target is the session high to the next extended level higher. *Since we typically only set up an eight-level field, you can simply add more levels of equal spacing to give you extended levels of interest as needed.* On your trading software if you have additional fields you can adjust your retracement or Fibonacci tool to reflect the extended values of 112.5 percent, 125 percent, 137.5 percent, or 150 percent for four upside additions and you can use −12.5 percent, −25 percent, −37.5 percent, or −50 percent for 4 downside additions.

The positive moods of you teammates on the momentum side of the action reflect from neutral: normal (level one—12.5 percent), interest (level two—25 percent), crush (level three—37.5 percent), and exalt (level four—50 percent). These make up the word or acronym NICE to serve as a reminder of your teammate's mood. The negative moods of those playing on the wrong side of the action reflect from neutral; manageable (level one—12.5 percent), edgy (–level two—25 percent), angry (level three—37.5 percent), and nasty (level four—50 percent). These make up the word or acronym MEAN to help remind you of your teammates on this side of the spectrum.

We have found that if you are aware of the mood of your teammates and your opponents that you will have a better feel for how much to place at risk on your trade. We have mentioned earlier the need to match personal risk to absorb the mini-shocks that price flow normally produces while in a trade. A normal price tolerance is what we have been calling one level (12.5 percent) of the expected four level (50 percent of total eight-level field) daily range expectation. *Setting a 1.25 percent risk tolerance to match 1L price movement for a stop loss along with a one- to two-level profit objective will begin to help you understand how many contracts you can place on the trade.*

All that is left after you establish how many you can allocate to the idea is to pinpoint where the entry is located on the field to help you determine how many of those contract you want to spread around the play.

## More than One: Scaling-In/Scaling-Out

Trading one contract at time is good for beginners to get a feel, but it is important to build your tolerance to trade two or more as soon as your confidence is ready. One contract is limiting, because many times entries and exits will not be selling the high of a move or buying the low of a move. Perfection on every trade is impossible. This leaves you with the fact that more times than not there will be slippage and imperfections upon entry and exit. Trading one creates the same mentality as all in or all out. Once you are entered, you have to live with the price and once you have exited you of course have to live with that price. This at times can be a good thing, but it also will at times find you leaving money on the table. *If you want to grow as a trader, you will eventually have to get off the one lot so building your tolerance on two or more as soon as possible will be the best approach overall. Trading more than one creates options as you can exit some or half of the position and let the others run.* Price typically doesn't always move to your target smoothly. It ebbs and flows along the way. Now if you are watching the action at your computer terminal, which most of us are, a scale-in or scale-out approach is recommended. If you are using a computer program or black-box approach you will tend to not be watching as much and adjusting is not an option as things are pre-set. We feel that you can capture more of the ebb and flow with a scale-in/scale-out style. Both styles are highly effective, but we feel that if you are going to watch, the tendency is to take a peek and adjust. Let's focus on not trying to dismiss the tendency to adjust as you watch, but rather help you develop some strengths of how to ease in and ease out of each trade.

When you enter the market, you instantly begin to learn about the range of price action as it begins to set high and low extremes. You soon can pinpoint areas where you can adjust and add back and take off along the ride to capture more of the move (sometimes multiple times) until price action has achieved the initial objective. As new windows become apparent, it also gives you opportunity to back off the idea, if it doesn't seem to be acting right over time. This can save you money with an early exit as the trade hits your time threshold.

Special Note: Adding to existing positions (as long as rules are still met) might be initially thought of as averaging or adding to a losing trade as you enter sells at higher levels or enter buys at lower levels. We however map entries according to what our risk allotment allows (1.25 percent) along the area that we identify to participate, full well knowing that we are

## Putting It All Together

not going to be perfect along the window. Not to get all military sounding, but armies do not place all of their troops on the front line. They send out scouts or what we call in our business *probe trades* to get a feel for the climate. A probe trades to us is two contracts to start. If the rules are still met and on the momentum side of the action and inside our risk tolerance and window, it is not adding to a loser as it is accounted for.

To gain further understanding you can look to how Mike prepares himself. He first knows his all-in number, which is 10 contracts and for the most part he understands whether right or wrong over the next couple of hours that he will experience approximately two-level (25 percent or range) risk with two-level (25 percent of range) potential reward. He adjusts the current two-level setting and understands how much a two-level risk/reward is if he had all 10 contracts running. This needs to correlate to 1.25 percent of his account. Mike doesn't let the trade run two levels against him as he begins to exit after one level against him. The added one level extra layer helps keep him calm throughout, so he can focus on price action and tops and bottoms that have been forming along the way. Now you can of course prepare for what your all-in setting may look like, as everybody's tolerance is different. If this is something new to you, take a look at how Mike prepares and adjust the concept to fit his style. He then spaces his entries up to 10 along the path of the window as price action is revealed.

He begins to cover (exit) a trade that he believes has gone bad after one-level stop loss, as he feels he has seen enough price action to have an idea. The extra cushion of preparing for an additional level of loss alleviates the thoughts about money. If you can handle two levels of loss going in and pulling the cord after one level, you will find that it doesn't sting as much when you look at the numbers later. He just plays a little game in his head to squash the money thoughts to keep his mind focused on what's important: price potential. So when prices are already beginning to travel near one level against the idea he will begin to exit the trade. On positive trades you most often get another chance to re-enter, take some off for profit, and then add back in when action looks good to reach his objective. Starting with two and adding up to 10 possible while discovering price tops/bottoms normally puts Mike in with a core of five most times. He may add up to 10 as the idea looks good, and peel some off to take profit in and let the other five ride. As he builds along the way up to five and things don't look so good in the first 15 to 30 minutes, he won't add up to 10 as he knows he is fighting the action as prices grind against the idea and signal he is on the wrong side. *Good trades tend to show positive immediate signs and bad trades tend to show negative immediate signs as well. Pay attention!* See Figure 11.19.

When a trade goes in your direction immediately it tends to be a good play but it most often doesn't move right to you objective. It comes back to

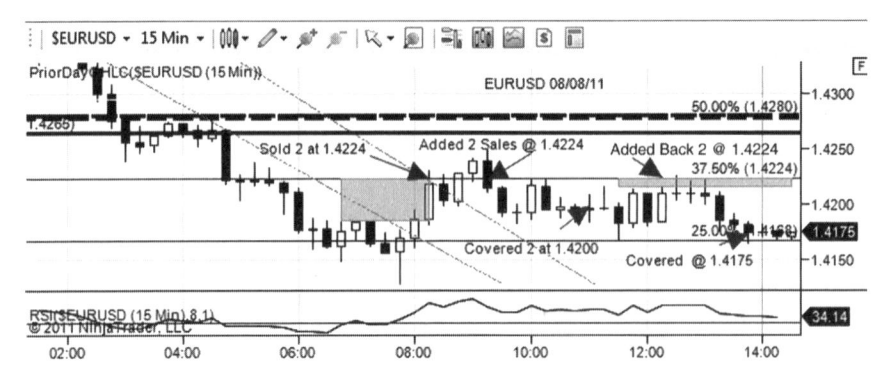

**FIGURE 11.19** Scale-In/Scale-Out USDCHF August 8, 2011

the entry spot and pauses and then goes to the target. This can shake you out of a move and leave you on the sidelines for the real ride. The scale-in/scale-out approach can help capture more money as the move develops, as the example shows.

## ONE GRENADE WILL GET YOU ALL

Mike's college football coach used to work with the special teams before practice actually started. Formal practice focused on offense and defense. The point Mike makes to students about special teams practice was that when we lined up for kick-off coverage, there were 11 players spread out along the width of the field. We all had a 1/11th responsibility when initially running down the field. As we gained a position on the returner with the ball we converged, but maintained our 1/11th responsibility accordingly. Coach Dau's Marine background really shined here when he often times yelled at a few defenders as they ran down the field to "Stay in your lane; one grenade will get you all!" He knew that if one defender broke his responsibility too early it would leave the entire team vulnerable for a long return or a touchdown for the return team.

Mike tells this story to clients that tend to be all-in-at-one-price traders. The fact simply is that our initial first entry is rarely the perfect spot (selling a top or buying a bottom). With this reality in mind we feel it is more appropriate to start scaling in to get a feel while at the same time gaining knowledge of the play so you could either conserve or potentially add bullets to better the trade positioning in accordance to the rules. The reward in the end may not always be as lucrative as the one time when you nail the entry on an all-in play, but it's rare that you hit one. We would rather prepare and practice to not put ourselves in a situation where one grenade will not get us all!

*Putting It All Together* **183**

## WHAT SIDE SHOULD I TRUST? BREAKOUTS VERSUS COUNTER

Once we have our thoughts about risk/reward, mood, and game plan set we simply favor a side based on our HR and NR. As far as current price trend is concerned, simply stated we would rather be long in an uptrend and short in downtrend. Questions tend to arise when an uptrend appears after only a slight pullback (one level) near a session high. Also on the flipside which way would you lean; short on a one-level pullback and flip to downtrend near a session low or take on a counter long play at session low support? When considering the momentum side play in these situations (long or short) the fact is that you will only have three rules: NR, HR, and WO. See Figures 11.20 and 11.21.

If you choose the counter side (long near a session low or short near a session high), you tend to have three rules as well (DR, WO, and RSI).

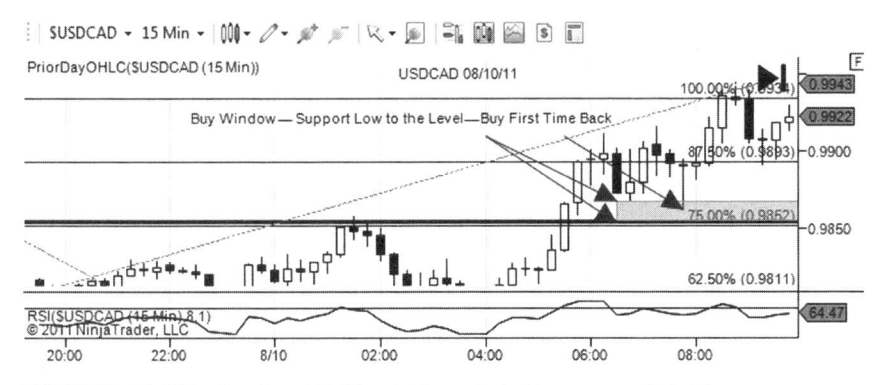

**FIGURE 11.20** One-Level Pullback Three-Rule Momentum Side Play

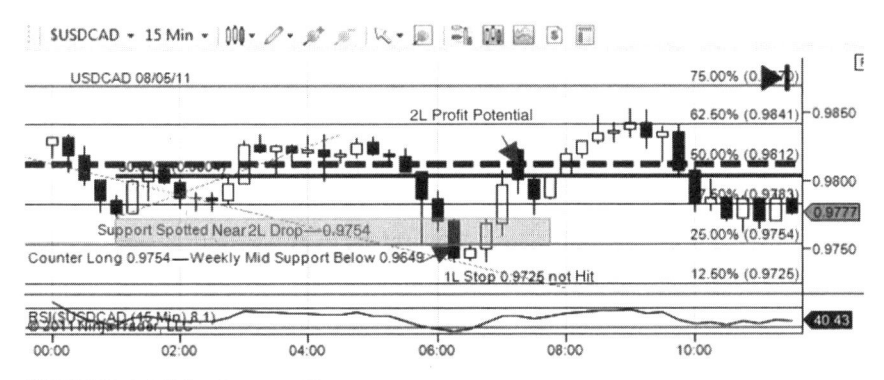

**FIGURE 11.21** Counter Play

Show caution on counter plays as a breakout in the momentum direction should always be in the back of our mind. You are counting on teammates to help you that have been losing money, so always be cognizant of your risk and time tolerance while participating on the counter trend side of the fence. Which side should you trust? If you are already in a trade, the play would be to definitely lighten up on the trade (take a portion or half off) or get out completely when you are not that confident.

When you considering an entry in either direction (counter or momentum), doing nothing is a viable choice. You have to be okay with the fact that you are doing nothing. All of our lives it is drummed into our heads that if we are not working we are lazy and in this case if we are not trading we are not making money. It's a tough pill to swallow. Remember that we are like firemen and policemen on call; we don't have to go out and start unnecessary fires or trouble. Wait for what you want!

If you pinned us down and said that doing nothing is not a choice; you have to make a decision (buy or sell), we would default to the momentum side play. The difference is that on a one-level pullback entry play (half of distance rule met), we would of course not play that zone with an all-in mindset. Scale in/scale out is the choice to gain a feel and perspective. We prefer to wait for a two-level pullback before even considering entry.

The reason for defaulting to the momentum side is that it is more likely for a break-out beyond session extremes when teaming with the winning side. The winning side has more energy physically, mentally, and emotionally to push for more. As you read further in this chapter, refer to the Weathering the Storm section to help entry and exit decisions. It clears up all of the confusion whenever or wherever you decide to play.

## TRADING THROUGH A BREAK OR WHILE YOU SLEEP

Everybody needs time to rest, relax, and recover. If you have a need to trade while you sleep, make sure that it doesn't ruin your focus and energy for the next session. Mike reminds himself of this all of the time. He found that when he has positions on overnight he tends to have restless nights of sleep, which sometimes diminish his ability the next day. The trick that he uncovered about himself was that if he were to go to sleep with pending orders working in his book or a position running, he needs to confirm the rules and judge the confidence in his entry spot. *In other words it needs to be what you want, no exceptions.* None of this middle of the road stuff like our friend Arthur took part in many times. Set up your risk parameters and realize that prices can move approximately four levels without any reports coming out overnight and more than eight if there are.

*Putting It All Together* **185**

## FIVE-SPEED TRANSMISSIONS

Just as in life, trading has a five-speed transmission. In life we need to keep feeding our energy so there is a need to sleep, sit down, stand up, walk, and run. Trading is no different! We all need to have fact (Rule 1, 2, 3) which falls in the realm of life's necessities ranging from sleep to walk and we need to build our energy and test our edge (Rule 4, 5) falling between the walk and run spectrum of life in order to grow into who we can and want to be. We will focus and expand on the concept of your energy in Chapter 12, Performance Evaluation.

## PRE-SESSION PREPARATION

At this time we think it is good to have a review of what we do before we sit down to trade. It is vital to go through a checklist to take care of all you can to ensure you are making a well-informed decision. The first thing is to always check the financial calendar, especially one that coincides with the time you are going to trade. As we outlined in the fundamental section it is important to play a market that is moving. Price movement creates opportunity, so focusing on the market(s) that tends to be moving when you trade is important.

Four PM PT/6 PM CT/7 PM ET is typically a time when you will start to see more activity on currencies related to the Japanese Yen (JPY), Australian dollar (AUD), and New Zealand dollar (NZD). It is their day session and over the next two to three hours is when all of the main reports of each respective country will be released. The Asian session afternoon overlaps into the London and European morning session, so those currencies interrelating with the Euro (EUR), British Pound (GBP), and Swiss Franc (CHF) tend to move best. Eleven PM PT/1 AM CT/2 AM ET is the time when currencies relating to EUR, GBP, and CHF come to life, and through this time the main reports of each respective country tend to be released.

The time that we trade the majority of the time is the U.S. session hours. Since the London and European afternoon session overlaps with the U.S. morning session those currencies relating to the USD such as EUR, GBP, and CHF tend to be most active. The United States is comparable in time zones with our neighbors to the north so the U.S. dollar/Canadian dollar (USDCAD) pair lands on our radar as well.

Since traders of all time zones tend to want to see what happens in the first two to three hours in the United States, so don't dismiss the chance for action on the USDJPY, AUDUSD, and NZDUSD. It's the day session for the United States, and the greenback is part of these pairs despite the

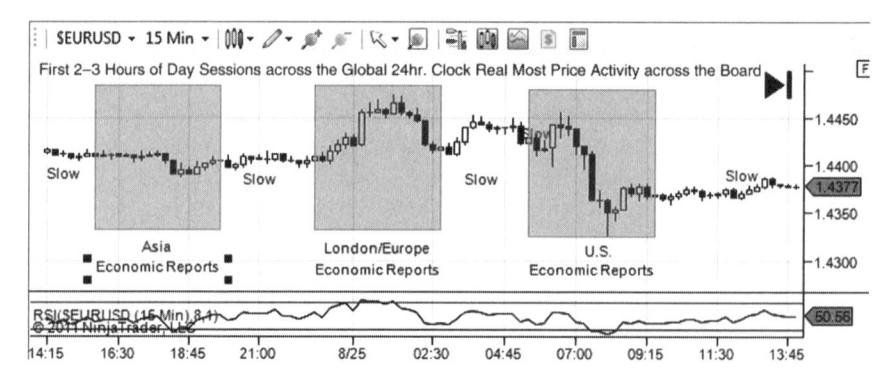

**FIGURE 11.22** Global Clock Most Active Around Reports

fact that it is their bedtime. All of the major reports released in the United States come out between 5:30 AM PT/7:30 AM CT/8:30 AM ET to 7 AM PT/ 9 AM CT/10 AM ET. Of course, eight times per year we have Federal Open Market Committee (FOMC) meetings to contend with as well. A good rule of thumb is to become familiar with the times that people wake up around the globe and count on the majority of the activity in the first two to three hours because that is when you have the most participants or in a sense two-thirds of the globe. See Figure 11.22.

The time overlap couples Asia with Europe and Europe with the United States. It may appear that the best seat in the house looks to be Europe and you may be right as they can take advantage of all the sectors around the globe during their daylight hours. *However, we feel that the United States has the best seat in the house; not because we live here but for the fact that we see two-thirds of the story before we trade.* We tend to have a clearer picture of how Asia and Europe views the action before we trade. *Greed and fear have no boundaries and the big dogs will always reveal their tell and how they are feeling. Since the market is bigger than us as individuals, it's nice to have that edge when making buy/sell decisions.*

If you decide to trade most often during the Asian session morning hours into the European overlap, it is important to have given some thought to how you are going to use and adjust the homework rule.

## ADJUSTING THE HOMEWORK RULE

Since you do not have much action to dissect at the start of the new session 4p PT/6p CT/7p ET, questions arise on how to deal with the homework rule. *We default to the RDS weekly and the previous day session midpoint to guide initial direction during the Asian session. After the first few*

*Putting It All Together* **187**

*hours of the new session settle into view, a transition to the current days session's midpoint is adhered to.*

We always want to see a preferred two-level move to make a case for long or short. If we are on the heels of a two-level rise and see a flip from uptrend to downtrend on the 15-minute chart at the start of the new day, we want to obviously make a case to go short. If the previous day's midpoint coupled with the RDS weekly is above the entry spot and in agreement with a short play, it helps confidence to participate as action tends to be right on the neutral rule at the start of the session.

The important point to factor in when faced with a decision at the beginning of a new day is to consider time of day and the currency pair. At the start of the Asian session, if the setup happens to be the USDCHF, you must understand that U.S. players want to go home and Swiss players are sleeping at this time. The two main components are not that interested at this time of day. You may have to wait this play out for the next several hours before CHF-interested players spring to life after a night's sleep before you see any real movement. Now if the setup happens to be the AUDUSD at the start of the new day that is a completely different situation. The Aussies are ready to roll at the start of their morning and movement is likely. This will help put a value on your time and instant-gratification thoughts as you focus on a market that has a better chance to move timely (a trader's friend) verses one that may be asleep for several hours.

### During the Session

We thought it might be beneficial to read what was on Mike's mind as he trades. The best way to do this is to look at some of the alerts he sends traders daily.

**RDS Trader Alerts Archive August 12, 2011 (all times Pacific):**

- 6:13:37 AM: good morning!! Today's reports and chart snapshot: http://www.rdsfx.com and
- 6:15:53 AM: not much movement across the board...USDCHF on radar again (Bullish bias)...hasn't pushed that far but minor support (one-level pullback) 0.7687...counter resistance showing up session high to 0.7829 (four-level range)
- 6:17:14 AM: buy order pending 0.7687 USDCHF
- 6:41:52 AM: consumer sentiment report in about 10 min.
- 6:53:45 AM: minor support forming EURUSD at session redline 1.4239 (weekly 1.4240)...don't really like redline setups...USDCHF looks best so far

*(Continued)*

**During the Session** (*Continued*)

- 6:55:20 AM: USDCHF moving back in uptrend on 15 min...any longs out there looking for session high to 0.7829
- 7:08:21 AM: prices sloshing around...slight downtrend now on USDCHF...careful any existing longs...I am waiting 7687 buy limit pending
- 7:10:04 AM: EURUSD trading thru 1.4240 mark...I'm going to watch that one...focus on USDCHF
- 7:34:52 AM: quiet Friday so far...
- 7:36:21 AM: USDCHF moving back in downtrend on 15 min...support still expected 1s time back in window down to 0.7687
- 7:41:42 AM: long four at 0.7687 USDCHF
- 7:42:48 AM: that's nice of them so far...
- 7:43:21 AM: going for a nice ride!!
- 7:44:13 AM: just took half off at 0.7707 (+20 on each)...still running long two from 0.7687
- 7:47:25 AM: very nice!! still running long...looking for session 0.7764 high to possible 0.7829 4L range target
- 7:51:45 AM: have a 0.7727 stop on remaining with 10 pip trailer to lock in +40 on remaining two long and will move it up if it keeps going
- 7:57:17 AM: glad I laid off EURUSD...hate redline trades...I will take the USDCHF...flat now...+120 total on entire long play
- 7:58:32 AM: going to leave on a high note and call it a day. Have a great weekend everybody!!

It's not all gravy and that easy, so we also would like to share the thoughts on Mike's mind when things started out rough. Losses are part of the game.

**RDS Trader Alerts Archive May 04, 2011 (all times Pacific):**

- 6:13:37 AM: good morning!! today's reports: ISM Non-Mfg Index 7:00 AM, EIA Petroleum Status Report 7:30 AM, ET, John Williams Speaks noon, FOMC Member Fisher Speaks 1:00 PM
- 6:14:23 AM: chart snapshot: http://www.rdsfx.com
- 6:15:56 AM: have interest in buying the EURUSD with a two-level fall to the 1.4856 expected support...targeting a move up to 14949
- 6:17:42 AM: watching NZDUSD as well...looking for some lower lows on 15min before entering a short play...but expecting resistance to

*Putting It All Together*

**During the Session** (*Continued*)

come in at 0.7959...targeting a move back down to session low to 0.7884

- 6:22:58 AM: seeing lower lows on 15 min NZDUSD...have sell limit pending at 0.7959 and buy limit pending EURUSD at 1.4856
- 7:41:07 AM: U.S. dollar gaining some strength
- 8:21:53 AM: long four at 1.4856 EURUSD
- 8:23:05 AM: stop below redline 1.4825...looking for 1.4887 to 1.4918
- 8:35:31 AM: took half off with some profit at 1.4866 with this stall here. Long two from 1.4856 looking for 1.4887 on remaining
- 8:53:57 AM: stalling but hanging in there...still running long
- 8:56:16 AM: EURUSD getting weak again...
- 8:57:00 AM: stop on remaining below redline 14825
- 9:01:54 AM: EURUSD coming back after hitting that last 1.4849 bottom...climbing again...would like to see some higher highs on 15 min
- 9:11:24 AM: stalling at 1.4863 bid on 15 min...starting to get heavy again
- 9:14:13 AM: looks like it's going to lunch
- 9:25:12 AM: brushing near 1.4825...glad I covered half on stall...1.4824 stop oco with 1.4887 profit
- 9:32:41 AM: stopped...think it will go up but I have worked it enough for me (1L against)...—24 total on trade
- 9:33:47 AM: probably just stopped myself on the low...but glad I covered some earlier...on to the next opportunity

Follow your game plan. It works, but it is not going to work every time. Remember that there are approximately 220 trading games a year and you are not going to win 220 and lose 0. At the first signs of failure most tear up their entire game plan after a loss. The strategy generally is not the culprit, but your stubbornness most often times is the reason. When trades start to go bad (one level against for us) we get out so we can live for another trade. Most fail because they think there will be no tomorrow, so they hang on to losing trades for hours upon hours that assuredly will get worse. Pre-trade always go in with a stop-loss in mind; just follow it! You set it for a reason and the reason is so you can have the emotional and financial energy to compete for the next opportunity. All trades do not work, but if you follow your plan the majority of them do, so don't fight the bad ones.

(*Continued*)

> **During the Session** (*Continued*)
>
> If Mike continued to hang with the long EURUSD play on May 4, 2011, it would have gotten worse. He started to feel it when he was mentioning U.S. dollar strength and using words like stall; all of these things didn't bode well for long EURUSD that day. He covered but you have to ask yourself, "Will you?" The dollars in your trading account are the most valuable commodity and if you burn it up on one bad idea, you will not be able to take advantage of the next opportunity.
>
> Our version of Murphy's Law becomes RDS Law:
>
> - Bad trades get worse
> - Good trades don't last forever.
>
> Questions of how long should I hold a trade, what's good, what's bad, and what's ugly always surface through the learning process. The next series of price-evaluation techniques should begin to help you identify the potentially good, bad, and ugly trades along the ride.

## WEATHERING ONE STORM

The normal ebb and flow of price movement over two levels (25 percent of field) on 15-minute chart lasts approximately two hours (eight 15 minute candles). Now this can take more or less time, but on average without any reports coming out it takes about eight 15 minute candles. Since prices do not always move directly to the desired objective smoothly, you sometimes get shaken off a positive trade a bit too soon. This can be frustrating to say the least. An easy fix would be to trade more than one contract at a time and cover part of or half of the trade along the journey. We of course believe that everybody needs to at one point or another get to at least two contracts. Forex as you know by now allows you to adjust to dime pips, so this isn't asking for too much when we say to trade two dimes a pip and build your tolerance from there. As you get confident and see account growth you can build the pip size and contract size.

Once you have your contract size in order, begin to concentrate on price action and begin to determine along the journey of the trade if the idea has potential to hit its target or fall short over time. Many times traders do not put a value on their time. This is so important! When you enter a trade the anxiety timer starts and you need to know your tolerance both in terms of money and time. As you see the ebb and flow of prices during a trade your emotions can and will shift from excitement (trade going in proper direction) to frustration (trade going in wrong direction) back to

*Putting It All Together* **191**

excitement and frustration. *On the emotion meter we refer to excitement as "clear skies" as the trade seems to be travelling as it should toward its intended path much like a smooth non-turbulent flight on an airline. In the frustration portion of price flow we refer to this as the storm much like when your flight needs to travel through a patch of bad weather, creating turbulence along the way.*

Excitement and frustration in relation to your position can be easily pinpointed on a chart. We will use our preferred 15-minute chart to help identify the entry and the holding time until an objective is met or the time allotment has expired. An unbiased technique is needed to help signal you as to whether or not the trade has potential to hit the target or fall short. *We can use price flips from uptrend to downtrend on our 15-minute chart to help identify where excitement and frustration exist.*

Assuming you have the HR, NR, DR, and a favorable RSI, we now patiently look for the window of opportunity to develop. You can speculate the bottom after two-level price drops, but we feel it is safer to let the big dog bulls resurface. Let them define a low that is confirmed after you start seeing higher highs on the 15-minute chart. The first time back into the window we execute our long position.

This is when the timer begins and if price snaps back into an uptrend (higher highs/lows), the excitement builds to shoot for our target (one level to two level). Along the path prices many times begin to pullback and show a downtrend (lower lows/highs) and frustration begins. If price doesn't stop out the trade (one level against) and the flow returns back to uptrend excitement, we begin to tell ourselves that we weathered a storm and price now in our eyes needs to respond and move towards our objective. If price action falls short of the target and lower lows/highs return (second storm), we feel the best thing to do is exit the trade. Time is nearing the normal patience tolerance of two hours as well and enough time has passed. Thoughts begin to turn to questions like why hasn't price moved to our target; it should have been there by now. See Figure 11.23.

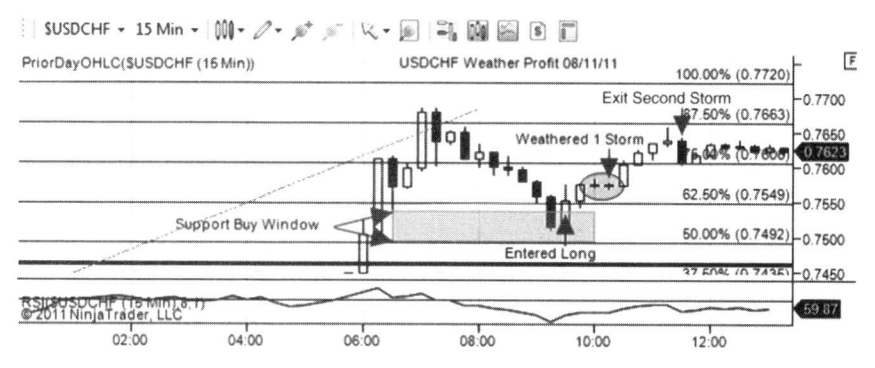

**FIGURE 11.23** Profit Weather One Storm, Exit Second Storm

**192**  THE RDS FOREX SYSTEM

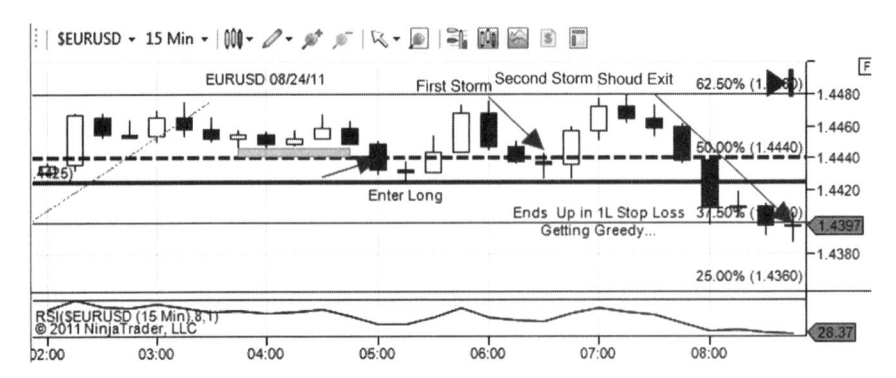

**FIGURE 11.24**  Turning Profit into Loss by Holding Past Second Storm

When working with a trade that seems to be struggling but not reaching the stop-loss area the same technique is used. The initial action of the trade most often tells the outcome. Trades that don't seem to let you up for air and get positive generally turn out worse. See Figure 11.24.

The same technique is applied to short side plays to help give you an un-biased filter to identify potential of the trade and balance it with time spent in the position.

A valuable method we noticed to help teach you how to prepare for length of time to wait for entry and length of time while entered in the position is to look at recent price action on a 15-minute chart. *Count how many 15-minute candles it took to move two levels in one direction and two levels in the other direction. You can then estimate with decent accuracy the total amount of time it may take before entry and holding time before exit.*

## PRICE EVALUATION: SLOPE OF STAND-OUT TOPS/BOTTOMS

We have been saying all along that price tells a story. The final blueprint of each candle upon completion should leave a mark in your mind to help remind you of what to do and what not to do as stand-out tops and bottoms are built during the session. When we have the rules on our side price tells us which side (long or short) to trust on that particular day. The location on the field upon entry helps define the mood of our teammates and opponents and signals how good we feel about a successful outcome.

An additional technique to help confirm the outcome is the direction of the slope of the stand-out bottoms and tops. This is using a simple trend

*Putting It All Together* **193**

line matched from window to window. Let's consider long side (buy) plays first. We all want to ride our winners and hit homeruns or have 100-yard touchdowns, serve aces in tennis or heave the last-second cross-court shot and sink the game winning basket. The probability of this outcome is small but we want to get you thinking about the times that it is possible to shoot for more than 1L to two-level runs.

It is not impossible to stretch a single to a double or a triple in trading. In order to accomplish this, you must be willing to weather more than one storm along the journey. The question to ask is: How bad are the storms? *As you ride your winner, look to see the slope of the windows on the 15-minute chart. When short you hope for the windows to be down trending and showing up lower over time and if long you want the windows to be sloping higher. This signals a nice solid trend. Gann considers a nice 45-degree angle to be a solid and healthy trend.*

We are sure that you have covered some trades and soon thereafter smacked the table in disgust as to how much money you left on the table as prices continued to move favorably if you had stayed with it. As you weather through the ebb and flow be smart along the way but be greedy when the signs tell you to be greedy. If the bottoms on long plays are getting higher, breathe through it and get greedy. Search for extension beyond session highs and possibly beyond the expected four-level outcome. You never know when a more than eight-level move is out there! See Figure 11.25.

Remember that price projections are predictions not fact. The levels you build whether using our style or some other version of them are based upon past data. The stand-out tops/bottoms, midpoints, and neutral areas are based on fact and reveal current mood. When greed and fear are in the air, the length of price moves are unpredictable. So when you have a

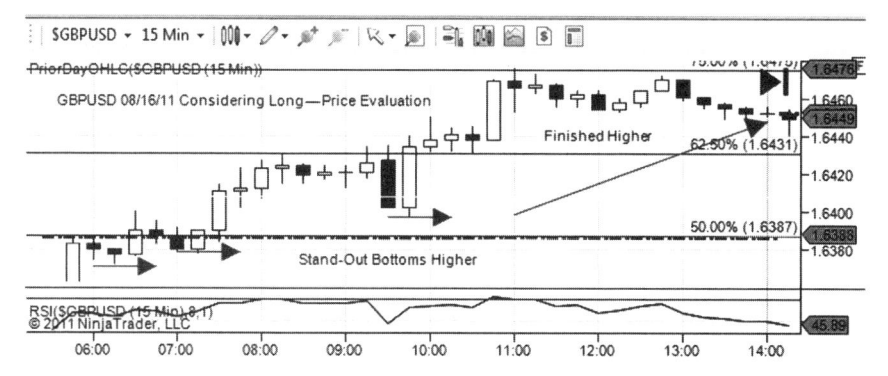

**FIGURE 11.25** Upward Slope Long—Higher Finish

**194** THE RDS FOREX SYSTEM

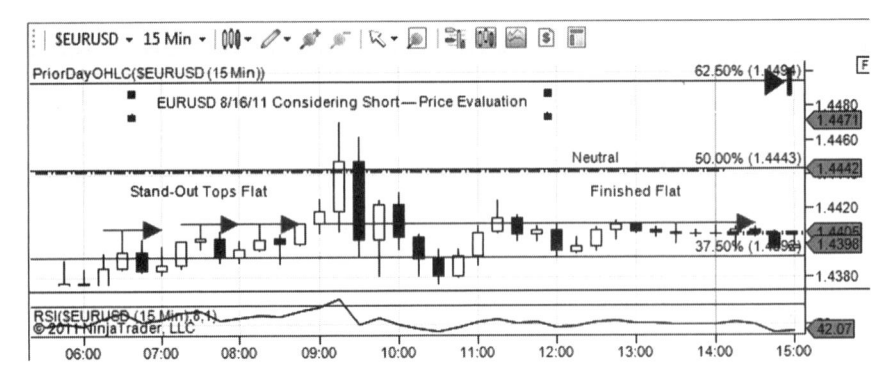

**FIGURE 11.26** Flat Slope Long—Flat Finish

positive long trade rolling and the stand-out bottoms are sloping upward, run with it!

When you notice that the bottoms are getting lower and you begin to weather more than one storm, this should signal with a smack to the back of the head that you are being stubborn when you should be fearful. The likely outcome is a lower finish. *When the stand-out lows are developing at or near the same point and looking flat, most often you are wasting your time as the likely outcome is a flat finish.* See Figure 11.26.

Stubbornness creates feelings of numbness and blocks your instincts. Be stubborn with greed when the signs are right and act instinctively to get out when signs of fear appear. See Figure 11.27.

The same price-evaluation technique can help your confidence in direction when tackling short side plays. If the stand-out tops are getting lower, you have a good one going and weathering through storms can be highly lucrative as the likely finish is lower. See Figure 11.28.

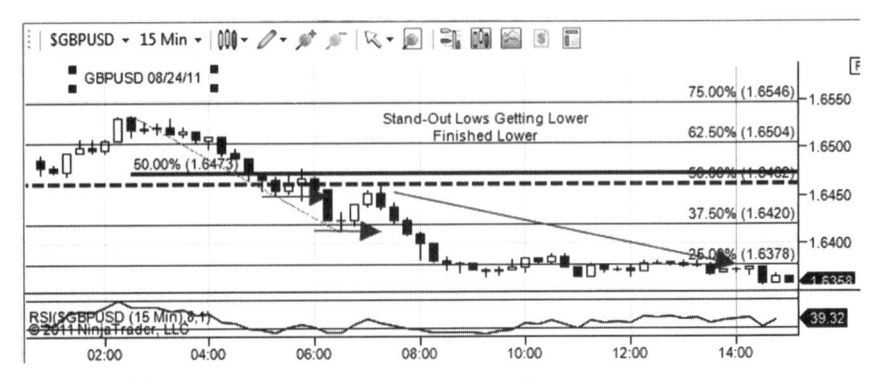

**FIGURE 11.27** Downward Slope Long—Lower Finish

Putting It All Together

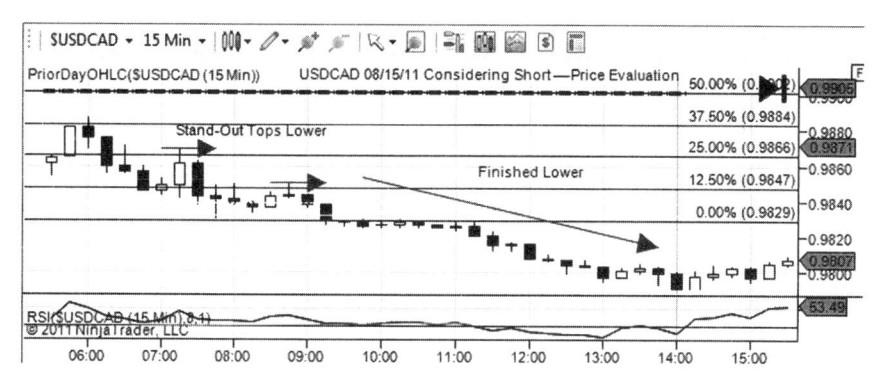

**FIGURE 11.28** Downward Slope Short—Lower Finish

If the stand-out tops are getting higher, prices are signaling that this isn't a great shot play as the likely finish is higher. If the slope of the tops is flat, the finish most times is flat. Don't waste your time.

Looking at the slope of the windows that have developed can be instrumental to aid confidence along the journey of any trade. As you enter the market it's important to have an amount on that allows you to think and evaluate the action along the way. *If you can't see or think, the problem oftentimes lies in the fact that you are trading too big. If you are not watching and indifferent—texting and chatting—often times you are trading too small and not reaching your potential.* Behaviorally these things will become more apparent as you read on to the next chapter about evaluating your performance.

# CHAPTER 12

# Evaluating Your Performance

When you get involved in the financial markets, you need to have a clear vision for your growth in business and in life. When you follow your instincts and commit, true growth appears. One of the hardest tasks a human being can take on is looking at one's self in the mirror. Really assessing the good, the great, and the space for improvement is quite a challenge and not one that most like to take. Whether you are open to this examination and introspective or not, as a trader you will be confronted with who you are every day. Your trades reflect you as a person, and how you handle each moment while you are in the market (or how you miss each opportunity due to your fears and second guessing). This may be a battle you didn't see coming, but trust us, it arrives and can pack a daily punch.

We were confronted with ourselves from the start. Our fears, stubbornness, anger, will to succeed, humor, self-consciousness, and a host of other emotions showed up loud and clear. When you are in the heat of a trade, some of these traits show up and can sabotage the entire plan. As we both look back on our careers to date, we can recall many instances early on when our performances were clouded by our emotions left unchecked.

As we mentioned previously "preparation contributes to timing and experience contributes to strategy." When we talk about preparation in this chapter we refer to physical, mental, and emotional work. All three need to be in place to succeed. We have learned to welcome our emotions, understand and manage them as they arrive. The markets are much bigger than us, we have to respect that and show flexibility. We have commissioned experts to teach us new tools to be flexible and better perform physically, mentally, and emotionally. We all have trading strategies, but not everyone has the other pieces in place to execute with success over and over.

New traders like to skip over this discussion because they have not experienced the emotional spiral that can decimate an account. They have not "seen it to believe it." And, they often (more often than we would like to see, unfortunately) think this will never happen to them, so they figure they don't need tools. This is another place to separate the peak performers from the average. In this chapter, Steph will tell her story in which her lack of a complete understanding of stress challenged her life.

## TWO INVESTOR PERSONALITIES

Let us introduce you to the two types of trader personalities: the Intellectual Investor (II) and the Emotional Investor (EI). These two types are inherent in all of us, so best to understand them both and recognize them quickly when they show up, especially the EI.

The II sets up the game plan, establishes risk/reward parameters, and makes the deal "I will follow my rules." This investor is intelligent, well thought out, and when he/she shows up, you will be satisfied with all of your trading decisions whether the trade is a winner or a loser. True success is found in executing your carefully laid plan.

The EI generally shows up unannounced while you are in a live trade and risking real money. He/she makes decisions that aren't necessarily in line with the plan and often takes you out of your trades in a completely different way than you got in. Did you ever get into a trade and then start asking your buddy what he/she thinks about where to get out? Once you start the polling process, you may as well get out. By asking someone else you are actually looking for a reason to stay in or get out that does not align with your original plan. Your EI is second guessing your II plan, and if you let the EI win, you will fail. If you happen to win in an instance where the EI prevailed, you will have experienced a very dangerous thing. Once you let the EI win, you will do it again and trust us, over time the EI always finishes last.

Steph recalls a day when she and her sister were computer trading side by side and they heard a loud, panic stricken voice in the trading room next door yelling, "Help! I'm stuck! Oh My God!" They both rushed to the side of a grown man who they knew to be an extremely intelligent and powerful all-state football player from The Ohio State University. He was just starting to trade one lots, live. He suffered from what we call the "fat finger syndrome" where you press the wrong button or click too many times on

*Evaluating Your Performance* **199**

the mouse. He got himself into a 100 lot by mistake and panicked. He sat frozen and Steph's sister, Dani, standing a mere 4'11' pushed this huge offensive lineman over, started clicking away on his computer, and got him out of the position in an instant. Luckily this man having come through our trading program knew this was a big problem and he called out for help instead of letting his EI take over and try to handle something he clearly couldn't. The EI would have convinced him to hang on to the trade to see what might happen. Often traders become numb when they have an incredibly large position on in relation to what they are accustomed to keeping. As software has become more sophisticated over the years, it is increasingly more difficult to make such an error.

Working with two personalities, it is important to evaluate them both. Evaluating the II is like a math equation, either you can solve for $X$ or not. In other words, either you follow the plan and can see the favorable results or don't follow the plan and again, can see the results. Evaluating the EI is a bit more subjective, and we will address this, as well.

## FOLLOWING THE PLAN

When the closing bell rang at 2:00 PM CT in the 30-year bond futures pit and 3:15 PM CT in the S&P pit, it was like a mass exodus. Traders and brokers raced to the turnstiles to release the day's stress by heading out to the golf course, the gym, or in many cases, the bars. What was left behind, not many people knew. The trading floor became as quiet as a church. The black rubber tile floors were covered from end to end with crumpled papers, gum, spit, chewing tobacco, shells from sunflower seeds, dental floss, fingernails, and even water bottles when they were allowed. The only ones who knew what this was like after the bell rang were the peak performers. These were the traders and brokers who wanted to win more than anything. They sat in complete silence on the steps of the pits and reviewed each and every trade they made. The janitorial staff knew them by name and swept around them each night. There were only a few of these peak performers. They were the ones with the lasting careers and bank accounts to show for it and it was obvious why. For one, they were willing to take the time to review.

We had both used this type of strategy with success during high school and college so this was easy for us from the start. In a small spiral notebook we could assess each trade, one by one. What worked, what didn't work, what was good, what was great, and what could be better were our concerns. The act of writing it down on paper made everything feel more real and we couldn't hide from anything. Each day we ask ourselves the following questions in regard to each trade based on the five Rotating Directional System (RDS) rules:

- When did we enter the trade?
- Did we enter when the II told us to?
- According to time of entry, were the majority of rules met?
- How much risk/reward did we experience compared to the day's events on the chart?
- How long did we hold the trade?
- Did we exit when our profit or loss thresholds were met?
- What was the profit/loss?
- Did the EI talk us into doing something the II didn't plan?
- Where did the market go after we got out?

These were questions with clear, black and white answers which we recorded in our notebooks. We solved for $X$ easily here. We knew right away if we followed our plans. We learned from our mistakes and remembered how it felt when we made good, solid decisions so we could capture that feeling and strive for it again and again. What wasn't so easy was asking about the EI.

## CHALLENGING THE PLAN

- Could we have done any better balancing the EI with the II?

This is a question we ask ourselves each day, but it is not always easy to answer or easy to admit if we let the EI win. No one wants to journal about a poor decision or an emotional decision or even relive it at all. Everyone wants to sweep the bad decisions under the rug. This is where the goodies lie, though.

As a new trader when you become honest with yourself about these trades, you grow to become a more seasoned, better trader. As seasoned traders the EI shows up less frequently during live trades. Many times during Steph's 10-year career on the trading floor the EI would show up after the trade was complete. Since the energy, good and bad, was intense on the trading floor she found it easy to get caught up in it. Sometimes it was fun to let the emotions run wild and yell and scream just because she could. It only became a problem when she couldn't calm down from the intensity. Steph would become attached to an emotion through her thoughts and hang onto the thoughts for far too long. She would come home from

*Evaluating Your Performance* **201**

work and recant a stressful trade with as much vigor when the situation occurred the first time. Mike would notice a large, protruding vein popping out of Steph's neck every time she would relive the days' events. Eventually Steph couldn't come down at all from the day's, week's, month's, and year's stress.

As a result of the situations that arose from years of unmanaged stress, we got to thinking about ways to address these issues.

The following story is only told here so that you, the reader and trader, understand why we have brought in more than just a trading strategy into our education program. Steph is not the only trader to fall from stress. We have watched a grown man have a mental breakdown and get carried off the trading floor, seen another man have a heart attack in the pit while everyone continued trading around him, and seen more men throw up on their keyboards than we care to share.

## STEPH'S STORY

Even though Steph was running three, four, or five miles a day, seven days a week, she could not stay healthy. First it was constant colds, followed by stomach issues. The stomach issues became bad enough that she went to a nutritionist. Right away, Steph cut out caffeine, drank more water, and began eating better. Frosted flakes for breakfast and a bagel and a piece of fruit for lunch just weren't cutting it. She was diagnosed with irritable bowel syndrome and was lactose intolerant. This meant her stomach was easily agitated by certain foods and stress. So again she cut out more food... no more popcorn, milk, cheese, ice cream, and even certain fruits and veggies were forbidden. This seemed to help for awhile.

The stress levels at work were exponentially rising, however. In the late 1990s she was filling orders in the NASDAQ 100 Futures pit which became the center of attention as the tech stock boom hit. With that came much larger orders to fill. Simultaneously the company that Steph worked for decided to open its doors to outside investors. This meant that she would have to fill orders for outside customers while continuing to manage her in-house customers. Over the years she had built an amazing relationship with her in-house clients, but this was new territory.

Soon Steph's stomach started to bother her again even though she was continuing to work out and eat right. She stopped teaching the pit-trading classes with Mike and her dad three nights a week and the pain still got progressively worse. She found herself at the doctor's office at least once a week. The doctor kept prescribing medication for Steph and sometimes it would help and sometimes it wouldn't. Steph got to know her doctor and the office manager so well that they all started to socialize outside work.

Finally one day Steph found herself lying on the dirty, disgusting trading floor because the stomach pain was so bad. She would watch for client orders on her handheld computer, jump up and fill them, and then lie back down. This was no way to live. She had gotten down to 90 pounds and found Ensure (the drink) was the only thing she could eat without having excruciating pain. She and Mike spent one evening in the emergency room because it got so bad. They doctors drugged her and sent her home. Mike had to carry her because she could not walk. One week later Steph was diagnosed with gall stones. Her doctor was shocked because she did not fit the typical description of someone suffering from gall stones. She was not over 40 years old at the time and was definitely not overweight. He didn't take into consideration her stress levels and how they were truly killing her.

As fast as she could get into surgery, she did. The stones were removed by laser while Mike and her mother sat vigil waiting for it to be over. Steph had a tough time coming out of the anesthesia and her recovery was slow. She did not have any strength and surely she couldn't go back to the trading floor. Two weeks vacation from the trading floor seemed to be an eternity, and perhaps the end to the stress story, but eventually Steph decided to go back and most importantly she didn't change anything. Eventually things got worse, much worse.

One week after the surgery with her stitches still in, Steph went to visit her mom in the hospital who had been battling breast cancer that had metastasized to her lungs. Her mom had fallen ill with pneumonia in the week after Steph's surgery and needed to be watched by the doctors. Four months later Steph's mom passed. It was the blow of all blows and Mike and Steph were crushed.

Steph went numb. She took a week off work and came back to the trading floor with one thought, "I quit." Her boss told her to stay. "Take a few months off and come back," he said. Steph knew she had come to the end of her career. This was the first time she made a big change, and unfortunately she was forced to do so.

This change would be something to celebrate, but Steph didn't have any energy to do anything, so she sat on the sofa for several months and went to therapy. She saw a psychologist twice a week and that was it. She was a shell of a person, going through the motions. It took her two months in therapy before she could even discuss her mom at all, or anything else. Interestingly she kept a journal during this time and it described nothing but her daily runs and what she ate. She left nothing on the pages about her thoughts or her feelings.

## Using Steph's Journal

Steph's lack of describing her emotions and the therapeutic work she did around this is where we got the idea to add thoughts and emotions to each trade's daily analysis. They play a huge role in life and trading and need to be addressed as much as the questions posed previously. We consider this:

- How did we feel when we entered the trade?
- Did we feel strong?
- Did we feel relaxed?
- How hard/easy was it for us to push the buy or sell button?
- Did we feel hesitant?
- Did we feel like we were sneaking something?
- Did we feel like we shouldn't be doing this?
- How did we feel about our exit?
- Were we happy we followed our plan?
- Did we feel anxious to get out?
- Did we feel confident?
- Did we feel stupid?

## Moving Forward

After a few months of sitting on her sofa and her therapist's sofa, Steph was ready for work again. This time she decided to do something less stressful, so she built a tutoring business. She tutored students in mathematics from the Latin School and the University of Chicago Laboratory School, both excellent private schools. Her stress levels stayed low and she stayed healthy, but after a few years, it became tedious. She needed something more challenging.

Steph's next move was to work as a project manager for an interior designer. Her first project was managing a 10,000 square foot home renovation. This was slightly challenging as she had never done this before and didn't know much about design. It was fun and she learned a lot, but after five years that didn't feel right anymore either, although she did stay healthy.

Steph then decided, based on her love for clothing, to challenge herself to a 100 percent-commission position at high-end retailer Neiman Marcus. She landed the job in the middle of the first interview and started the following week. It took six months for the @*^# to hit the fan. She was introduced to ethically questionable and miserable people (both coworkers and clientele). The stress to make the numbers was not too alarming, but she could not believe the lying and cheating and stealing and soon she was feeling pain again. This time she knew to move faster. It was too late, though. She, again, had to have surgery, this time to remove painful uterine fibroids.

Steph was determined to find a way to handle the stress. She knew she was strong. She spent three years in the S&P 500 Futures pit with 600 yelling, adrenalin pumped men and eight women, but why did she keep falling? This time she went to a psychologist to explore her issues. She needed some expertise and guidance and felt she was not living on purpose and wanted to know more. She adored this therapist as he helped other traders before her and never sugar coated anything. Without really knowing what she was saying, she kept telling him she was out of balance.

In 2006, after Steph left Neiman Marcus we took a week off and went to Los Angeles. At the time Mike was already trading off the floor and had restructured the education program so he could run it and teach it online to clients all over the world. He taught himself how to build a web site and to provide his long-time clients with the support and resistance numbers online.

The trip to LA was awesome and it dawned on us that we were not tied to the trading floor anymore. We could live wherever we wanted. When we returned to Chicago, Steph talked to her therapist about this idea. He wasn't surprised that we had fun. Who wouldn't have fun at the Beverly Hills Hotel, eating out at fabulous restaurants, and exploring an exciting city? He strongly recommended we go back and explore more, this time staying at a low rent hotel and not spending as much money on the material things. We ended up going back and staying in someone's small Pilates studio that was closed for the holidays. It was actually an old apartment that had not been redone since the 1970s. We slept on an air mattress with a hole in it and showered in the little stall. It definitely wasn't the Beverly Hills Hotel, but we were still in love with LA, so we went back, put our home up for sale, and moved eight months later.

Whether its trading or life you never know what the outcome will be but that doesn't mean you shouldn't try and it also doesn't mean you should go all-in during the learning phase either. This is truly why we love Forex with $0.10 in the beginning, just as our testing the waters on an air mattress helped us discovery and try LA. We could have landed in Los Angeles and gotten over-extended by buying a house out of the gate without knowing if this was the spot we wanted to be. This is the same lesson when trading. Playing with professional dollars just because you want to do it in the beginning is not always the best approach

## FIND YOUR GIFTS

After more than 40 years of being in Chicago, both of us were rejuvenated. We felt spirited to drive cross country and excited for the new experiences that awaited us. We had no idea the things we were going to be introduced to and tools to share with our fellow students and traders. The move and the exposure to new ideas have been great gifts.

The three biggest gifts have been:

1. Physical fitness
2. Exposure to new things
3. Continuing education

## Physical Fitness

As you have heard we feel it is important to stay fit. In the beginning we needed this to have the stamina and endurance to stand in the trading pits wedged shoulder to shoulder, yelling and screaming, for all those years. Today as screen traders we still need to be fit, but for other reasons. When you are active, you work many muscles including your heart. You are able to stay focused longer and have more patience as a result. Staying active can increase your desire to eat better and, in turn, provide better nutrition for your muscles and organs. Sitting at a computer for hours, your body can become lethargic and you need to have stable energy to focus without your mind wandering.

As you know, Steph thought this was all she needed until she realized her out of balance meant she was only focusing on one part of herself in the mind, body, spirit trio.

## Exposure to New Things

In the move to LA, we realized the veil was lifted in regard to what others thought of us. We weren't expected to do this or that, or react in a certain way. We found we were able to just be ourselves and really pick and chose who, what, when, where, how and why for ourselves. There was no more keeping up with the Joneses, which was a relief. It was liberating. And, we were exposed to things that we hadn't found in Chicago.

It was a pleasure to see, when a friend brought us to visit spiritual leader Reverend Michael Beckwith, that a church existed open to all walks of life and based on just being the best person you can be. We were introduced to restaurants with smaller, more reasonable portions that were dedicated to using organic and healthier foods. We found hip hop yoga and challenged ourselves to our first marathon which we did accomplish! It was fun to meet people in "the industry" as they often call the entertainment world. We saw our first taping of shows like Entourage and Ellen and even got to be on several cable shows.

We often find ourselves looking at each other while experiencing something new in LA and saying, "Wow, what do you think our family and friends back in Chicago would think?" And, we just laugh knowing that we have expanded ourselves in so many ways.

## Continuing Education

Dr. Linda Bedessian, D.C., is one of the most special gifts to come our way. Steph met her at a women's networking event in the first six months after we moved to LA. They spoke several times before they really had a deep conversation. She told Dr. Linda she was about to see a physical therapist because her legs and hip were hurting and she didn't know why. At the time Steph had been working for the same Philanthropic Consultant she worked for in Chicago and knew the stress levels were acceptable. Dr. Linda gifted Steph an initial visit and analysis for free. She also asked Steph if she wanted to put a bandage on her leg pain or get to the bottom of it. Steph, of course, wanted to get to the bottom of this. She was tired of quick-fix, patch-job methods to fix her ailments that seemed to help but only short term. Dr. Linda told her to make a decision... physical therapy or something new. So, Steph took the leap of faith. She loved the first session so much, she told Dr. Linda she wanted to pay her the $450 even though it was a gift. Dr. Linda refused payment and suggested Steph take the money and give it to a great cause. Steph gave the money to the non-profit arm of the women's networking group where she and Dr. Linda met and proceeded to work with Dr. Linda at her Beverly Hills office twice a week.

Dr. Linda practices what is called Spinal Network Care (NSA) and Somato Respiratory Integration (SRI), developed by Donald Epstein, D.C., and often referred to as *care*. She graduated from UCLA with a bachelor of science in biology, got her D.C. from Life Chiropractic College West, and studies under Donald Epstein on a continual basis. Although Dr. Linda is a chiropractor, she does not practice the traditional spinal adjustments (cracking), which Steph had previously experienced and decided was not for her. To Steph, care is like the evolved version of therapy (both mental and physical) and spinal study. The only reason the practitioner has to be a doctor of chiropractic is because the work focuses on the spine and the nervous system. Care involves the use of breath, energy and gentle touch along the spine, to relieve the nervous system of tension and stress that is stuck and reuses this tension to create positive results.

The markets are based on many things, including a mindset of the masses. What afflicts one eventually gravitates and afflicts the other. Remember that the markets are run by human beings and we tend to be creatures of habit. Who/what contributes to this mindset? Many factors are involved including the media, the governments, our families including past and present members, friends, teachers, and so on, and they all help us

*Evaluating Your Performance* **207**

develop fears and anxiety. Overall we make most decisions based on emotion and then deal with the ramifications of those decisions. What happens when emotions get out of control is where the pain lies.

When pain shows up we look to specialists to heal it. Each specialist is just that, a specialist. They look at a certain symptom with knowledge and treat that symptom. Have you ever known someone with extreme pain pay visits to every specialist they can find? They first reach out to the oncologists, then the rheumatologists and the gastroenterologists, the endocrinologists and the cardiologists, but don't forget about the pulmonologists, and the endless list of other specialists. Then they try the acupuncturists and the massage therapists, the physical therapists, and the body workers. What we have noticed is that hardly anyone looks at the person's life and the stress they have endured or are currently enduring. Getting to the bottom of it is what we feel is the tipping point to true healing and growth.

Storing tension and emotion, the nervous system acts as the hub of our bodies. The nervous system is the only system in the body where the cells cannot regenerate themselves. This means your body handles stress and emotions the same way today as it did when you were younger. Clearly the tactics you use at age 50 should be different than the ones you used when you were five, but how does the body know to make the change? It doesn't, and the stress and emotional swings just build and build until your body can't take it anymore. Have you ever had the urge to cry, but held back? As adults we are not supposed to cry, so we hold it in. Think about how your body feels when you hold in a cry. It's a lot of built up energy and if you don't release it, it gets stored somewhere.

This storage of tension builds along your spine causing muscles to tighten and pull differently on one side or the other. You will notice this via pain in your neck, shoulders, or upper and lower back. Unaddressed pain can lead to heart disease, high blood pressure, diabetes, thyroid issues, anxiety, insomnia, cancers, wrinkles, gall stones, fibroids, weight problems, fatigue, depression, and so on as a result of the built-up tension. These are the visible reactions. What about the things you don't realize while under stress like the release of glucose by your liver to provide energy for muscles, the slowdown of your digestive system, and the release of cortisol, which depresses your immune system? Many undetected symptoms occur while enduring stress until they finally rear their ugly head.

After several months of working with Dr. Linda, Steph ultimately figured out what the pain in her legs and hip was. Mostly it was coming from handling situations in the same way that she always had. These tactics were becoming obsolete for her and her body was signaling her with pain to let her know some changes needed to be made. As a result, when she would feel the pain come on, she would think about situations in the previous days in which she might have experienced stress. Every time she recalled

**Behavior**

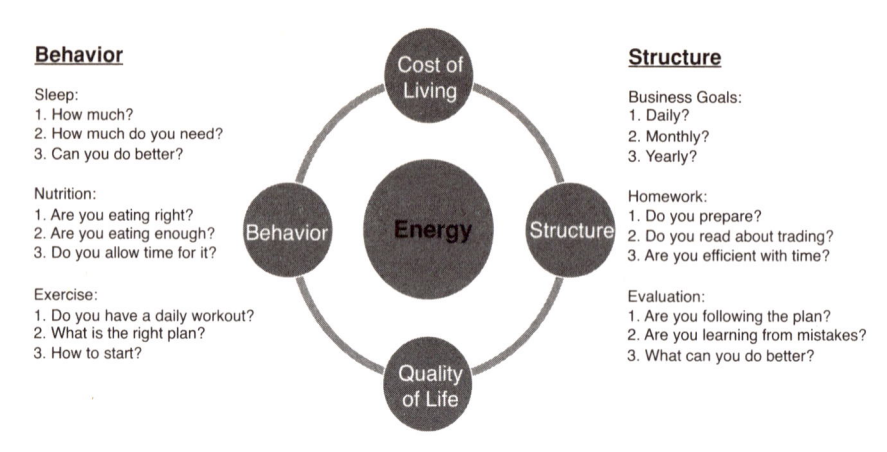

Sleep:
1. How much?
2. How much do you need?
3. Can you do better?

Nutrition:
1. Are you eating right?
2. Are you eating enough?
3. Do you allow time for it?

Exercise:
1. Do you have a daily workout?
2. What is the right plan?
3. How to start?

**Structure**

Business Goals:
1. Daily?
2. Monthly?
3. Yearly?

Homework:
1. Do you prepare?
2. Do you read about trading?
3. Are you efficient with time?

Evaluation:
1. Are you following the plan?
2. Are you learning from mistakes?
3. What can you do better?

**FIGURE 12.1** Financial, Physical, and Mental Energy

the exact situation and went through it in her head in a more positive way, the pain would dissipate. As Steph progressed in the work, she noticed more and more positive effects like handling situations better with less anger and not feeling the need to relive each stressful situation over and over at the same level, like she used to do on the trading floor.

Mike started to notice these changes and decided to try out Dr. Linda's services, too. He found access to more emotions and balance to his thoughts. He was able to release feelings he was holding onto from old experiences. He started incorporating some of the breathing techniques Dr. Linda taught us into his trading and noticed positive results. He also took away tools he was taught which led him to incorporate a goals map for our clients. This map looks at trading and life to find balance as shown in Figure 12.1.

## FOUR LEVELS OF CARE

Dr. Linda taught us the four levels of care starting with discovery, transformation, awaken, and finally integration. Care is not necessarily progressive, as we can experience any level at any moment in time. However, as we learn about each level, we are able to live through our experiences with more tools and can move through difficult situations with grace and ease.

Part of care involves breath work and energy that can be practiced on our own. We often check in with our bodies to see what it needs. The first exercise Steph learned was from the discovery level and it shocked her because it took a long time for her to connect to it. We find ourselves

*Evaluating Your Performance* **209**

doing this all the time now as we have become quite good at it. We will explain it here:

> As we build up tension in our spines, oxygen struggles to make it up and down the spine completely. It will skip over the tension spots and form an unhealthy spine lacking oxygen in these areas. The goal is to get the oxygen (or breath) into the spine and thus create total connection.
>
> There are three areas of our spine that we address in this exercise: The upper chest, the rib cage where the ribs meet in the middle, and the belly. We perform the exercise on the front side of our body.
>
> First we place one hand on top of the other. The palm of the top hand should be touching the backs of the fingers of the bottom hand, and the underside of the fingers of the top hand will be over the backside of the bottom hand.
>
> We then place both hands in position on top of our upper chest and breathe in and out deeply, isolating this area. No other area in the torso should be moving while doing this. (The first few weeks of practice, Steph could not get this area to move.)
>
> Next we move our hands down to the rib cage area and breathe in and out deeply, again isolating this area. Some people have a difficult time getting this area to isolate. Finally we move down to the belly and practice the same instructions as above. When we found we could isolate each area and get breath into each place we realized our spine was getting more breath than it had gotten in years.

## LOOKING AT THE BIG PICTURE

As we have driven our point home, evaluating your performance is just as important as the performance itself. We take our strategy, execute it, and then we need to evaluate and adjust. Not every performance is perfect, and the EI needs to be managed. We encourage ourselves to be kind and patient with ourselves and others. The goals map gives us a great picture on balance. We start with energy in the center and the four satellites around it—cost of living, structure, quality of fife, and behavior. Everything revolves around energy and if you don't have energy you have no way to accomplish anything.

### Cost of Living

We have had clients come to us over the years with various different reasons to get involved in trading. The most important thing to understand is that there are no guarantees in trading. You can, in fact, lose more money than you originally invest, although with newer, sophisticated computer parameters this happens less frequently. When clients say they want to make $500 or $1,000 a day, which is an acceptable goal, they need to give themselves at least three to six months to get used to the idea of trading at these values before thinking about making money at this rate. Rarely does a trader make this kind of money in the first year. Things to consider before beginning the journey of a trader are:

- Do you have enough money to live while you learn?
- How much are you willing to commit to the idea?
- Is making money creating stress in your life?

Only you can answer number one and number two best for yourself. If you answered "yes" to number three, now is not the time to start trading unless you are treating it like a hobby.

## Structure

Some people are better with structure than others. For those who work well with structure, consider daily, monthly, and yearly goals. For those who don't like structure, start with the questions in the Behavior section.

As you set out to embark on a trading career, we expressed earlier what might be reasonable to expect. Keep a spreadsheet with your goals and actual results to see how you are faring. In terms of preparation, consider these:

- Are you preparing on a regular basis?
- Are you keeping a journal?
- Do you read about trading?
- Are you efficient with your time?

Remember the peak performers are doing these things. Where do you fall?

## Quality of Life

It is understandable in the beginning if this piece is not considered due to focusing heavily on learning, however, it should not be forgotten. As soon as you feel you understand the strategy well enough to look at your screen and within seconds be able to identify if you should buy, sell, or do nothing,

*Evaluating Your Performance* **211**

you should revert to this part of the map. Without the fulfillment of these pieces here, life becomes empty and there is no reason to make money.

- Do you spend time with those you love?
- Do you spend time enjoying life?
- Do you give to the causes that move you?

If you answered "no" to any of these, it might be time to consider at least one. We get so charged and our weekends go from "okay" to "amazing" when we find something new and fun to do, or at least do something we love doing. It's not all about picking up the dry cleaning and going to the bank every Saturday morning.

## Behavior

For those of you who don't prefer structure, consider these questions and leave the structure questions for last.

- How much sleep do you get?
- How much sleep do you need?
- Can you do better?
- Are you eating right?
- Are you eating enough?
- Do you allow time for it?
- Do you have a daily exercise routine?
- What is the right plan for you?
- How can you start, if you don't exercise now?

## Some Other Questions to Consider

You might want to consider how you perceive yourself and the markets/economy.

- Do I rise to challenges?
- Can I do this?
- Do I have to be highly intelligent to trade?
- Can I do this without understanding my emotions?
- Do I care what others think of me?
- Am I willing to do what it really takes?

- Is it possible to make as much money in a falling stock market as a rising one?
- Can a retail trader make any money?

Perceptions are just stories we create in our minds based on previous experiences. Sometimes these stories are beneficial and oftentimes they constrict us from moving forward.

## CONCLUSION: STAYING POWER

If you really want to become a trader you are going to have to take a good, hard look inward. You need strength to do this and a good support system. The need to examine yourself may not be necessary or obvious in the beginning, but as you start to trade live and journal your behavior you will be confronted with who you are on each trade. Every one of our clients is surprised when they move from the demo account to the live account. This explains everything. Trading with real money is very, very different than it is with play money, and you will never learn anything about trading until you trade live. *That* is the day you can call yourself a trader.

And, even if you think Steph's story "could never happen to me" at our cores we are all human and don't have too many different ways to handle stress. Ultimately it catches up since our nervous systems don't regenerate naturally, and we have to find ways to reuse that stress and tension in a positive way instead of always resorting to medication and surgery, also known as bandages.

When choosing a market to trade; remember our story about the client that could only tolerate $50 on an idea and was forced out of the professional market plays due to the volatility and pip (tick) risk being too high for the length of time he needed to hang with the trade. Staying power is so important! You need time to learn and grow, so don't blow your capital before you even have a solid chance at understanding the markets, let alone who you are or who you can be as an individual investor. There are many choices when it comes to markets, and Forex seems to fit every risk tolerance in the beginning and is a great place to start and grow. As you grow to the professional risk tolerance ranks you will have the tools and versatility to stay with Forex and add the other professional Commodity Futures or Currency Futures markets to your list. As sectors of the economy go in and out of style you will be armed with the tools and a solid strategy that will enable you to transfer the knowledge as we have and bring your game to any market.

Our definition of true happiness is actually trying all of the things in life that you say you wanted to try. The result doesn't define happiness, but the act of trying does! Whatever you decide to try, you can't win, if you don't play!! Prosperity is at your fingertips! All you have to do is grab it!!

Trade strong! Trade smart! And always have enough to trade tomorrow!

# Resources

There were many resources we turned to in the writing of this book, and most are the same resources we often recommend to traders who want to know more about Forex trading, business strategy, technical analysis, or possibly just need a dose of inspiration. Listed here are books, films, and web sites we recommend to readers, categorized by topic.

## BOOKS

### Business Strategy

Grimm retold by Kimmel, Eric. *Seven at One Blow*. New York: Holiday House, 1998.

Sun Tzu. *The Art of War*. New York: Barnes and Noble, 2003.

### Inspiration

Epstein, Donald. *The 12 Stages of Healing*. San Rafael, CA, 1994.

Harp, David, with Smiley, Nina. *The Three Minute Meditator*. Oakland, CA, New Harbinger Publications, 1990.

Jeffers, Susan. *Feel the Fear and Do it Anyway*. New York, Fawcett Books, 1987.

### Technical Analysis

Gann, W.D. *How to Make Profits in Commodities*. Lambert-Gann Publishing, Pomeroy, WA, 1951.

Copsey, Ian. *Integrated Technical Analysis*. New York: Wiley, 1999.

Frost, A.J. and Prechter Robert R. *Elliot Wave Principle*, New Classics Library, Gainseville, GA, 1996.

### Trading

Falloon, William D. *Charlie D: The Story of the Legendary Bond Trader*. New York: Wiley, 1997.

Hoffman, Mickey and Basetti, Gerry. *Pit Trading, Do I Have the Right Stuff*. Trader Press, 1999.

## FILM

*Floored*. DVD, Trader Film LLC, 2008.

## WEB SITES

### Trading

*RDS Trader* by Michael Radkay, http://www.rdstrader.com
    Education: http://www.rdstrader.com/education
    Schedule: http://www.rdstrader.com/schedule
    Connectivity: http://www.rdstrader.com/connectivity
    Platform: http://www.rdstrader.com/platform
    Charts: http://www.rdstrader.com/charts
    Patterns: http://www.rdstrader.com/patterns
    Reports: http://www.rdstrader.com/reports
    Glossary: http://www.rdstrader.com/glossary
    Overtime: http://www.rdstrader.com/blog/
*DTI Trader* by Tom Busby, http://www.dtitrader.com
*Traders Coach* by Bennett McDowell, http://www.traderscoach.com
*Trading Pit History.com*, Debrouillard Group, http://www.tradingpithistory.com
*University of Trading* by Mickey Hoffman, http://www.universityoftrading.com
What Business is Wall Street In, *Blog Maverick; The Mark Cuban Weblog* by Mark Cuban, http://www.blogmaverick.com

### General Information

Econoday: http://www.econoday.com
Federal Reserve: http://www.federalreserve.gov
Whitehouse: http://www.whitehouse.gov

# About the Authors

**Michael Radkay**
After receiving a BA in Economics from Lake Forest College in May 1989 and enjoying four years of Forester Football as first-string strong safety and punt returner, Mike has dedicated the last 20 years of his life to the Futures and Forex industry. Mike felt this was a great way to transition his competitive spirit to the workplace. He started as a runner in the 30-year bond futures pit at the Chicago Board of Trade and worked his way up to becoming a broker for a top brokerage firm by 1993. In 1997 Mike became a self-funded, self-employed trader.

After trading hours from 1993 to 2004 Mike was instrumental in building and delivering the curriculum used by the University of Trading, a school that set the foundation for traders of all skill levels. This firm employed 25 to 50 employees and housed more than 200 traders. In 2004 he transitioned from the trading pit to the computer screen and rebuilt his entire program to cater to the screen trader. In 2007 Mike moved to Los Angeles to start his own trading education company, RDS Trader LLC. Mike has been a frequent contributor for Northwestern University and UCLA Continuing Studies Programs, the CME Group, Trader Kingdom, Forex Connect, FX Instructor, Traders Coach, and in early 2010 Mike and his wife, Stephanie, built the new DTI-FX division. Mike offers his experience and skills as a Futures/Forex trader, broker, mentor, CBOT/CME Group (acronym RDS), and NFA (#0250761) member to his clients. The proprietary method taught to his students is known as the Rotating Directional System (RDS). This method has helped him achieve success specifically as a trader and generally in all aspects of investing. *Web site: www.rdstrader.com*

**Stephanie Radkay**
After receiving a BA in Mathematics at Indiana University in 1990, Stephanie joined the rough pits of the Chicago Mercantile Exchange as a clerk for a major international options and futures firm. In 1993 she began her broker career as the only woman in the major market index futures pit.

At the same time, she also joined her husband, Mike, after trading hours at the University of Trading to teach eager learners to pit trade. By 1995 she was awarded the task of filling orders in the S&P500 futures pit. At the time, this pit community had 600 men and five women. In 1998, Stephanie left the S&P 500 futures pit and followed the Tech Boom to fill orders in the NASDAQ 100 futures pit.

By 2000, Stephanie decided to take a break from trading and in 2008 she returned to her love for the trade and to help build RDS Trader, the screen trading education company that Mike was building. In early 2010 Stephanie and Mike joined forces with DTI to head up their new DTI-FX division. Stephanie is known as TIGR to her fellow traders and brokers at the Chicago Mercantile Exchange and "Eats Stress for Breakfast" according to the *Chicago Tribune* feature article (September 14, 1997). She brings her experience and knowledge of trading, teaching, and managing stress to all of our clients. *Web site: www.rdstrader.com.*

# Index

9-11, 70–72
*The 12 Stages of Healing*, 215

**A**
adjustments, 146
analysts, fundamental, 35
average range, 144–145

**B**
Basetti, Gerry, 216
basics, chart, 112–114
bear day adjustment, 146
bearish hook, 116
Bedessian, Linda, 206–208
behavior, 208, 211
big dog bottoms/tops, 55–58
Blog Maverick, 2
Bollinger Bands, 153
break, trading through, 184
breakouts, counter versus, 183–184
Buffett, Warren, 44
bull day adjustment, 146
bullish hook, 116
Busby, Tom, 216
Bush, George W., 72–73
buy location, 174–182
buy window of opportunity, 149–151

**C**
candle, outside, 116
candlestick chart, 123–124
care, levels of, 208–209
carry interest, 14–15
CFD. *See* Contract for Difference
*Charlie D: The Story of the Legendary Bond Trader*, 215
chart basics, 112–114
chart patterns, 114–118
chart, candlestick, 123–124
checklist, pre-trade, 119–120
Chicago Mercantile Exchange, 13
circle of influence, 50–52
closing price, neutral rule and, 131–133
CME. *See* Chicago Mercantile Exchange
competition, know, 26
computer trading, 1–4
　preparation questions, 6–7
continuing education, 206–208
Contract for Difference, 29
controlled rage, practicing patience with, 21–22
Copsey, Ian, 215
cost of living, 209–210
counter, breakouts versus, 183–184
Cuban, Mark, 2–3, 216
currencies, by region, 62
currency futures, 13–14

**D**
Debrouillard Group, 216
decision maker, 32–33
decisions, results of, 40–46
demand, supply and, 77
demo traders, 20
discipline, 102–103
distance rule, 160–161
distance run, 146–148
Dodd-Frank Reform Act, 30

**219**

double bottom/top, 117
downtrends, 55–58
DR. *See* distance rule

**E**
economic reports
 dates of, 36–40
 times of, 38
economics degree, 66–67
EI. *See* emotional investor
electronic trading, 1–4
 preparation questions, 6–7
Elliot Wave Principle, 215
emotion, intellect versus, 20
emotional investor, 198
employment reports, preparing for, 80–84
energy, 208
entry, 165–166
Epstein, Donald, 206, 215
experience, strategy and, 105

**F**
failure, reasons for, 8–11
Falloon, William D., 215
fear, greed and, 67–68, 105
Federal Funds Interest Rate, 75–76
Federal Funds target rate, purpose of, 77–80
Federal Open Market Committee, 35, 75–76
 preparing for, 80–84
Federal Reserve
 bank presidents, 39
 board members, 39
 policy statements, 37–38
Feel the Fear and Do It Anyway, 215
Fibonacci, 141–142
field building, forecasting and, 137–138
field, adjusting to neutral rule, 143–144
financial energy, 208
first hour magic, 118, 121–122
first-hour rhythm, 121
five-day concept, 134–135
five-day cycle, 138–139
flight to quality, 22

Floored, 19, 216
FOMC. *See* Federal Open Market Committee
football field, trading as, 88–92
Ford, Henry, 1
forecasting, field building and, 137–138
foreign exchange market, 13
forex, growing with, 31–32
Frost, A. J., 215
fundamental analysts, 35
fundamental events, surprise, 69–70
futures contract, 13–14
futures
 currency, 13–14
 learning, 101–102

**G**
Gann, W. D., 215
Gecko, Gordon, 3
geo-political events, surprise, 69–70
Goose, 1
greed, fear and, 67–68, 105

**H**
Harp, David, 58, 215
high-frequency programmers, 27–28
high-frequency trading, 26–29
Hoffman, Mickey, 216
homework rule, 123–129, 160–161
 adjusting, 186–187
homework
 weekly, 126–128
 yearly, 128–129
hook, bearish/bullish, 116
hot currencies, by region, 62
*How to Make Profits in Commodities*, 215
HR. *See* homework rule

**I**
IBKR. *See* Introducing Brokers
II. *See* intellectual investor
IMF. *See* International Monetary Fund
independent thinker, 32–33
ingisms in trading, 6–8
instant gratification, 59

# Index

*Integrated Technical Analysis*, 215
intellect, emotion versus, 20
intellectual investor, 198
International Monetary Fund, purpose of, 77–80
Introducing Brokers, 27–28
intuition, trusting, 63–64
investor personalities, 198–199

## J
Jeffers, Susan, 215
journal, 203

## K
keys to success, 103–107
Kimmel, Eric, 215

## L
learning, winning and, 106–107
leverage, 15–17
longevity, risk management and, 105

## M
M pattern, 117
MACD. *See* moving average convergence divergence
market profile, 161–164
market tolerance, mapping, 65–66
market, trading more than one, 23–24
Maverick, 1
McDowell, Bennett, 216
measured move, 137
measurement, zones of, 139–141
mental energy, 208
micro pip traders, 20
missing a move, fear of, 74
momentum side timing, 160–161
move
 fear of missing, 74
 measured, 137
moving average convergence divergence, 153

## N
neutral rule, 129–146, 160–161
 adjusting the field to, 143–144
 closing price and, 131–133

neutral side setup, 175–176
new things, exposure to, 205–206
news, reading, 73–74
NR. *See* neutral rule
NSA. *See* Spinal Network Care

## O
OCO. *See* one-cancels-other
one-cancels-other, 59–60
OTC. *See* over the counter
outside candle, 116
over buying/selling, 154
over the counter, 13

## P
parity, 48–49
 price and, 55–58
patience, practicing with controlled rage, 21–22
patterns, chart, 114–118
perseverance, 170
personal questions, 7
personal risk tolerance, 96–97
personal time tolerance, testing, 63–65
personalities, investor, 198–199
physical energy, 208
physical fitness, 205
*Pit Trading, Do I Have the Right Stuff*, 216
plan
 challenging, 200–201
 following, 199–200
policy statements, Federal Reserve, 37–38
pre-trade checklist, 119–120
Prechter, Robert R., 215
preparation
 pre-session, 185–186
 timing and, 104
price, 54, 109–110
 parity and, 55–58
 sentiment and, 131
price evaluation, 192–195
price movement, 190–192
price range, predicting, 84–86
price response chart, 76

profit, 165–166
profit objective, 166–167
programmers, high-frequency, 27–28

**Q**
quality of life, 210–211
questions, asking, 52–54

**R**
Raday, Stephanie, stress and, 201–208
Radkay, Michael, 216
rage, practicing patience with, 21–22
range bound, 161–164
range, average, 144–145
RDS risk calculator, 97–101
   using, 100–101
Reba, Greg, 19
relative strength index, 153–157, 161
relative strength index formula, 154–156
reports, economic, 36–40
risk, 94
   managing, 94–96
risk allotment, 98
risk breakdown, 97
risk calculator, 97–101
   using, 100–101
risk management, longevity and, 105
risk tolerance, personal, 96–97
RSI. *See* relative strength index
rule
   homework, 123–129
   neutral, 129–146

**S**
scaling in or out, 180–182
screen trading, 1–4
   preparation questions, 7
sell location, 174–182
sell window of opportunity, 151–153
sentiment, price and, 131
*Seven at One Blow*, 215
sleep, trading through, 184

Smiley, Nina, 215
Somato Respiratory Integration, 206
Spinal Network Care, 206
SRI. *See* Somato Respiratory Integration
stand-out tops and bottoms, 192–195
stochastic, 153
Stone, Oliver, 3
stop loss, 165–170
strategy, 67
   experience and, 105
structure, 208, 210
success, keys to, 103–107
supply, demand and, 77

**T**
technical analysis, 109–110
technical charts, 112–114
technology questions, 7
thinker, independent, 32–33
*The Three Minute Meditator*, 58, 215
time, 109–110
timeframe, 118–121
timing, preparation and, 104
tolerance to market, mapping, 65–66
trade thought process, 157
traders
   demo, 20
   types of, 92–93
trades, forcing, 24–26
trading card, 95
trading software, 59–60
trading
   ingisms in, 6–8
   as a football field, 88–92
   electronic, 1–4
   high-frequency, 26–29
trending, 161–164

**U**
U.S. Government Officials (2011), 39
uptrends, 55–58

**W**
W pattern, 117
waiting, 74

# Index

waiting game, 133–134
weekly homework, 126–128
window of opportunity rule, 50, 148–153, 160–161
window of opportunity
  buying, 149–151
  selling, 151–153
winning, learning and, 106–107
WO. *See* window of opportunity

## Y

yearly homework, 128–129
yearly homework rule, yearly neutral rule and, 135–137
yearly neutral rule, yearly homework rule and, 135–137

## Z

zones of measurement, 139–141